GREAT AMERICAN QUILTS 2001

Edited by
Patricia Wilens

Great American Quilts 2001

Book Division of Southern Progress Corporation
P.O. Box 2463, Birmingham, Alabama 35201

Published by Oxmoor House, Inc., and Leisure Arts, Inc.

We're Here for You!
We at Oxmoor House are dedicated to serving you with reliable information that expands your imagination and enriches your life. We welcome your comments and suggestions. Please write us at:

Oxmoor House, Inc.
Editor, *Great American Quilts 2001*
2100 Lakeshore Drive
Birmingham, AL 35209

To order additional publications, call 800-633-4910.

ISBN: 0-8487-1985-9
ISSN: 0890-8222
Printed in the United States of America
First Printing 2000

Editor-in-Chief: Nancy Fitzpatrick Wyatt
Senior Crafts Editor: Susan Ramey Cleveland
Senior Editor, Copy and Homes: Olivia K. Wells
Art Director: James Boone

Editor: Patricia Wilens
Contributing Copy Editor: Susan S. Cheatham
Contributing Designer: Barbara Ball
Illustrator: Kelly Davis
Senior Photographer: John O'Hagan
Photo Stylists: Linda Baltzell Wright, Cathy Harris
Publishing Systems Administrator: Rick Tucker
Director, Production and Distribution: Phillip Lee
Book Production Manager: Theresa L. Beste
Production Assistant: Faye Porter Bonner

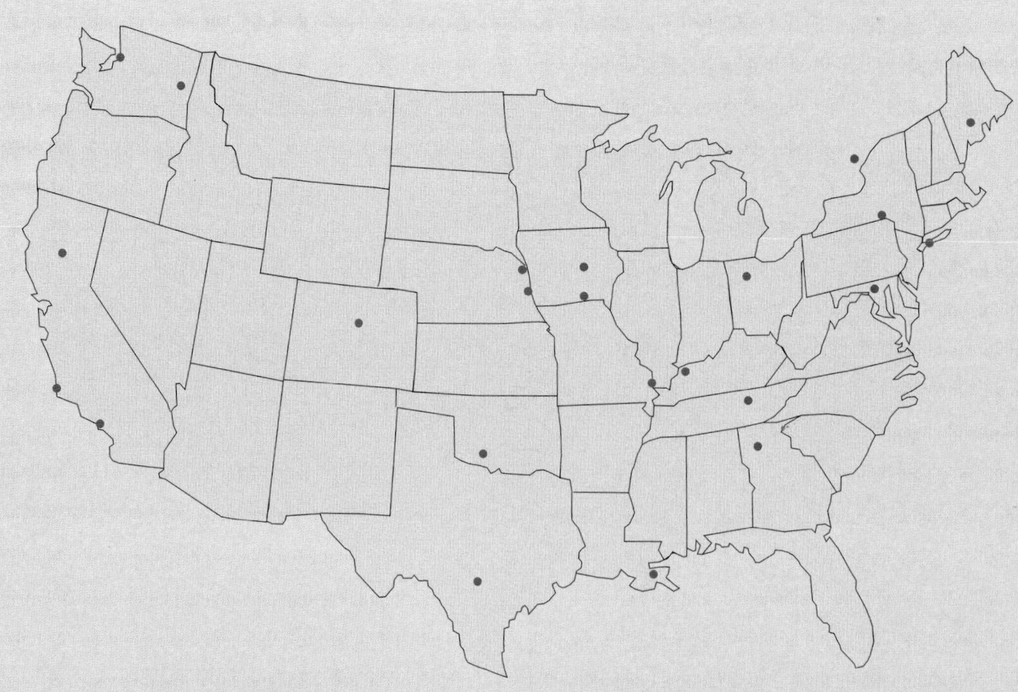

Where do Great American Quilts come from? They come from north and south, east and west, and lots of places in between. This year's book features quilters from 16 U.S. states and one from Canada. If your state isn't represented here, perhaps you can make a mark on next year's map. (We'd love to hear from states not represented in our history—Delaware, South Dakota, and Montana—as well as Washington, D.C., and the territories.) To submit a quilt for consideration, send a snapshot with your name, address, and phone number to *Great American Quilts*, Oxmoor House, 2100 Lakeshore Drive, Birmingham, AL 35209. Deadline for the 2002 edition is January 8, 2001. We cannot return photos.

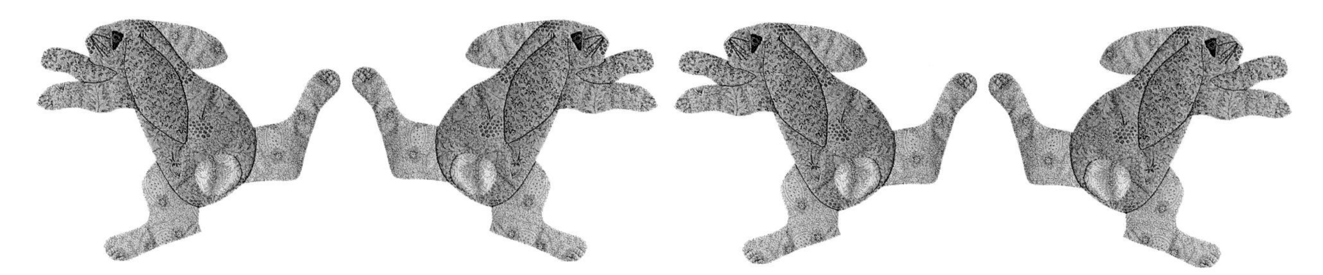

15 Years of *Great American Quilts*

The traditional gift for a 15th anniversary is crystal. It might have taken a crystal ball to predict, way back in 1987, that *Great American Quilts* would endure so long.

Loyal readers have made *Great American Quilts* the long-running success that it is. Over the years, you've appreciated 465 quilts, made by 347 individuals and 51 groups from 47 U.S. states and one Canadian province. (See map note, below left.)

This year's quilts are all that 21st-century quilts should be—innovative, yet rooted in tradition. The quiltmakers include renowned professionals and exciting new talent. Look for the bumblebee illustration that indicates a quilt made by a guild or bee.

This year's theme chapter is **Quilts for All Seasons,** with quilts that celebrate the changing splendor of nature. *Spring Delight* evokes the softness of delicate blossoms. *Lime & Chile* sizzles with summer heat, while *Oak & Acorn* glows with the mellow hues of autumn. *Carolina Lily* closes the year with traditional Christmas colors.

Quilts Across America showcases innovative design from coast to coast. If you like rotary cutting, you'll appreciate *Concertina* and *Celestial Garden,* which is also an exercise in paper-foundation piecing. Fabric lovers and scrapaholics will enjoy *Bali Snails* and *Blowin' in the Wind.*

Classic design, enhanced with today's techniques, is the focus of **Traditions in Quilting.** You'll appreciate the elegance of Jennifer Patriarche's blue-ribbon quilt, *The Frequent Flyer*, and the exuberance of *Rainbow Riot.* Harken back to folk-art style with *Cockscombs, Tulips & Berries.*

Designer Gallery is a veritable Noah's Ark. Birds, fish, rabbits, even buffalo are interpreted in fabric by talented artists. *Prairie Thunder* and *Dancing in the Rain* are powerful images of wildlife, while *Moon Dance* is a hare-raising experience. On the domestic front, *All Dogs Are Good* celebrates our most faithful companion.

Contributor Jan Magee says it means a lot to her that her quilt is in this year's book. "*Great American Quilts* helped me become a quiltmaker," she says. That means a lot to us, too. We hope to help and inspire quiltmakers for years to come. Thank you for sharing 15 years of great quilts and good friends.

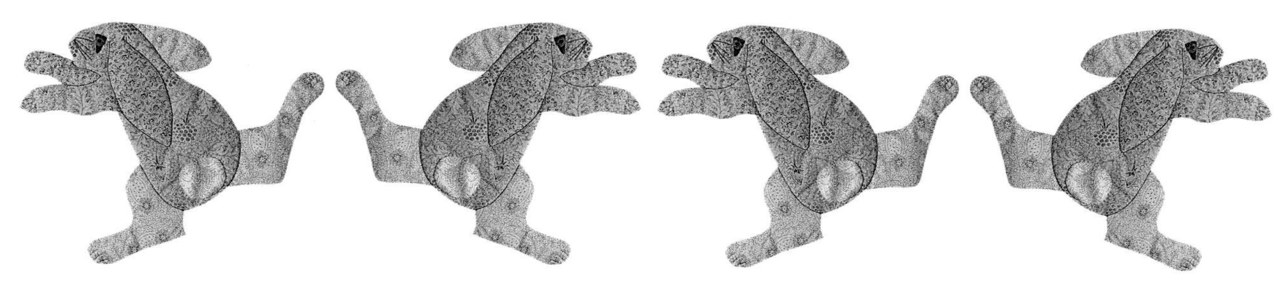

C O N T

Quilts for All Seasons

Quilts Across America

Quilt Smart

Traditions in Quilting

Designer Gallery

Quilts for All Seasons

Night Lights

Spring Delight

Lime & Chile

The Pepper Quilt

Oak & Acorn

Carolina Lily

Yvette Magee

Harahan, Louisiana

Yvette Magee once took the bus all the way from New Orleans to Collins, Mississippi, to see her husband's grandmother "put in" a quilt. She was honored to be allowed to take a few stitches.

Though she loved sewing, Yvette didn't make a quilt until the 1970s when her mother-in-law gave her an appliqué kit. "I applied the flowers the only way I knew how, with a buttonhole stitch like my husband's grandmother did," Yvette says. Before that top was finished, Yvette took classes with Marion Maerke, the late founder of the Gulf States Quilting Association. "That's when my quilting journey really began," she says.

"I get a thrill out of perfectly matched seams."

In the 20 years since, Yvette has made at least 10 bed-size quilts. They are mostly machine-pieced because "with four children, faster is better." But she loves to quilt the tops by hand. "When I have a few minutes, I can sit down and collect my thoughts while my fingers are engaged in a productive pursuit," she says.

Yvette describes herself as a very precise person. "I get a thrill out of perfectly matched seams, even if I have to rip a few times to accomplish it," she says. "Not everyone understands those feelings of satisfaction in a well-executed piece."

Yvette gets encouragement from the Cotton Pickin Quilters, a member chapter of the Gulf States Quilting Association, of which she is a past treasurer. In addition to the social benefits, she says, "I truly cherish all the things I've learned from my fellow quilters through the years."

Night Lights

1999

Yvette Magee collected teal, purple, and hot pink fabrics, intending to use them for wearables. But she liked the idea of setting bright stars against a dark background "so they appear to be floating in space," she says. The stars in Yvette's quilt glitter against the inky blackness of a moonless winter night's sky.

Quilting black fabric with black thread was a challenge that required a spotlight and a new pair of glasses.

Yvette made this quilt in a class led by Gayle Wallace, a fellow member of the Gulf States Quilting Association. The quilt uses quick-piecing techniques that make it "a fun project that goes together very quickly," Yvette says.

Night Lights won a third place ribbon at the 1999 Gulf States Quilting Association show in New Orleans.

Night Lights

Finished Size

Quilt: 84½" x 84½"
Blocks: 25 (12" x 12")

Materials

10 (18" x 22") fat quarters assorted bright fabrics
6 yards black (includes binding)
½ yard bright print for middle border
2½ yards 90"-wide backing fabric

Pieces to Cut

Instructions are for rotary cutting and quick piecing. See tips for diagonal-corners technique, page 12. Cut pieces in order listed to make best use of yardage. Rotary-cut all strips cross-grain. When possible, pieces are listed in order needed, so you don't have to cut everything all at once.

From each *fat quarter*

- 1 (2" x 18") strip, cut along 18" length of fabric, and 7 (2" x 20) strips, cut from remaining width. Set aside 4 (2" x 20") strips for nine-patch strip sets and remaining 4 strips for B star points.
- 1 (3½" x 20") strip. From this, cut 4 (3½") A squares. (You'll need a fifth square from 1 fabric to get a total of 41 for blocks and sashing.)

From black fabric

- 25 (2" x 40") strips. From these, cut 50 (2" x 20") strips for nine-patch strip sets.
- 4 (3½" x 90") lengthwise strips for outer border.
- 25 (3½" x 27") strips. From 20 of these, cut 40 (3½" x 12½") sashing pieces. Add remaining strips to next cut.
- 10 (3½"-wide) strips. From these and 27"-long strips remaining from previous step, cut 100 (3½" x 5") C pieces.
- 8 (2"-wide) strips for inner border.
- 8 (2½"-wide) strips for straight-grain binding.

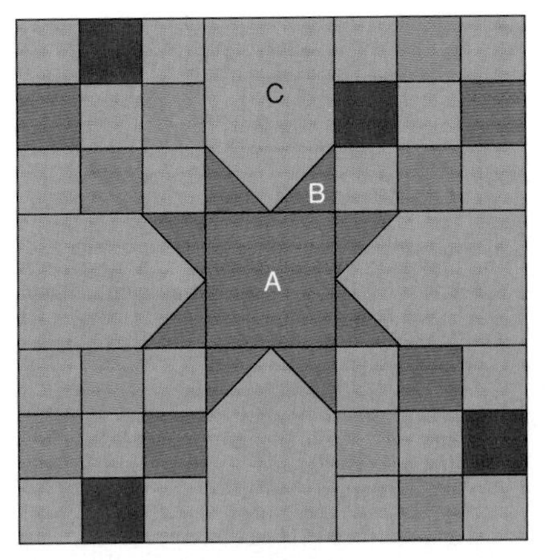

Star & Nine-Patch Block—Make 25.

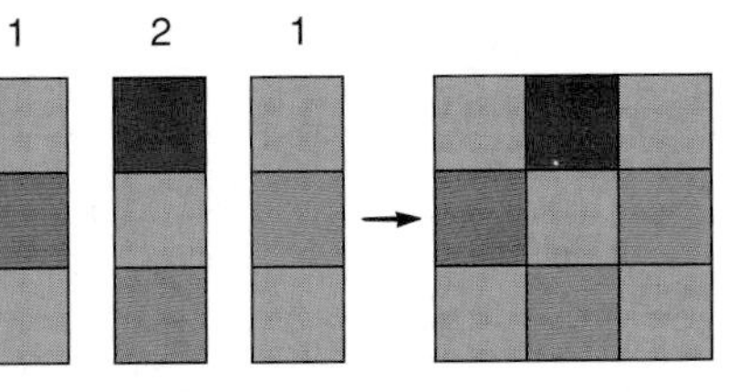

Diagram A

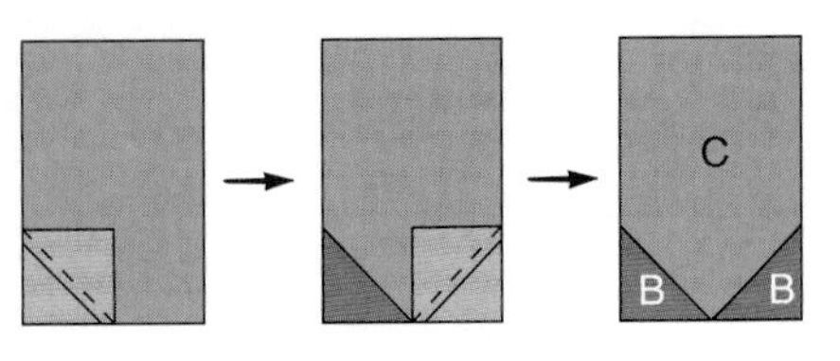

Diagram B

Block Assembly

See page 12 for instructions on Diagonal-Corners Quick-Piecing Method.

1. Select 2 (2" x 20") strips of each colored fabric. Sew black strips to both sides of each strip to get 20 of Strip Set 1. Press seam allowances toward black.

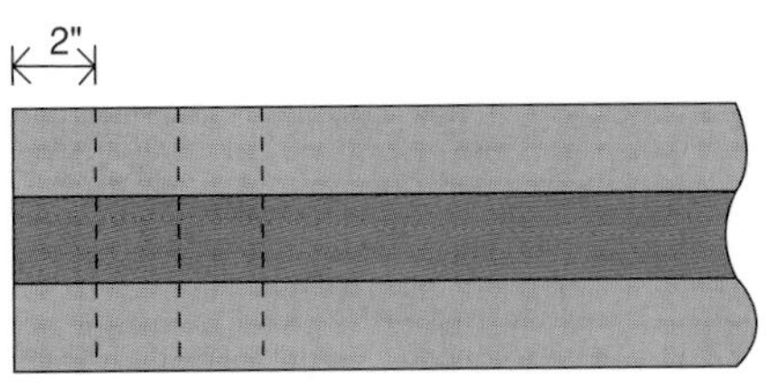

Strip Set 1—Make 20.

Strip Set 2—Make 10.

2. Stitch colored strips to both sides of remaining 2" x 20" black strips to get 10 of Strip Set 2. Press seam allowances toward black.

3. Cut 10 (2"-wide) segments from each strip set to get a total of 200 Strip Set 1 pieces and 100 Strip Set 2 pieces.

4. For each nine-patch, select 2 Strip Set 1 segments and 1 Strip Set 2 segment. Join segments to make a nine-patch *(Diagram A)*. Make 100 nine-patches.

5. Select 4 black Cs and 1 colored strip for star points. Cut 8 (2") B squares from strip. Use diagonal-corner technique to sew 2 B squares to each C piece *(Diagram B)*.

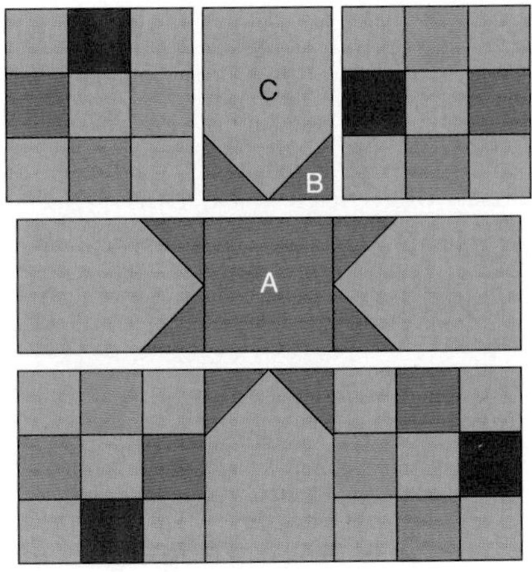

Block Assembly Diagram

6. For each block, select 4 nine-patches and a set of 4 B/C units and a matching A square. Join units in 3 rows *(Block Assembly Diagram)*. Join rows to complete block.

7. Make 25 blocks.

Quilt Top Assembly

1. Lay out blocks in 5 horizontal rows with 5 blocks in each row. Rearrange blocks as needed to achieve a nice balance of star colors across quilt.

2. When satisfied with layout of blocks, position remaining colored A squares in sashing rows, again striving for a balance of color and fabric.

Row Assembly Diagram

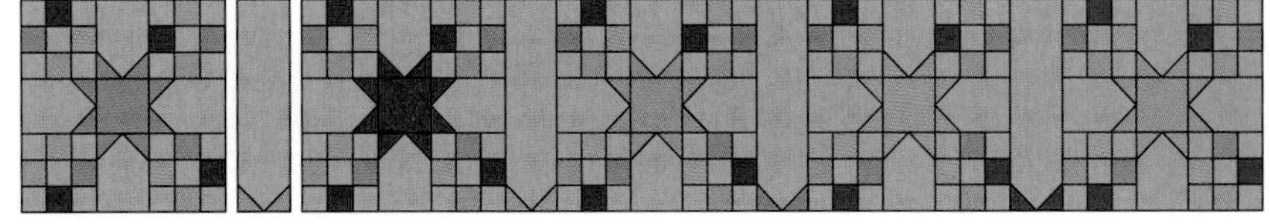

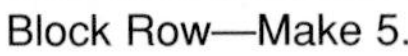

Block Row—Make 5.

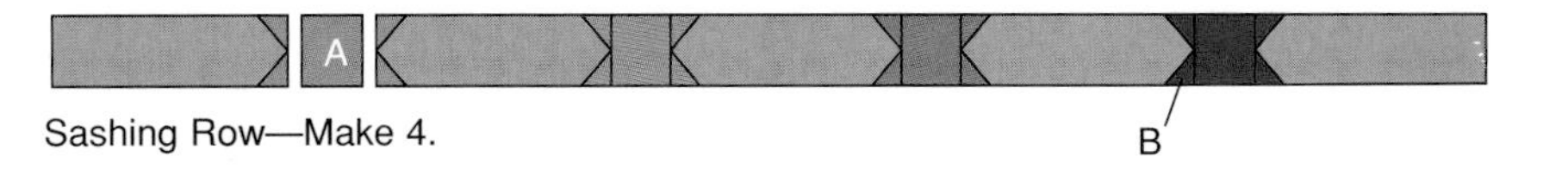

Sashing Row—Make 4.

3. From remaining colored strips, cut 8 (2") B squares to go with each colored sashing square. Use diagonal-corner method to sew 2 B squares to 1 or both ends of each sashing strip as needed *(Diagram B)*. As each sashing strip is completed, add it to layout between blocks and between block rows, so that each sashing square is surrounded by 8 star points *(Row Assembly Diagram)*.

3. Join units in each row. Join rows to complete quilt center.

❖QUILT SMART❖

Diagonal-Corners Quick-Piecing Method

The diagonal-corners technique turns squares into sewn triangles with just a stitch and a snip. This method is especially helpful when the corner triangle is very small, because it's easier to handle a square than a small triangle. And by sewing squares to squares, you don't have to guess where seam allowances match, which can be difficult with triangles.

1. A seam guide helps you sew diagonal lines without having to mark the fabric. Draw a line on graph paper. Place the paper on the sewing machine throatplate; lower needle onto line *(Photo A)*. (Remove presser foot if necessary to see what you're doing.) Use a ruler or a T-square to verify that line is parallel to needle or edges of throatplate. Tape paper in place. Trim paper as needed to clear needle and feed dogs.

2. Match small corner square to 1 corner of the base fabric, right sides facing. Align top tip of the small square with the needle and the bottom tip with seam guide. Stitch a seam from tip to tip, keeping bottom tip of small square in line with seam guide *(Photo B)*.
3. Press corner square in half at seam *(Photo C)*.
4. Trim seam allowance to ¼" *(Photo D)*.

Repeat procedure as needed to add a diagonal corner to 2, 3, or 4 corners of base fabric.

A

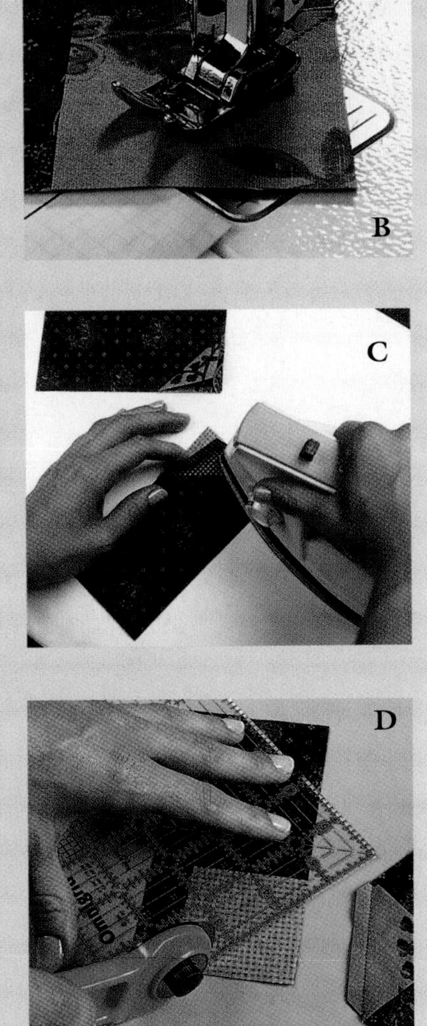
B
C
D

Borders
1. From print border fabric, cut 8 (2"-wide) strips. Join pairs of strips end-to-end to get 4 (88"-long) borders.
2. Join 2"-wide black strips in same manner. Sew a black border strip to each print border.
3. Sew a 3½" x 90" black strip on remaining side of each print border strip, centering length of outer strip. Press all seam allowances toward black.
4. Sew borders to edges of quilt. Miter border corners.

Quilting and Finishing
1. Layer backing, batting, and quilt top. Baste.
2. Quilt as desired. On quilt shown, patchwork is outline-quilted. A purchased stencil was used to mark a Celtic knot design quilted in black areas formed by sashing and adjacent blocks. Parallel lines, 1½" apart, are quilted in sashing strips and borders.
3. Make 9½ yards of straight-grain binding from reserved strips. Bind quilt edges.

Color Variations

Night Lights is such a quick and easy quilt to make, and it can shine in many different color schemes. Here are a few ideas to take to your scrap bag.

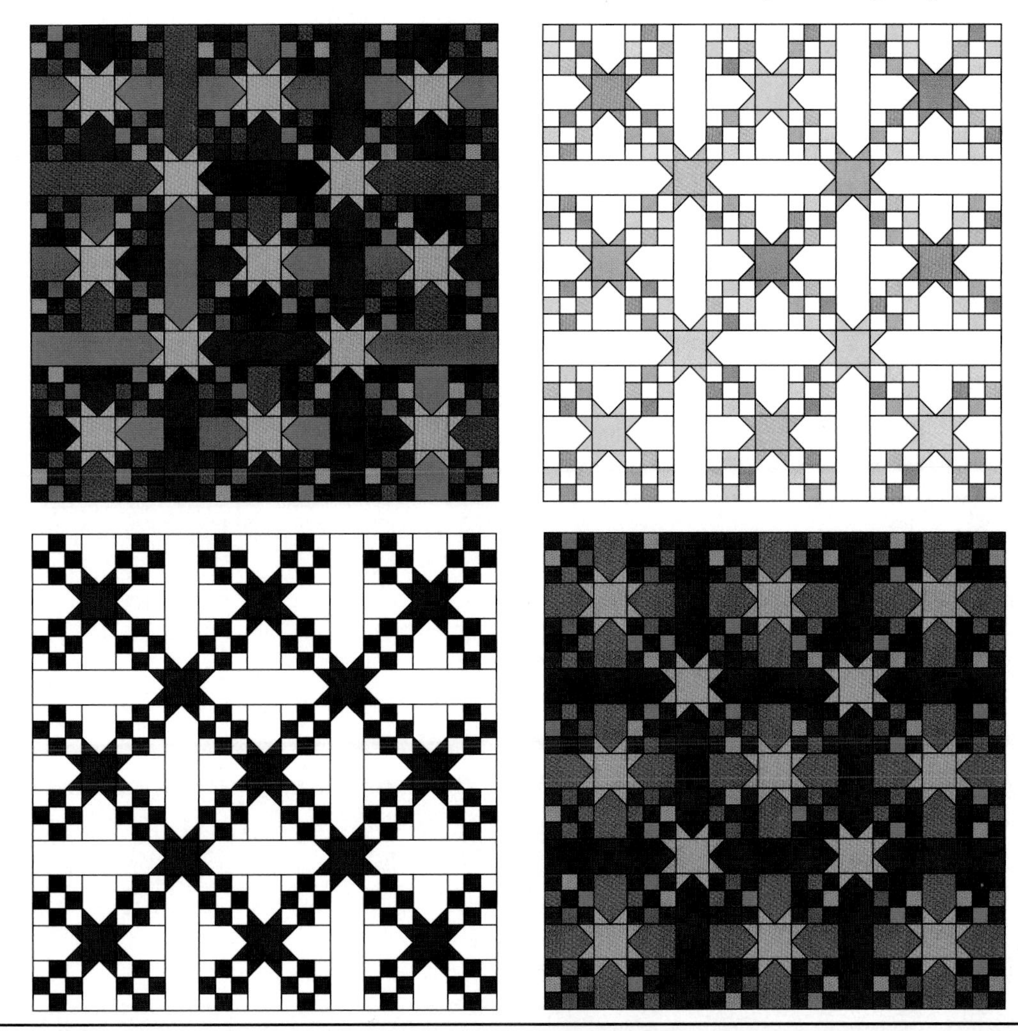

❖QUILT SMART❖

Make a Signature Patch

It's important to sign and date your quilt for posterity. Most antique quilts offer few clues about their origin, leaving empty pages where there could be history about individuals and family.

Incorporating a name or a date in the quilting is a time-honored method, as is embroidering them on the quilt top or backing. Andi Perejda of Arroyo Grande, California, appliquéd a leftover block on the back of *Perennials* (see page 129), adding information about the origin of the vintage materials used in the quilt.

A practical label is a piece of fabric, hemmed on all sides, on which you write or embroider desired information. For writing, use a fine-tipped permanent pen. Press freezer paper to the back of the fabric to stabilize it for writing; then peel it off when the writing is complete. Hand-sew the label to the quilt back.

Milltown Quilters
Columbia, Maryland

Monday is quilting day for the Milltown Quilters. The current members, 71 strong, meet weekly to share their lives and the love of quilting. "We've been quilting together for more than 25 years!" says member Lynn Jourdan.

The Milltown Quilters are involved in various projects to share their quilts with the community, including making friendship quilts for numerous charities. The members met their greatest challenge a few years ago when they made an oversized quilt for a local production of the play "The Quilters" in less than four weeks. That quilt is now loaned to productions across the country.

"We've been quilting together for more than 25 years!"

In alternate years, the Milltown Quilters put on a quilt show to share their work with the public. A portion of the proceeds from the raffle quilt is donated to the church that houses their weekly meetings, and the balance is dedicated to bringing national and local teachers in for education programs.

Spring Delight
1999

The Milltown Quilters' *Spring Delight* heralds a time of blue skies and perky tulips, when something new comes along nearly every day.

Lynn Jourdan originally designed the tulip block for a sampler quilt. But just when the group started to wonder what pattern to use for their next raffle quilt, one member brought in a block she'd made from Lynn's design.

"Everyone fell in love with the swirling tulip appliqué on a sky blue background," Lynn says.

The decision made, members refined and redrafted the block to set it on point. Shoppers scoured local shops for just the right fabrics. Milltown member Pat Brousil distributed instructions for making her dimensional dogwood blossoms. Then the sewing began and 12 blocks were soon set together within a flowing vine border.

The quilting designs (see patterns, pages 20 and 21) were inspired by graceful curves on a picture frame.

Spring Delight won second place/group quilts at the 1999 Maryland State Fair. It is owned by raffle winner, Mr. Leslie "Bug" Flowers, Jr., of Cary, North Carolina.

Spring Delight

Finished Size
Quilt: 81½" x 102½"
Blocks: 12 (14" x 14")

Materials
7 yards blue fabric*
2½ yards green print (includes binding)
1 yard dark green for vines
1⅛ yards *each* white and light pink for dogwood blossoms
¾ yard pink
½ yard yellow
⅛ yard light green for yo-yos
Small scraps of assorted dark green print fabrics for leaves
3 yards 90"-wide backing
Template material
¼"-wide bias pressing bar
* *Note:* Prewashed fabric must be full 44" wide for yardage to be adequate. If fabric is narrower, you need at least another yard.

Pieces to Cut
Make templates for patterns A–G on page 20. Cut pieces in order listed to make best use of yardage. Whenever possible, pieces are listed in order needed, so you don't have to cut all fabric at once. Cut all strips cross-grain except borders as noted.

From blue fabric
- 6 (14½"-wide) strips. From these, cut 18 (14½") squares.
- 2 (10" x 110") and 2 (10" x 90") lengthwise border strips.
- 3 (22¼") squares. Cut each square in quarters diagonally to get a total of 10 setting triangles (and 2 extra).
- 2 (12") squares. Cut each square in half diagonally to get 4 corner triangles.

Spring Delight Block—Make 12.

From green print
- 4 (7½"-wide) strips. From these, cut 48 of Pattern B.
- 11 (1¼"-wide) strips. From 9 of these, cut 24 (1¼" x 14½") strips and 2 (1¼" x 16") strips for sashing.
- 1 (32") square for binding.
- 8 (1¼" x 32") sashing strips, cut from piece leftover from binding square.

From dark green
- 3 (4½"-wide) strips. Trim a 4½" triangle from 1 corner of each strip *(Diagram A)*. Measuring from cut edge, cut ¾"-wide diagonal strips as shown to get a total of 84 strips for flower stems.
- 1 (20") square for border vine.

Use remaining dark green fabric for A and E leaves.

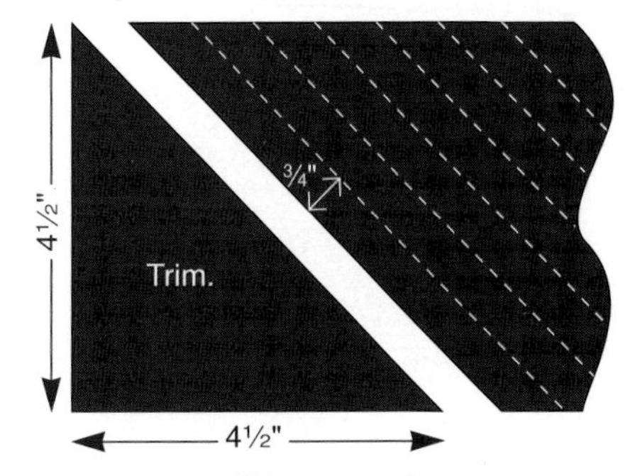

Diagram A

From white and *light pink*
- 16 (2½"-wide) strips of each color. From these, cut 64 (2½" x 10") strips of each color for dogwood blossoms.

From pink
- 53 of Pattern C.
- 53 of Pattern D.

From yellow
- 39 of Pattern C.
- 39 of Pattern D.

From light green
- 64 of Pattern G.

From green scraps
- 96 of Pattern A.
- 82 of Pattern E.

Block Assembly
1. Fold 1 blue square in half vertically, horizontally, and diagonally and crease to make placement lines for appliqué.
2. Align vertical and horizontal creases with lines of pattern (page 20). Lightly trace pattern details onto fabric square.
3. For each block, select 8 A, 4 B, 2 yellow C, 2 yellow D, 2 pink C, 2 pink D, and 4 dark green stem strips.
4. Referring to *Block Diagram*, position a prepared D piece on vertical and horizontal placement lines about 1⅛" from center point of block. Pin C, A, and B pieces in place.
5. Fold each stem strip over bias pressing bar, right sides out, centering raw edges on 1 flat side of bar. Press. Tuck 1 end of stem under C piece; then curve stem around to A leaves.
6. When satisfied with placement of all pieces, start with stem and appliqué pieces in place in alphabetical order.

7. Referring to Quilt Smart on page 18, make 4 dogwood blossoms for each block. Sew blossoms in place to complete block.
8. Make 12 blocks.

Quilt Top Assembly

1. Lay out blocks and setting squares in 6 diagonal rows *(Quilt Assembly Diagram)*. Insert 14½" sashing strips between blocks and at ends of each row as shown. Do not add setting triangles yet.
2. Join blocks and sashing strips in each row.
3. For rows 1 and 6, join a 16" sashing strip to outside edge of block. Complete these rows with setting triangles and corner triangles as shown. Press seam allowances toward sashings.
4. Piece 32" green strips end-to-end to make a sashing strip long enough for each block row. Sew pieced sashing strip to edge of row as shown *(Quilt Assembly Diagram);* then add setting triangles and corner triangles to complete each row. Press seam allowances toward sashing.
5. Join rows to complete center section of quilt.

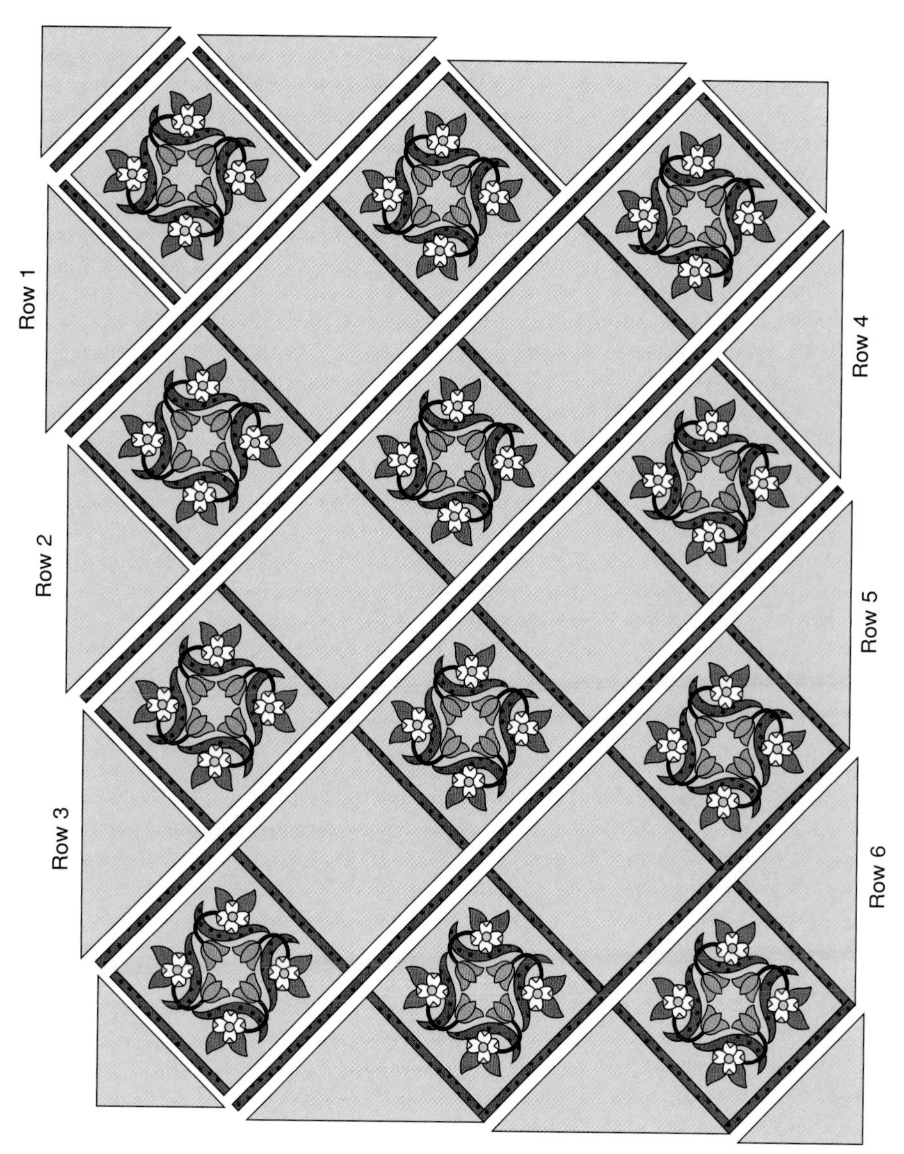

Quilt Assembly Diagram

Borders

1. See page 141 for tips on sewing a mitered border. Stitch border strips to quilt edges and miter corners. Press seam allowances toward border.
2. On each edge of quilt, find center of each setting triangle and place a pin 1½" above border seam line. These indicate low points of vine. For high points, measure from border seam line at sashing corners to place a pin 3" from raw edge of border.
3. Follow directions on page 144 to make 11 yards (396") of ¾"-wide continuous bias from 20" square of green print fabric.
4. Fold bias around pressing bar, right side out, centering raw edges on flat side of bar. Press entire length of continuous bias.
5. For each side border, cut a length of bias 110" long. Match center of bias strip with center of border and pin. Curve bias from pin to pin, creating hills and valleys. At corners, curve bias around to opposite side of mitered seam.
6. For top and bottom borders, cut bias strips 88" long. Starting at center, pin bias in place.
7. Referring to photo on page 19, pin 16 dogwood blossoms on vine. Pin leaves and flowers in place, adding curving stems as shown. Pin pink C/D tulips at corners, straddling miter. There should be about ½" between tips of C pieces at corners. Pin E leaves on vine as shown or as desired.
8. When satisfied with placement of all border elements, appliqué vine and pieces in place. Press.

❖QUILT SMART❖

3-Dimensional Dogwood Blossoms

1. On wrong side of 1 (2½" x 10") white piece, trace 4 of Pattern F. Leave space between petals for seam allowance.

2. Match marked piece with a light pink strip, right sides facing. Stitch on drawn line of each petal, leaving bottom of each petal open.

3. Cut out petals, adding a scant ¼" seam allowance around stitching. Trim tip of petal to ⅛". Turn right side out and finger-press.

4. Thread hand-sewing needle with 24" of white thread. Hand-sew gathering stitches through both layers, ⅛" from bottom edge of first petal. Pull to gather petal. Backstitch to secure gathers. Do not clip thread. Use same thread to gather remaining 3 petals.

5. Arrange 4 gathered petals in a circle *(Diagram 1)*. Tack first and last petals together at base of petals; knot thread to secure. Tack flower in place on background fabric, white side up.

6. Turn under seam allowance on each G circle. Use matching thread to hand-sew a gathering stitch ⅛" from raw edge of circle *(Diagram 2)*. Overlap first and last stitches.

7. Pull thread to gather circle tight *(Diagram 3)*. Secure end of thread with backstitches or knot. Flatten gathered circle with gathers in center as shown.

8. Use thread end to sew yo-yo in place at center of flower.

9. Fold over tips of each petal to expose pink fabric; tack in place.

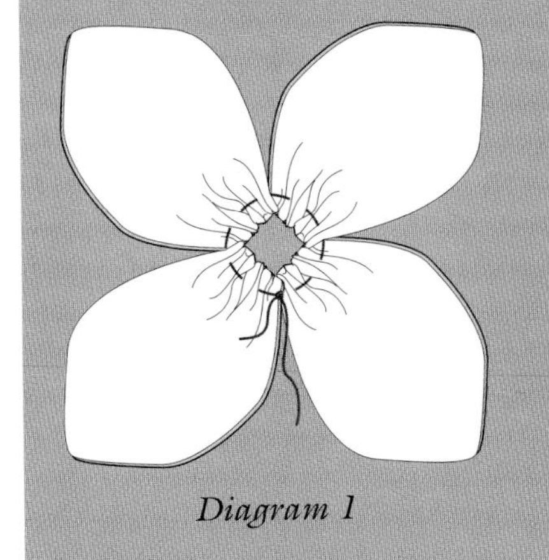

Diagram 1

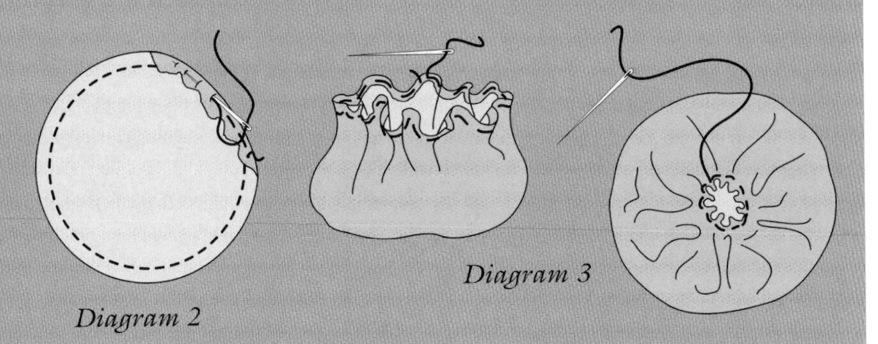

Diagram 2

Diagram 3

Quilting and Finishing

1. Mark quilting designs on quilt top. On quilt shown, appliqué and piecing are quilted in-the-ditch. Each appliquéd block has a 1¼" grid of cross-hatching quilted in the center and a heart pattern quilted around appliqué (see block pattern, page 20). Quilting pattern for open blocks is on page 21. Border is quilted in straight lines, 1¼" apart.

2. Layer backing, batting, and quilt top. Quilt as desired.

3. Make 10½ yards of bias or straight-grain binding. Bind quilt edges.

Color Variations

If blue leaves you cold, plant your *Spring Delight* quilt in some other color scheme. Our ideas for alternative background colors are sunny summer yellow and dramatic black.

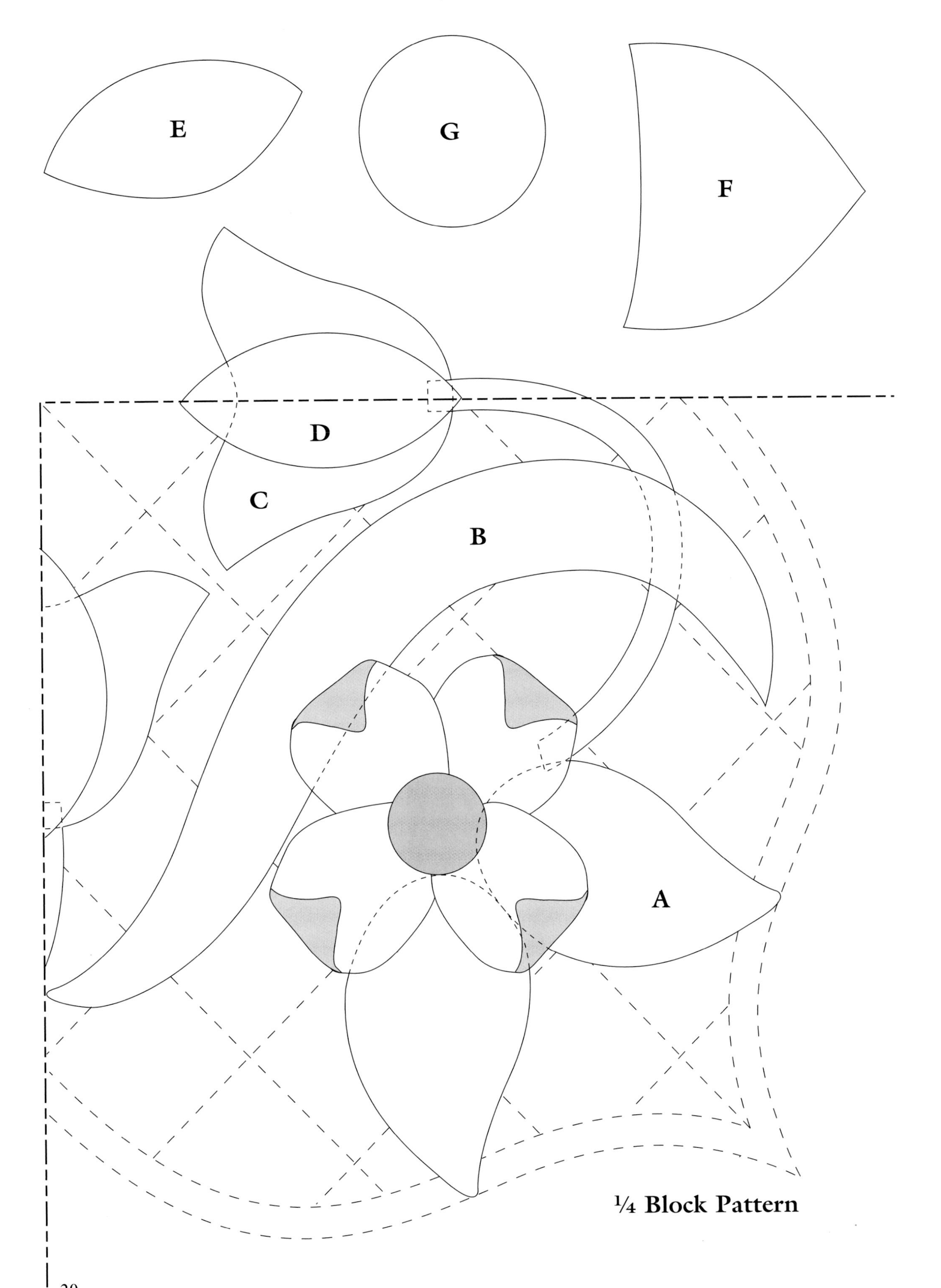

¼ Block Pattern

Quilting Design

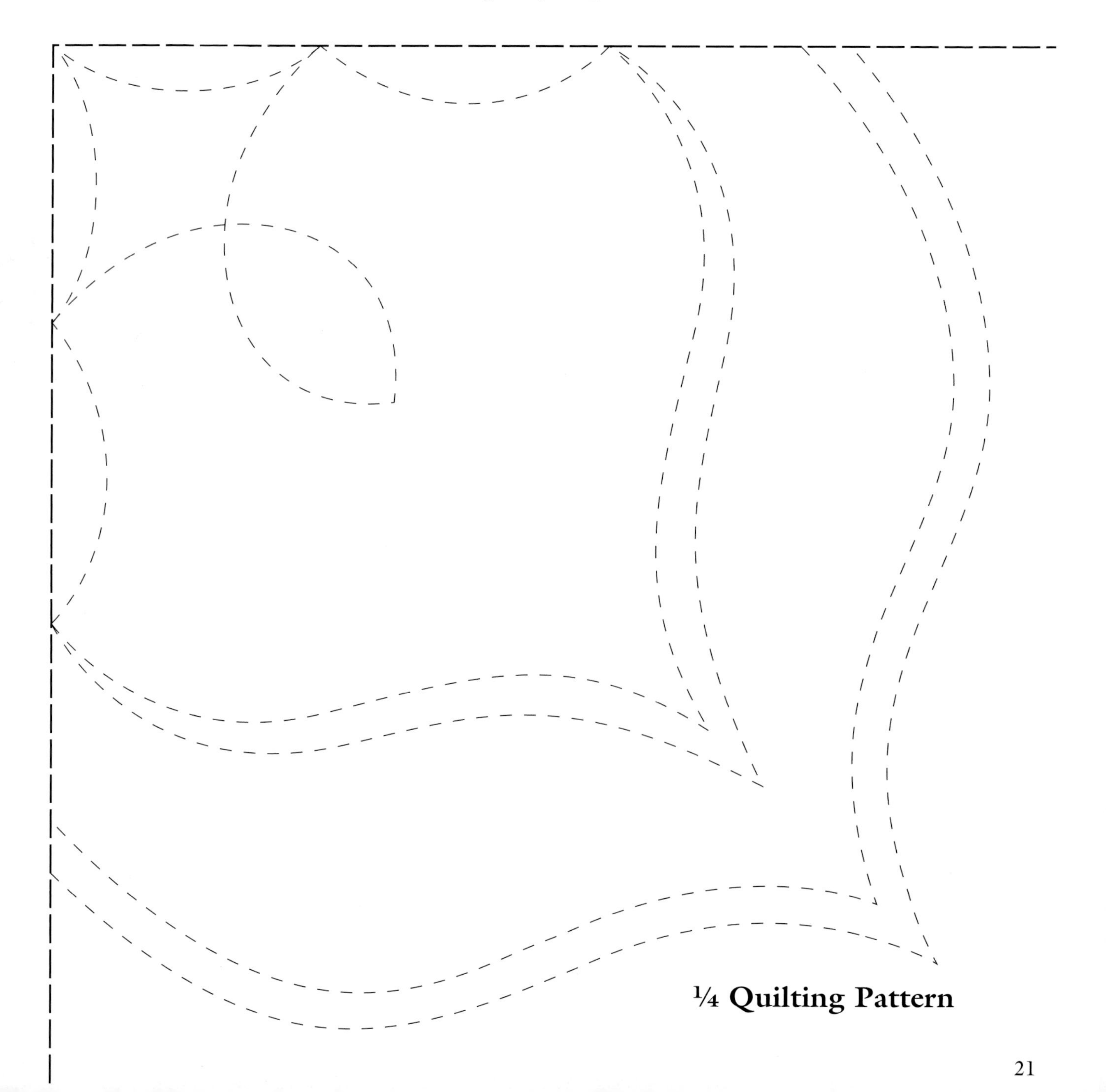

¼ Quilting Pattern

Jan Magee

Denver, Colorado

Few people are as lucky as Jan Magee—her art and passion for quilting recently became her profession as well.

From a contributor to *Quilter's Newsletter Magazine,* Jan became features editor there in late 1999. "Now, all my waking hours are centered around quilting," Jan says. "I'm surrounded by the traditions, innovative techniques, and the world's finest quilts."

"All my waking hours are centered around quilting."

Jan took her first quilting class in 1988. The teacher was machine-quilting authority Harriet Hargrave, so it's not surprising that Jan fell in love with machine techniques. And the graphic possibilities in quilts appealed to her art background. No stranger to sewing, Jan says, "I've always loved the process. Making quilts adds emotional and aesthetic layers to the process, making it a life's passion."

Spending the day surrounded by wonderful quilts fuels Jan's own works. "I'm always eager to get home to translate all that inspiration into my own designs and art quilts," she says.

Jan is a member of the Columbine Quilt Guild, Front Range Contemporary Quilters, and the Colorado Quilting Council.

Lime & Chile

1999

Hot, hot, *hot!* A fondness for hot peppers, hot weather, and hot color stirred Jan to make this sizzling wall quilt. Even if the weather doesn't get all that hot in Denver, Jan's penchant for peppers gives her quilts real spice.

Lime & Chile is one of a series of pepper quilts. Jan says she finds inspiration in the shapes and colors of the multifaceted pepper. And she loves to delve into her collection of fabrics to find the right ones for the many pepper varieties.

The offbeat block in *Lime & Chile* gave Jan a challenge. "Any four-sided figure can be set together," she says. "I hoped a skewed block would provide an energy to match the subject matter. It did!"

Lime & Chile was juried into the 1999 International Quilt Association show and the 2000 American Quilters' Society show.

Lime & Chile

Finished Size

Quilt: 64" x 67"
Blocks: 25 (11½" x 11¾")

Materials

13 (18" x 22") fat quarters of assorted bright green fabrics*
25 (8") squares for chile backgrounds
25 (4½") squares for chiles
25 (2½") green squares for chile stems (optional)
2⅛ yards border fabric
¼ yard fabric for border stripes
1⅜ yards muslin
¾ yard binding fabric
3⅞ yards backing fabric
Paper-backed fusible web (optional)
25 sheets (12" x 14") of lightweight tissue or tracing paper
14" x 20" sheet template plastic

**Note:* Recommended yardage for purchasing guidelines. Quilt shown has far more than 13 fabrics; use as many as your scraps allow. Yardage requirements may vary, so estimated yardage includes enough fabric to cut at least 1 more strip set if needed.

Paper Foundations

Note: You can make this block without a foundation, but we recommend this method.

1. Trace Pattern X (page 27) onto plain white paper.
2. Using a photocopy machine, enlarge drawing 169%. Make a template of enlarged pattern.
3. Trace template outline onto tissue paper. Use a ruler to mark a ¼" seam allowance around outside edge of each outline.

Block A—Make 13.

Block B—Make 12.

Chile Appliqué

1. Make templates of chile, stem, and Pattern X. Mark outline of Template X on wrong side of each 8" square. Mark a ¼" seam allowance around outside edge of each outline. Cut out patches on outer line.
2. For traditional appliqué, trace chile template onto *right* side of each 4½"-square chile fabric. Cut out chiles, adding a 3/16" seam allowance around each piece. For Block A, appliqué chiles onto 13 patches as shown on pattern. For Block B, turn remaining 12 patches upside down and appliqué.
3. For fusible appliqué, turn chile template over and trace reversed image onto paper side of fusible web. Follow manufacturer's instructions to fuse web to wrong side of chile fabrics. Cut out chiles on drawn line. For Block A, fuse chiles onto 13 patches as shown on pattern. For Block B, rotate remaining 12 patches upside down and fuse. Set sewing machine to a small zigzag stitch and machine appliqué each chile in place.
4. Stems can be appliquéd by hand or by machine in same manner. On quilt shown, Jan Magee used machine embroidery to fill a traced outline of each stem. Complete stems as desired.

Block Assembly

1. From fat quarters, cut approximately 108 (22"-long) strips, varying strip widths from 1" wide to 2½" wide.
2. Use strips of different widths to make a strip set about 16" wide *(Diagram A)*. Make 12 strip sets, varying fabrics.
3. Cut vertical slices from 2 or 3 strip sets to begin with, again varying widths or angles of each cut as shown.
4. Position 1 chile patch right side up on a foundation. Patch does not have to be centered.
5. Select 1 strip-set slice and place it against 1 side of chile patch, right sides facing. Sew ¼"

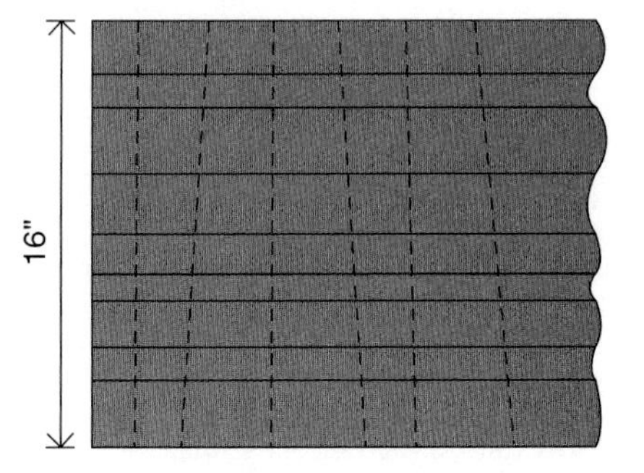

Diagram A

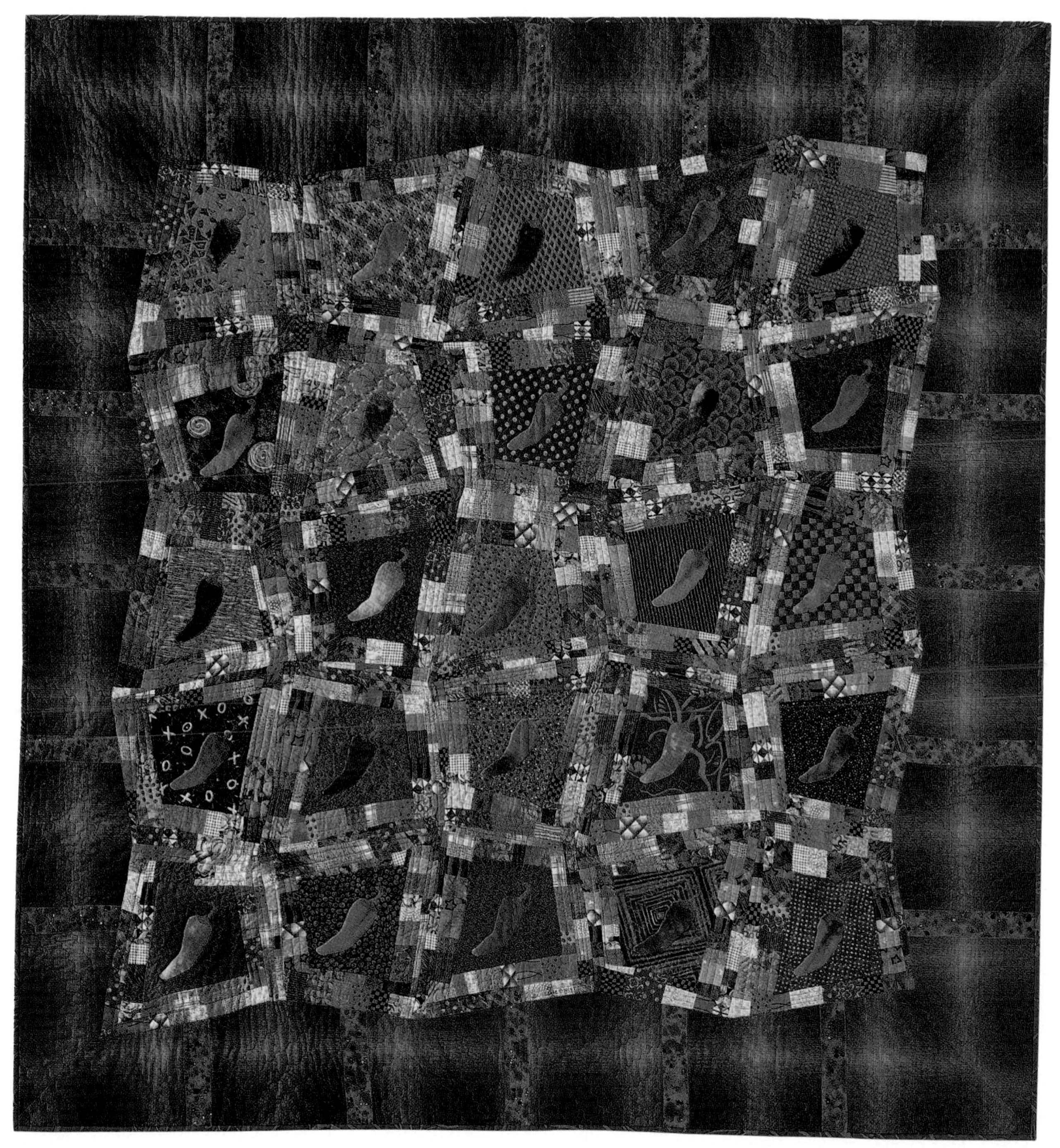

seam through fabric and paper. Press strip to right side; then trim slice at both ends to align with chile patch *(Diagram B)*.

6. Add another slice to next side of chile patch in same manner *(Diagram C)*. Continue adding slices of different fabrics and widths, log-cabin style, around center patch *(Diagram D)*.

7. Add a second round of green slices in same manner, covering remaining area of foundation. Trim any excess fabric even with outside edge of foundation.

8. Make 13 of Block A and 12 of Block B. Do not remove foundations yet.

Diagram B

Diagram C

Diagram D

Quilt Top Assembly

1. For Row 1, join 3 of Block A and 2 of Block B *(Row Assembly Diagram)*, stitching on drawn seam lines of adjacent foundations. Be very careful not to stitch *into* any seam allowance so seams will be free for setting-in rows. Make 3 of Row 1.

2. For Row 2, join 3 of Block B and 2 of Block A as shown. Make 2 of Row 2.

3. Referring to photo, join rows 1-2-1-2-1, setting in each angled seam across row. (See page 77 for tips on sewing set-in seams.)

4. Gently tear foundations off back of each block, being careful not to tear stitching. Press.

Row Assembly Diagram

Borders

1. Press muslin. Trim muslin to 44½" x 47½".

2. Cut 4 (10"-wide) lengthwise strips from border fabric. Mark center of each strip.

3. Referring to page 141 for tips on stitching a mitered seam, sew border strips to muslin and miter corners *(Diagram F)*. Trim excess fabric from mitered seam and press.

4. Lay assembled blocks on border foundation. Use pins to mark border strips at center (more or less) of each outside block. This is where stripes are placed.

5. For traditional appliqué, cut 25 (2" x 8½") stripes and turn edges under; for machine appliqué, cut 25 (1½" x 8½") stripes. Position stripes on borders and appliqué.

6. Pin assembled blocks on border foundation. Turn under seam allowance on outside edge of blocks. Make sure raw edges of border and stripes are covered and no muslin is showing. Appliqué by hand or by machine.

Quilting and Finishing

1. Assemble backing. Layer backing, batting, and quilt top. Baste.

2. Quilt as desired. Quilt shown is machine-quilted with wavy lines in border, contrasting rows of zigzag stitch in chile patches, and concentric lines on blocks that echo shape of center patch.

3. Make 7½ yards of bias or straight-grain binding. Bind quilt edges.

Diagram F

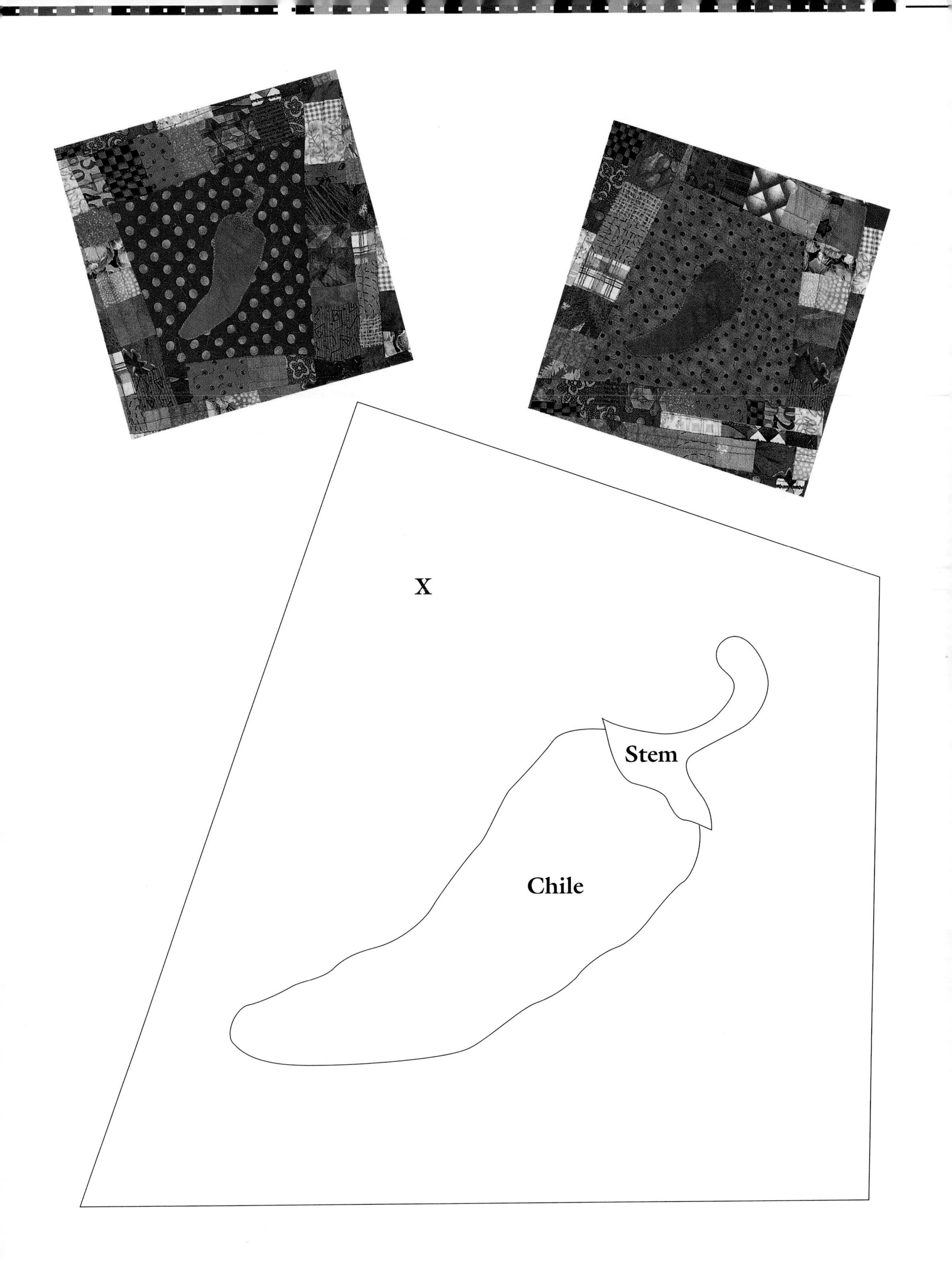
X
Stem
Chile

Susan Bradley
Boerne, Texas

Susan Bradley's passion for fabric and color comes from within. Unlike those who learned at a mother's knee, there is no history of quilting in Susan's family.

"I have no idea where the love of fabric comes from," muses Susan. "But it is as much a part of me as the color of my eyes." A clinical social worker by day, Susan spends free time immersed in color. "I love my work, but its results are intangible and sometimes transient," Susan says. So traditions mean a lot to Susan. She says, "The history of women and quiltmaking adds a connection to the past, which I value." Her quilts "will be part of that ongoing history long after I am gone."

Susan is a long-time member of the Greater San Antonio Quilt Guild.

The Pepper Quilt
1998

Other plants may wither under the summer sun, but hardy pepper varieties thrive in Tom Bradley's garden.

Bell, jalapeño, Thai, and habanero peppers bring festive color into the Bradleys' home. Susan says, "I love to put them in white bowls around the house, like other people display flowers."

Susan called on the clear, bright colors of these garden favorites for *The Pepper Quilt.* Using piecing techniques for feathered stars popularized by Marsha McCloskey, Susan machine-pieced 16 blocks in different combinations of hot red, cool green, and sunny cheddar-colored fabrics.

Susan created an original design for the border, which is appliquéd by hand. Cross-hatching and feathered wreaths of meticulous hand quilting complete the quilt.

In 1999, *The Pepper Quilt* was Best of Show at the Greater San Antonio Quilt Guild's biennial show and won a second place ribbon at the International Quilt Association's Houston show.

The Pepper Quilt

Finished Size

Quilt: 81¼" x 81¼"
Blocks: 16 (16³⁄₁₆" x 16³⁄₁₆")

Materials

16 (5½") squares for star centers
16 (5") squares for star inner triangles*
16 (3½" x 42") strips for star points*
32 (1¾" x 42") strips for star feathers, contrasting feathers, and diamonds*
5½ yards beige tone-on-tone background fabric
¾ yard green for vines
Assorted small scraps of green, red, and gold fabrics for border leaves and flowers*
1 yard binding fabric
2½ yards 90"-wide backing
Template material
¼"-wide and ⅜"-wide bias pressing bars

* *Note:* As in all scrap quilts, these yardages are recommendations. Use your own scraps and fabric placement as desired.

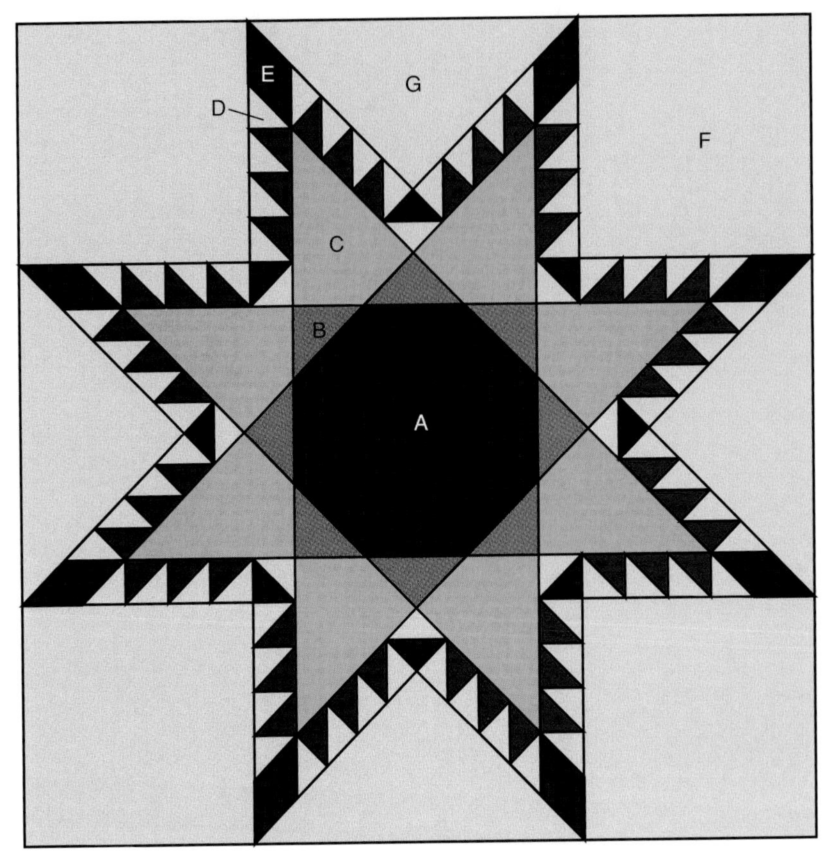

Feathered Star Block—Make 16.

Pieces to Cut

Because of their odd size, we recommend traditional cutting for most pieces. Make templates for patterns on pages 33 and 34.

Cut pieces in order listed to make best use of yardage. Pieces are listed in order needed for each star, so you don't have to cut all the fabrics at once. Save remaining scraps for border leaves and flowers.

From each *star center fabric*
- 1 of Pattern A.

From each *inner triangle fabric*
- 8 of Pattern B.

From each *star point fabric*
- 8 of Pattern C.

From each *of 16 feather fabrics*
- 24 (1¾") squares for D.

From each *of 16 feather fabrics*
- 4 (1¾") squares for D.
- 8 of Pattern E.

From background fabric
- 4 (8½" x 90") lengthwise strips for border.
- 2 (8" x 42") strips. From these and fabric leftover from border, cut 16 (8") squares. Cut each square in quarters diagonally to get 64 G triangles.
- 21 (1¾" x 42") strips. From these and fabric leftover from previous steps, cut 576 (1¾") squares for D feathers.
- 8 (5¼" x 42") strips. From these, cut 64 (5¼") F squares.

Block Assembly

In this block, partial seams allow us to avoid set-in seams. In diagrams, brackets indicate seams that are partially sewn and completed later. Begin and end these seams with backstitching.

1. For each block, select 1 set

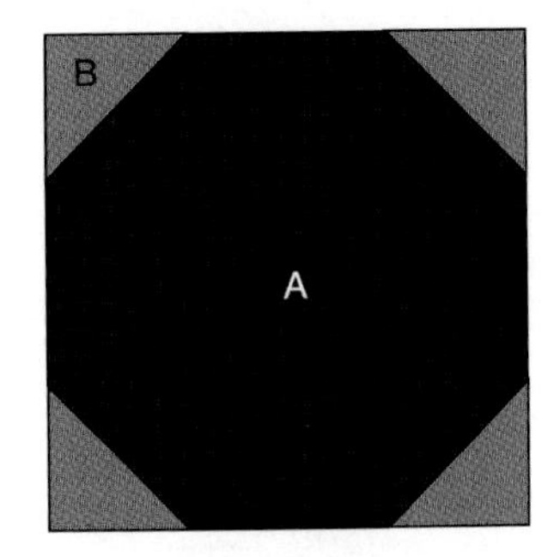

Diagram A

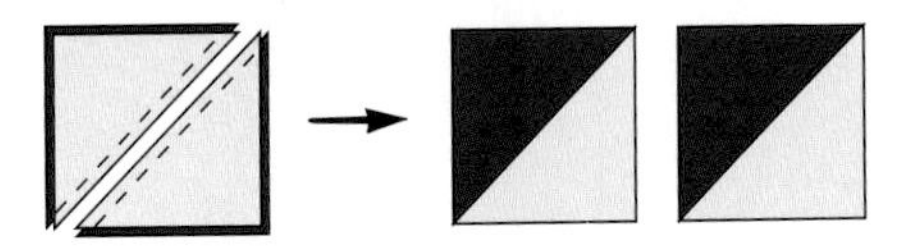

Diagram B

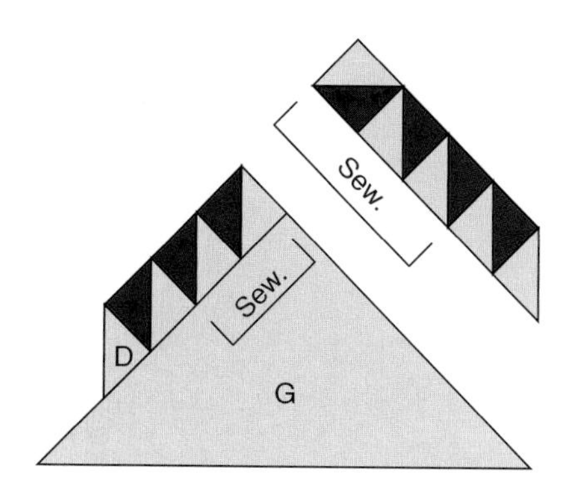

Diagram C

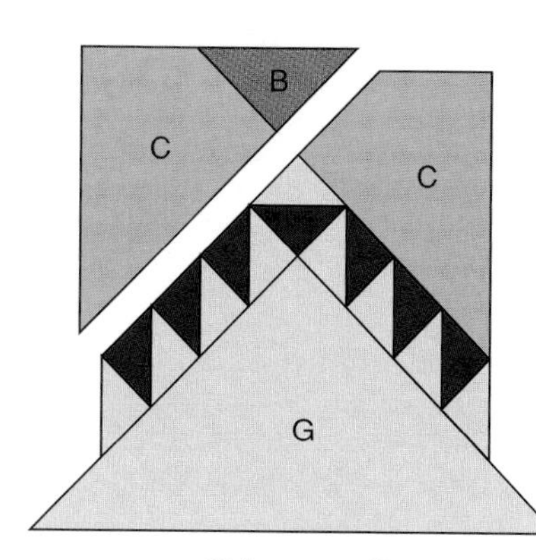

Diagram D

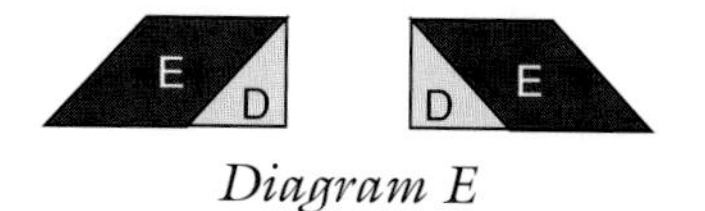

Diagram E

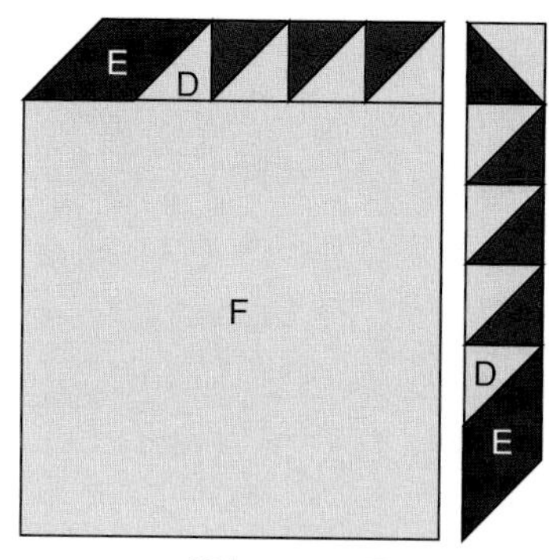

Diagram F

(8 matching pieces) *each* of B, C, and E. Choose matched sets of 24 D squares for feathers, 4 contrasting D squares (for star corners), 1 A, and 36 D squares of background fabric. You will also need 4 *each* of F and G.
2. Sew B triangles to each corner of A *(Diagram A)*. Press seam allowances toward Bs.
3. Match each colored D square with a beige D square, right sides facing. Cut squares in half diagonally through both layers *(Diagram B)*. Chain-piece seams to get 48 D triangle-squares for feathers and 8 D triangle-squares for star corners. Press seam allowances toward darker fabrics.
4. You should have 8 beige D squares left. Cut these in half diagonally to get 16 D triangles.
5. For side unit, select 6 D triangle-squares. Join 3 squares in a row; then add a D triangle to 1 end *(Diagram C)*. Starting at corner, sew row to 1 leg of G with partial seam as shown. Press seam allowance toward G. Join remaining triangle-squares; then add a D triangle and a contrasting D triangle-square to row as shown. Join row to second leg of G with partial seam.
6. Sew a C piece to 1 side of unit *(Diagram D)*. Press seam allowance toward C. Sew a B triangle to second C; then add B/C unit to remaining edge as shown to complete side unit. Make 4 side units.
7. For corner unit, join D triangles and E diamonds *(Diagram E)*, making 2 mirror-image units as shown. Join 2 rows of 3 D triangle-squares as before. Add D/E units to row ends as shown *(Diagram F)*. Sew 1 row to F. Add contrasting triangle-square to remaining row; sew row to adjacent edge of F as shown to complete corner unit. Make 4 corner units.
8. Join 2 side units to sides of center unit *(Block Assembly Diagram)*. Press seam allowances toward center. Sew corner units to remaining side units, making 2 rows as shown. Press seam allowances toward corners.
9. Join rows. Then complete partial seams as shown.

Block Assembly Diagram

Quilt Top Assembly

1. Referring to photo (page 32), lay out blocks in 4 horizontal rows, with 4 blocks in each row. Arrange blocks to get a pleasing balance of color and contrast.
2. Join blocks in each row. Then join rows.

Borders

1. See page 141 for tips on sewing a mitered border. Stitch border strips to quilt edges and miter corners. Press seam allowances toward border.
2. Cut a 25" green square for vine. Follow directions on page 144 to make 13 yards (468") of 1"-wide continuous bias.
3. Fold bias around ⅜"-wide pressing bar, right side out, centering raw edges on flat side of bar. Press entire length of bias.
4. Start pinning bias on border at any point. Referring to photo, meander vine up and down each border, bringing some curves up over border seam line into open

areas of blocks. Note that no 2 corners are quite alike, so just let it flow. Leave vine pinned until other border pieces are in place.

5. From remaining green fabric, make 9½ yards (342") of ⅝"-wide continuous bias for smaller vines. Fold and press bias strip on ¼"-wide pressing bar.

6. From scraps, cut any number and combination of leaves and flowers (see appliqué patterns on page 34). Pin leaves and flowers in place, adding curving stems of narrow bias as desired. Pin a leaf or flower over bias ends to conceal them.

7. Arrange appliqué pieces until you have a configuration that you like. When satisfied with placement, appliqué all pieces in place. Press.

Quilting and Finishing

1. Mark quilting designs on quilt top. On quilt shown, blocks are quilted in-the-ditch and a rosette is quilted in center of each star (see pattern, page 33). Feathered wreath quilted in open areas is a commercial stencil—visit your local quilt shop to look for something similar that is 8"–9" in diameter. Remaining areas of

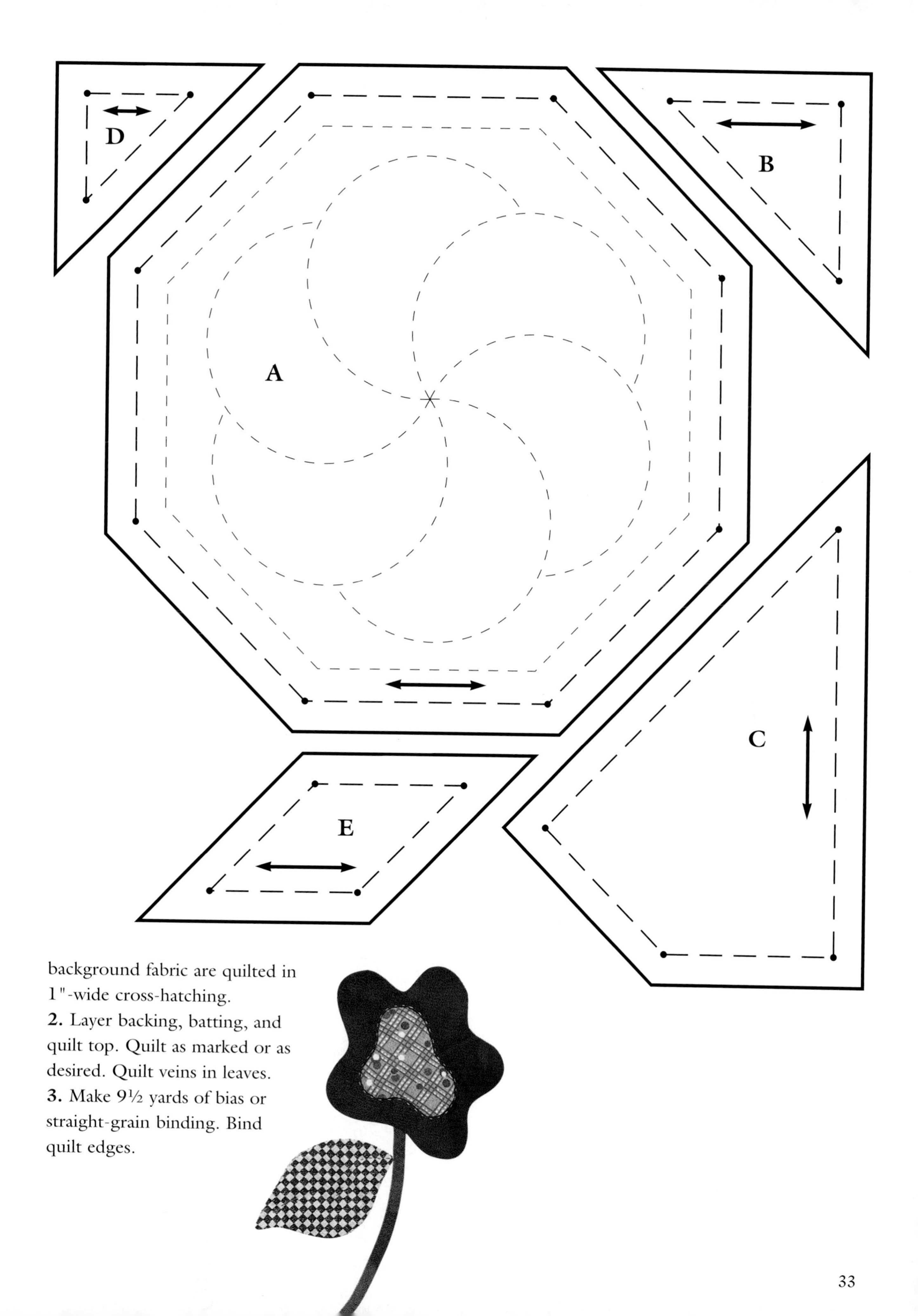

background fabric are quilted in 1"-wide cross-hatching.

2. Layer backing, batting, and quilt top. Quilt as marked or as desired. Quilt veins in leaves.

3. Make 9½ yards of bias or straight-grain binding. Bind quilt edges.

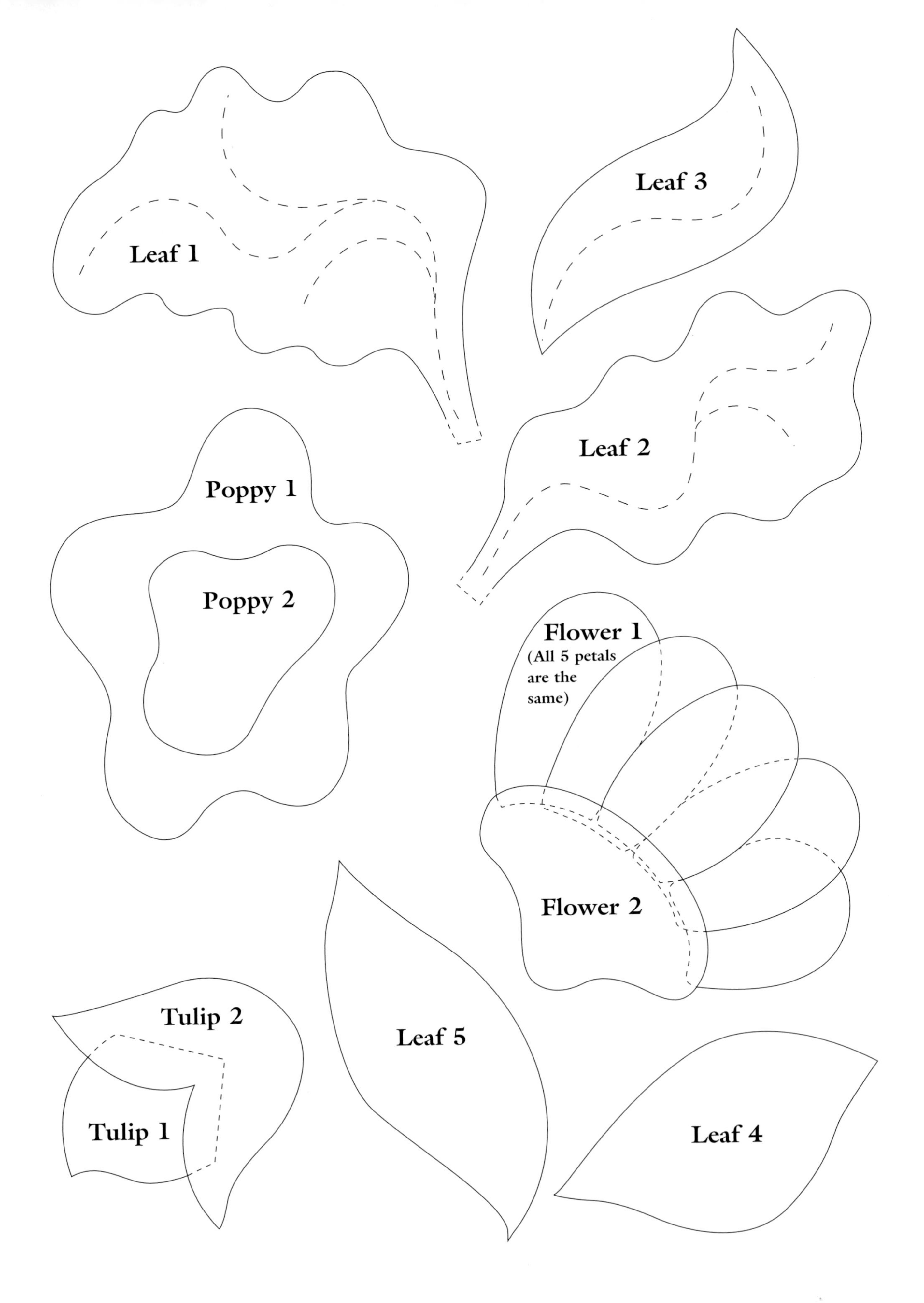
Leaf 1
Leaf 3
Leaf 2
Poppy 1
Poppy 2
Flower 1
(All 5 petals
are the
same)
Flower 2
Tulip 2
Tulip 1
Leaf 5
Leaf 4

Anita Shackelford

Bucyrus, Ohio

Awards and acclaim are all very well and good, and Anita Schackelford's quilts have earned her plenty of both. But her quilts also represent Anita's love of quiltmaking techniques and an abiding respect for the history and traditions of quilts.

"I've been in love with quilts all of my life," Anita says. She learned the basics in the late 1960s from a favorite aunt who was, and still is, a quilt lover and collector. From there, Anita honed her skills "just by doing what I thought made sense." With the revival of quilting's popularity in the late 1970s, Anita became a nationally known teacher and show judge.

"I've been in love with quilts all of my life."

Appliqué is Anita's favorite style of work. She often uses 19th-century dimensional techniques to create original designs and enhances them with fine quilting. She has twice won the Mary Krickbaum Award given annually by the National Quilting Association (NQA) for best hand quilting.

The author of three books published by the American Quilter's Society (AQS), Anita is an NQA member and is currently on the faculty of that group's Quilting Judging Seminar. She is also a charter member of AQS and is active in the American Quilt Study Group, The Appliqué Society, and The Baltimore Appliqué Society, as well as local and regional guilds.

Oak & Acorn

1997

The quiltmaker's love of fabric is evident in this tribute to autumn, the season of richest and deepest color.

A panoply of 115 fabrics, the quilt's fabrics are mostly fall favorites of brown, gold, green, and orange. But Anita added their complementary colors to deepen the palette.

Anita created this original appliqué design for her book *Appliqué with Folded Cutwork* (1999). The appliqué is done in a machine blanket stitch, using contrasting color threads for additional accent.

Oak & Acorn won second place in the scrap quilt category at the 1998 National Quilting Association show and first place/combination quilting at the 1999 Kaleidoscope of Quilts in Toledo, Ohio.

Oak & Acorn

Finished Size
Quilt: 82" x 91"
Blocks: 56 (9" x 9")

Materials
56 (9½") squares for block backgrounds
56 (9") squares for appliqué
2½ yards outer border fabric
⅝ yard gold fabric plus 1 (2½" x 40") strip of second gold fabric for inner border
1 yard binding fabric
5½ yards backing fabric or 2¾ yards 90"-wide backing
Freezer paper or translucent template material
Lightweight paper-backed fusible web (optional)

Freezer-Paper Appliqué
1. Trace half-pattern onto dull side of freezer paper. Do not add seam allowance. Turn paper to trace second half of pattern. Cut out pattern on drawn line.
2. Press shiny side of freezer paper onto right side of 1 appliqué fabric. Cut out appliqué, adding a 3/16" seam allowance all around. Leave pattern in place.
3. Fold 1 background square in half crosswise, lengthwise, and

Oak & Acorn Block—Make 56.

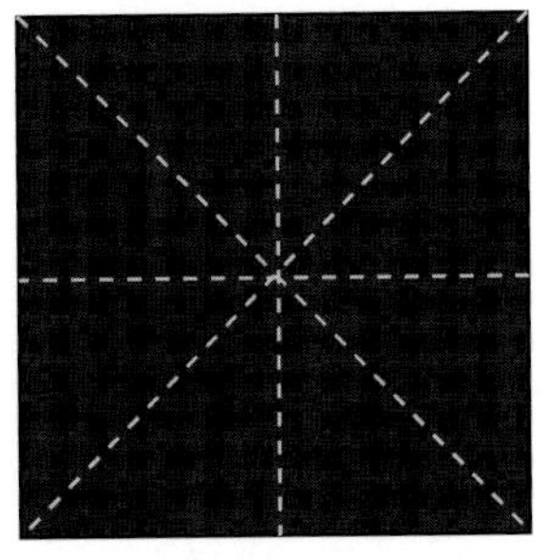

Diagram A

diagonally *(Diagram A)*. Crease folds to make placement guides.
4. Lay appliqué on background square, matching center line of pattern with folds on background square. Pin appliqué in place. Remove paper template when appliqué is complete.
5. Re-use freezer-paper template until it looses its stick (4 or 5 blocks); then make another template. Make 56 blocks.

Fusible Appliqué

1. Trace half-pattern onto template material, including dotted center line. Do not add seam allowance. Turn template to trace second half of pattern. Cut out template on drawn line.
2. Cut an 8½" square of fusible web. Following manufacturer's instructions, fuse web onto wrong side of 1 appliqué fabric.
3. Trace template onto paper side of square. Cut out design on traced line. Remove paper backing and fuse appliqué onto right side of 1 background fabric, being careful to center design on background square.
4. Work a blanket stitch or other decorative stitch over raw edges by hand or by machine.

Quilt Top Assembly

1. Referring to photo, lay out blocks in 8 horizontal rows, with 7 blocks in each row. Arrange blocks to get a pleasing balance of color and contrast.
2. Join blocks in each row. Then join rows.

Borders

1. From main gold fabric, cut 8 (2½" x 32") strips. Piece 2 strips for each inner border.
2. From second gold fabric, cut 4 (2½") squares. Sew a square to both ends of 2 border strips. Stitch borders to top and bottom edges of quilt, easing to fit.
3. From second gold fabric, cut 4 (2½" x 7") strips. Sew these to end of remaining borders. Stitch borders to quilt sides.
4. Cut 4 (7¾" x 84") lengthwise strips from outer border fabric.
5. Measure length of quilt top through middle, including inner borders. Trim 2 outer borders to match length. Sew borders to quilt sides, easing to fit.
6. Measure width of quilt top through middle, including outer borders. Trim remaining borders to match width. Sew borders to top and bottom edges of quilt.

Quilting and Finishing

1. Assemble backing. Layer backing, batting, and quilt top.
2. Quilt as desired. Quilt shown is outline-quilted and a large cable is quilted in outer border. A triangle pattern is quilted in inner border.
3. Make 10 yards of straight-grain or bias binding. Bind edges.

Color Variations

The *Oak & Acorn* design is particularly suited for autumn colors, but that doesn't mean your fabrics can't reach for other seasons. Other ideas shown here are Christmas colorations, pastels, or a monochromatic theme.

Golf is a good walk spoiled.
Golf is an awkward set of bodily contortions designed to produce a graceful result.
Golf is a game whose aim is to hit a very small ball into a very small hole, with weapons singularly ill designed for the purpose.

Sharlot Steen

Elk Horn, Iowa

Sharlot Steen remembers her Grandma Miller was a quilter. "I would sit under the stretcher bars while she and my mother tied her simple one-patch quilts," Sharlot says. "I was fascinated by the many colors and patterns she could make with simple squares."

Now Sharlot is passing the love of quilting on to yet another generation. Her daughters, Meredith and Monica, grew up with quilts and are making their own. "Their college friends are always interested to see what we're working on," Sharlot says, "They often suggest they'd love to have one for graduation or a wedding gift."

"I was fascinated by the many colors and patterns."

Sharlot's adventures in quilting took off when she took a class at a local shop. A stay-at-home mom then, she quickly caught the quilting bug. Sharlot intended her first quilt to have elaborate hand quilting, but "by the time I'd quilted four blocks, I was tired of sitting at that frame," she recalls. "I had visions of seven or eight quilts I wanted to make, and here I was *stuck* with this quilt in the frame." She got the quilt done in time, but has never liked it—she says it's folded up somewhere, "aging."

Once the student, Sharlot is now the teacher at Prairie Star Quilts in Elk Horn. "I meet so many wonderful people from teaching classes," she says. "I especially enjoy teaching at retreats." Sharlot also designs quilts and markets her own pattern line called The Feathered Heart.

Carolina Lily

1998

Sharlot Steen's favorite quilts are golden oldies. "I love traditional patterns that have been passed from generation to generation," she says.

Carolina Lily is Sharlot's latest tribute to the timeless quilts of the 19th century. The classic red and green fabrics continue to please today's quilt lovers at Christmas time.

"I'm happy to see the reproduction fabrics available today that make it possible to achieve the look of old quilts," Sharlot says.

Carolina Lily, quilted by the Manning Catholic Sewing Group, was exhibited at the 1999 National Quilters Association show in Omaha.

Carolina Lily

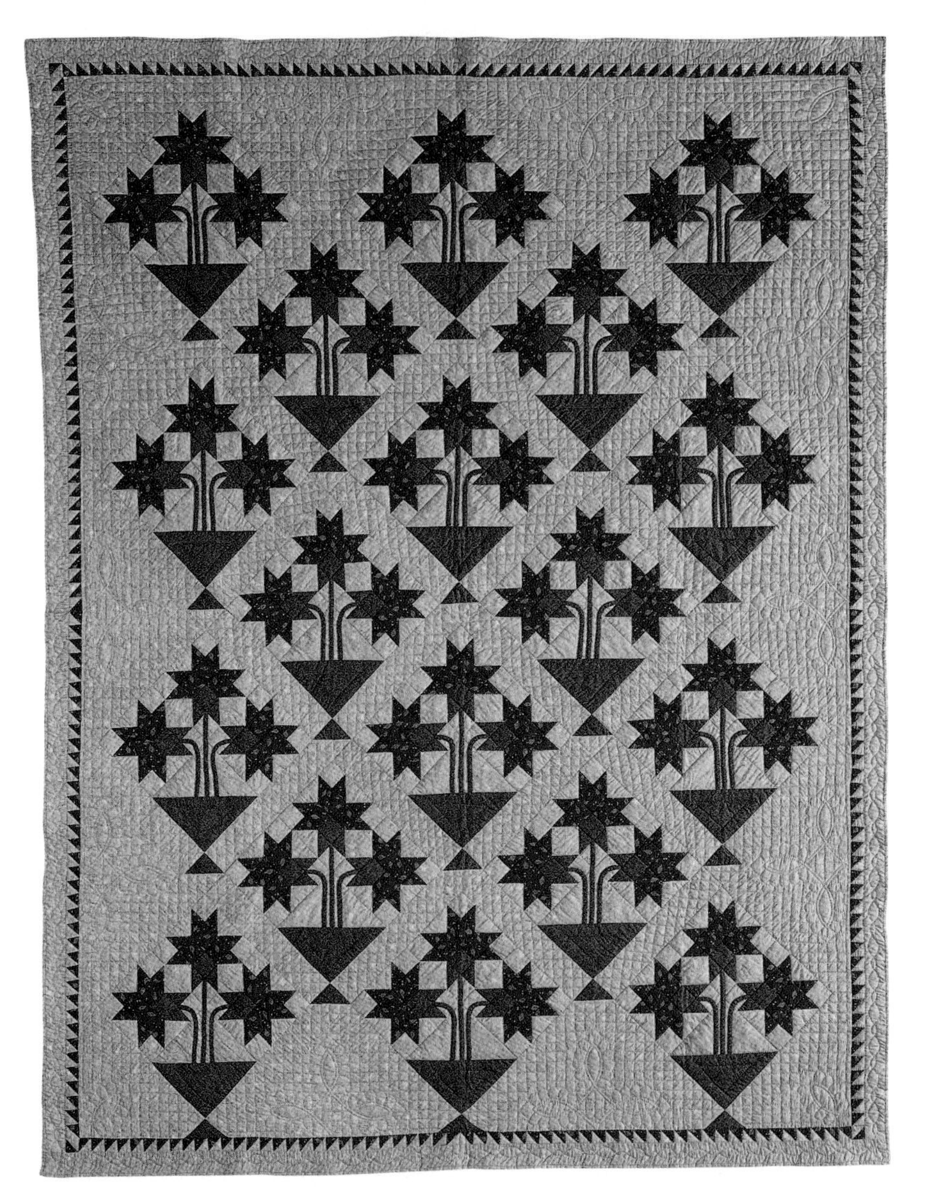

Finished Size

Quilt: 78⅝" x 105½"
Blocks: 18 (14" x 14")

Materials

8¼ yards tan fabric
2¾ yards red fabric
2 yards green fabric
3⅛ yards 90"-wide backing fabric
½"-wide bias pressing bar

Pieces to Cut

Instructions are for rotary cutting and quick piecing (see tips for diagonal-corners technique, page 12). Cut fabrics in order listed to make best use of yardage. Cut all strips cross-grain. When possible, pieces are listed in order needed, so you don't have to cut everything at once.

From tan fabric

- 10 (3"-wide) border strips.
- 12 (2¼"-wide) strips. From these, cut 216 (2¼") A squares for blocks.
- 12 (4"-wide) strips. From these, cut 216 (2¼" x 4") C pieces for blocks.
- 2 (7⅞"-wide) strips. From these, cut 9 (7⅞") squares. Cut squares in half diagonally to get 18 E triangles.
- 4 (14½"-wide) strips. From these, cut 48 (3¼" x 14½") sashing strips and 2 (3¼") sashing squares.
- 2 (21"-wide) strips. From these, cut 3 (21") squares and 2 (10¾") squares. Cut larger squares in quarters diagonally to get 10 setting triangles (and 2 extra). Cut smaller squares in half diagonally to get 4 corner triangles.
- 1 (32"-wide) strip. From this, cut a 32" square for binding. From remainder, cut an 8¼" x 15½" piece for sashing triangle-squares and 4 (5⅛") squares. Cut squares in quarters diagonally to get 11 edge triangles (and 1 extra).
- 3 (10½"-wide) strips. From these, cut 17 (6½" x 10½") pieces for triangle-squares.

From red fabric

- 3 (4"-wide) strips. From these, cut 54 (2¼" x 4") D pieces.
- 3 (10½"-wide) strips. From these, cut 17 (6½" x 10½") pieces for triangle-squares.
- 21 (2¼"-wide) strips. Set aside 3 strips for A squares. From 18 strips, cut 324 (2¼") B diagonal-corner squares.

Carolina Lily Block—Make 18.

From green fabric

- 9 (2¼"-wide) strips. Set aside 3 strips for A squares. From 6 strips, cut 108 (2¼") B diagonal-corner squares.
- 2 (7⅞"-wide) strips. From these, cut 9 (7⅞") squares. Cut each square in half diagonally to get 18 E triangles. From remainder of strip, cut a 5⅛" square. Cut this square in quarters diagonally to get 3 edge triangles (and 1 extra).
- 1 (8¼"-wide) strip. From this, cut an 8¼" x 15½" piece for sashing triangle-squares. Use leftover piece for stems.
- 3 (6½"-wide) strips (and remainder of previous strip) for stems.

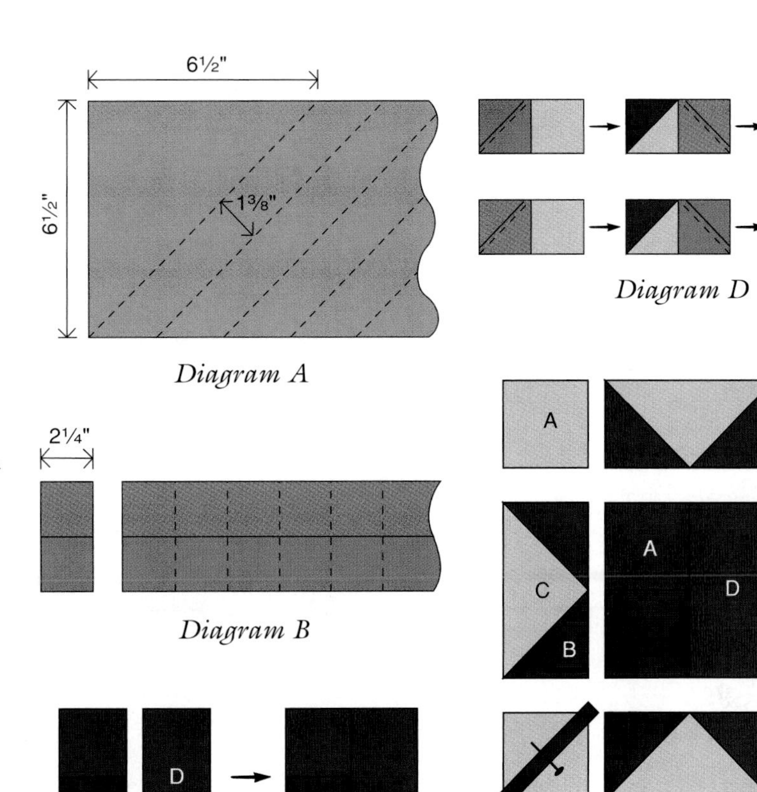

Diagram A

Diagram B

Diagram C

Diagram D

Diagram E

Preparing Bias Stems

1. On 1 long edge of each 6½"-wide strip, measure 6½" from corner. Trim triangle as shown *(Diagram A)*. Measuring from cut edge, cut 1⅜"-wide bias strips as shown. Cut a total of 54 bias strips for stems, each about 9" long.

2. Fold each bias stem over pressing bar, right sides out, centering raw edges on flat edge of bar. Press.

Block Assembly

See page 12 for instructions on Diagonal-Corners Quick-Piecing Method.

1. Join 3 pairs of red and green 2¼"-wide strips *(Diagram B)*. Press seam allowances toward green. From these strips sets, cut 54 (2¼"-wide) segments for block centers.

2. Sew a D unit to right edge of each red/green segment *(Diagram C)*. Press seam allowances toward D.

3. Use diagonal-corner technique to sew B squares to each tan C piece. For each block, make 6 units with red and green corners (3 of each as shown in *Diagram D)*. Make 6 units with both red corners.

4. For each flower quadrant, select 4 tan A squares, 1 A/D center unit, 1 bias stem, and 4 diagonal-corner units *(Diagram E)*. Arrange units in 3 horizontal rows as shown. Pin bias stem on 1 tan square as shown.

5. Join units in each row, sewing stem into seam. Press seam allowances away from diagonal-corner units. Join rows to complete quadrant. Press. Make 3 flower quadrants for each block.

6. Join tan E triangle and 3 flower quadrants in 2 rows *(Block Assembly Diagram)*, keeping bias stems out of seams. Then join rows.

7. Press stems in place on tan triangle and pin. Appliqué stems.

8. Sew green E triangle in place to complete block. Trim excess stems from seam allowance.

9. Make 18 blocks.

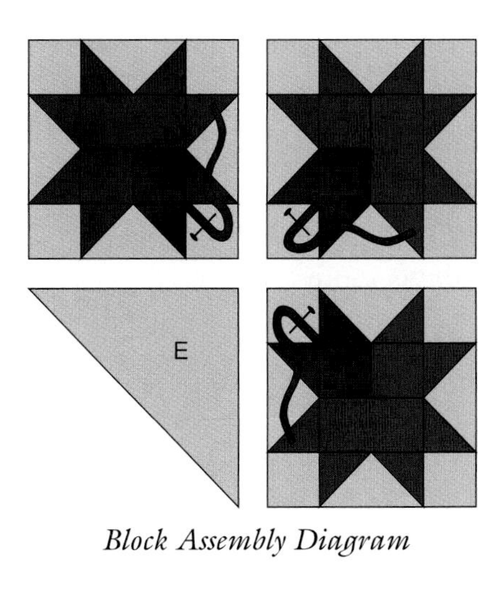

Block Assembly Diagram

Quilt Top Assembly

1. To make sashing squares, use $8\frac{1}{4}$" x $15\frac{1}{2}$" pieces of tan and green fabrics. On wrong side of tan fabric, draw a 2-square by 4-square grid of $3\frac{5}{8}$" squares, leaving a 1" margin on all sides *(Diagram F)*. Draw diagonal lines through squares as shown.

2. Match marked tan piece with a green piece, right sides facing. Sew a $\frac{1}{4}$" seam on both sides of diagonal lines as shown. Press.

3. Cut on all drawn lines to get 15 triangle-squares (and 1 extra). Press seam allowances toward green.

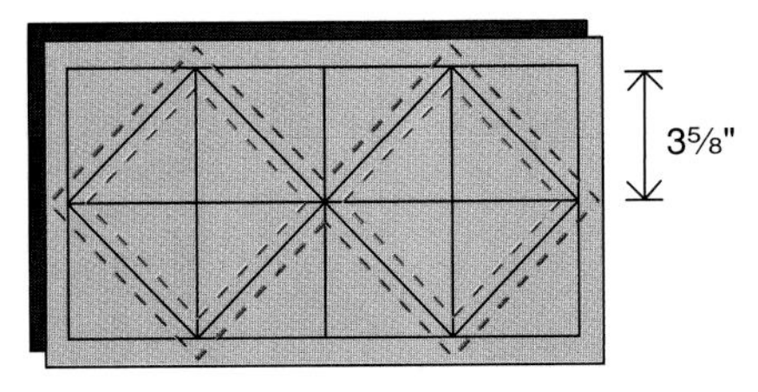

Diagram F

4. Lay out blocks in 6 diagonal rows as shown, alternating blocks and sashing strips *(Quilt Assembly Diagram)*. End rows with setting triangles as shown. Between block rows, lay out sashing strips and sashing squares in rows, ending each row with edge triangles as shown.

5. When satisfied with placement of all units, join units in each row. Press all seam allowances toward sashing strips.

6. Join rows to complete quilt center. Sew corner triangles in place as shown.

Quilt Assembly Diagram

Borders

1. For border triangle-squares, use $6\frac{1}{2}$" x $10\frac{1}{2}$" pieces of tan and red fabrics. On wrong side of tan fabric, draw a 2-square by 4-square grid of $2\frac{1}{8}$" squares, leaving a 1" margin on all sides. (This is the same grid as shown in *Diagram F,* but with smaller squares.) Draw diagonal lines through squares as shown.

2. Match marked tan piece with a red piece, right sides facing. Stitch a $\frac{1}{4}$" seam on both sides of diagonal lines. Press.

3. Cut on drawn lines to get 16 triangle-squares from each grid. Stitch 17 grids to get 268 triangle-squares (and 4 extra). Press seam allowances toward red.

4. Select 74 triangle-squares for each side border. Join squares in a vertical row, changing direction of squares in middle of row (see photo, page 42). Press. Stitch borders to quilt sides, easing to fit as needed. Press.

5. Join 58 triangle-squares in a horizontal row for top border, changing direction of triangles in middle of row. Add a triangle at each end of row as shown. Sew border to top edge of quilt, easing to fit. Assemble and join bottom border in same manner.

6. Measure length of quilt through center of quilt top. Join 3 (3"-wide) tan strips end-to-end for each side border; then trim border strips to match measured length. Sew borders to quilt sides, easing to fit as needed.

7. Measure quilt width through center of quilt top. Join 2 tan strips end-to-end for top border; then trim border strip to match measured length. Sew border to top edge of quilt. Repeat for bottom border.

Quilting and Finishing

1. Layer backing, batting, and quilt top. Baste.

2. Outline-quilt patchwork. Add lines of quilting through center of each D piece to make center unit look like a four-patch. On quilt shown, sashing and setting triangles are quilted with cross-hatching. Purchased stencils were used to mark knot and cable quilting designs in setting triangles and border.

3. From reserved fabric, make 10½ yards of bias or straight-grain binding. Bind quilt edges.

Color Variations

After the frosty tones of winter, you might like to see a *Carolina Lily* grow in the pretty hues of spring, summer, and fall. Here are some ideas for alternative color choices.

Quilts Across America

Memories of Provence

Dogwood Star

Bali Snails

Concertina

Celestial Garden

Blowin' in the Wind

Marti Michell
Atlanta, Georgia

In 1970, 5-year-old Stacy Michell helped her mother, Marti, pick out fabrics that Marti made into little shorts and tops for Stacy. Marti used the scraps to make a patchwork Prairie dress. Today, Marti wonders, "Who would have guessed that would be a life-changing decision?"

Back then, Marti was teaching sewing classes, but her students quickly forgot about dressmaking when they saw Marti's patchwork. "The next thing I knew, I was in the quilting business," she remembers. In 1972, Marti and her husband, Dick, started Yours Truly, Inc., a manufacturer of kits, patterns, and supplies for quilters. "Those were the early days of the current quilt revival, and many of the authors we introduced are now prominent in the industry," she says.

"If I had more free time, I'd spend it quilting."

Since the Michells sold Yours Truly in 1985, Marti has been a popular author, designer, and teacher. "I love developing easier, better methods (for quiltmaking) and communicating them to others," Marti says. "I'm one of the lucky people who makes a living doing what I love. If I had more free time, I'd spend it quilting!"

Marti and Dick now operate a new company, manufacturing a line of acrylic templates, tools, and books. And Stacy, all grown up now, owns Shades Hand-Dyed Textiles, which provides beautiful specialty fabrics for quilters.

In 1991, Marti was the first recipient of the Michael Kile Award, presented by her peers to honor creativity and excellence in the quilting industry. She is the current president of the International Quilt Guild.

Memories of Provence
1997

When Marti Michell travelled to France in 1996, fabric shopping had to be a part of the tour. *Memories of Provence* uses fabrics she found in that Mediterranean region.

"The fabrics take me back to the wonderful times of that trip," Marti says. "I can still tell which section I hand-pieced in a café in Avignon."

Marti packed a rotary cutter and templates so she could start piecing during the trip. "Hand piecing is not a big part of my repertoire," she says, "but I found this an ideal carry-along project."

The Sunburst is a traditional design, made contemporary by Marti's fabrics. She manufactured a template set for it because "I wanted templates for a design that you couldn't cut with a ruler." (See next page for information on ordering templates.)

Memories of Provence

Finished Size

Quilt: 54" x 54"
Blocks: 9 (13⅛" x 13⅛")

Materials*

15 (11" x 18") or more pieces gold, red, green, and blue print fabrics for block piecing and sashing squares*
14" square print fabric for center block background (On quilt shown, flower is center motif of background fabric)
1⅛ yards muslin
⅝ yard dark green print for alternate block backgrounds
18" x 22" (fat quarter) *each* red and gold prints for sashing
1¾ yards border print for outer border (On quilt shown, dark green on either side of paisley is part of same fabric)
⅛ yard gold for inner border
½ yard dark green binding fabric
3¼ yards backing fabric
Template material (optional; see information below about ready-made acrylic templates)

**Note:* As in all scrap quilts, these yardages are recommendations. Use your own scraps and fabric placement as desired.

If you prefer to use pre-cut acrylic templates for this block, look for Perfect Patchwork Templates from Marti Michell, including the Sunburst set, at your local quilt shop or write to Michell Marketing, P.O. Box 80218, Chamblee, GA 30366. Ask for Set F.

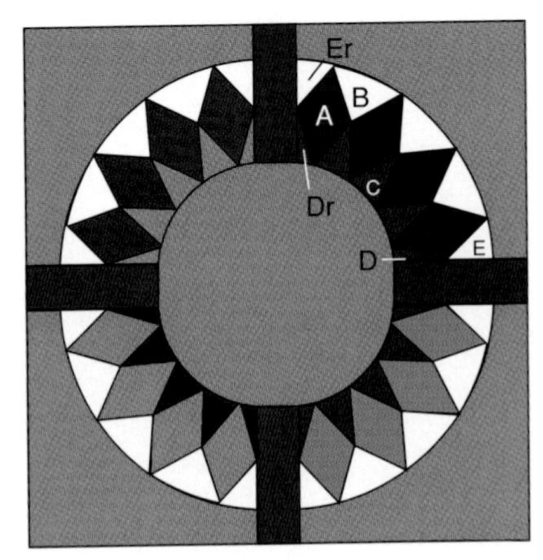

Center Block—Make 1.

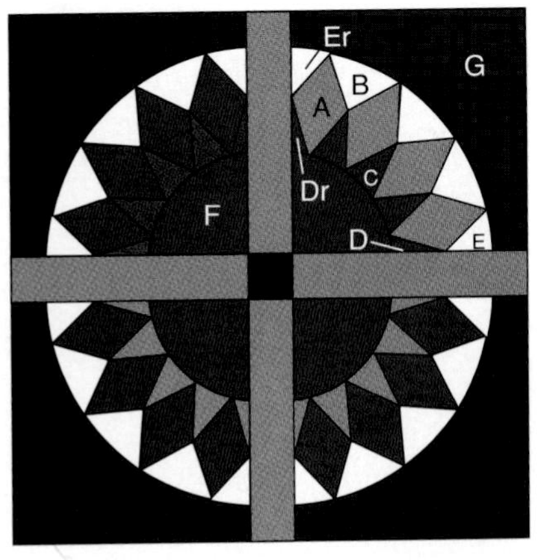

Sunburst Block—Make 4 with green background and 4 with muslin background.

Pieces to Cut

Make templates of patterns A–G (pages 52 and 53) or use precut acrylic templates.

From assorted print fabrics

- 36 sets of 4 matching A diamonds.
- 36 sets of 3 C triangles and 1 each of triangles D and D reversed, all of matching fabric.
- 8 sets of 4 matching F pieces.
- 8 (1⅝") sashing squares.
- 4 (1⅝" x 4") sashing strips for center block.

From red and gold prints

- 16 (1⅝" x 6½") sashing strips of each color.

From muslin

- 108 of Pattern B.
- 36 *each* of E and E reversed.
- 16 (6½") G squares.

From dark green print

- 16 (6½") G squares.

Block Assembly

Instructions are for machine piecing. To be successful with this design, it is crucial to have an accurate ¼" seam allowance and to sew dot-to-dot. (See Quilt Smart at right.)

1. Sew a C triangle to 1 side of an A diamond. (This is the only diamond seam you sew edge-to-edge.) Press seam allowance away from diamond. (Pressing each seam makes adding the next piece easier. Hand piecers can finger-press, reposition the pieces, and continue sewing.)

2. Match A and B with wrong sides facing. Sew with A on top so you can see previous sewing line. Begin sewing at center dot, where all 3 pieces meet. Sew to outside dot. Press seam allowance away from diamond.

3. Make 3 A/B/C units *(Diagram A)*. Press seam allowances consistently in same direction.

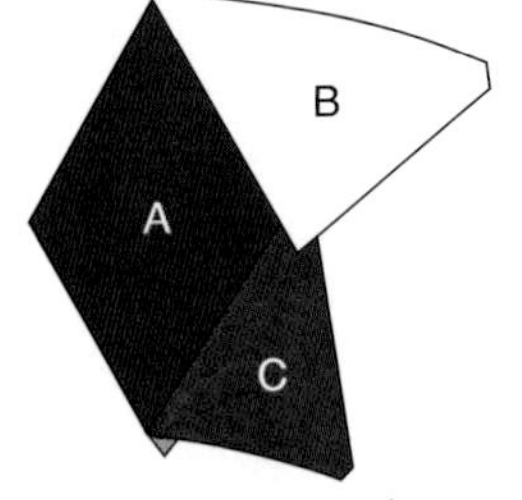

Diagram A

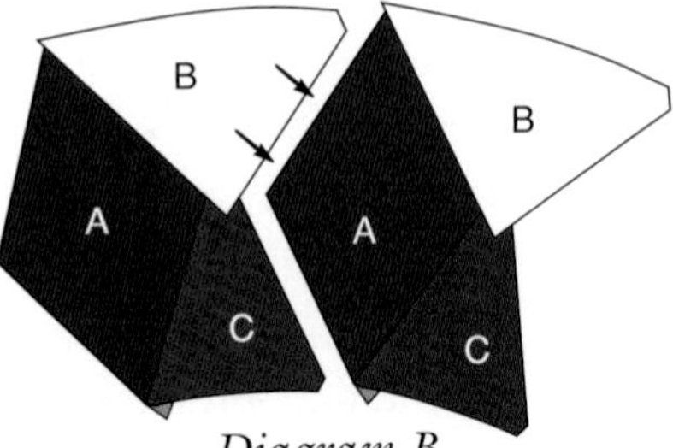

Diagram B

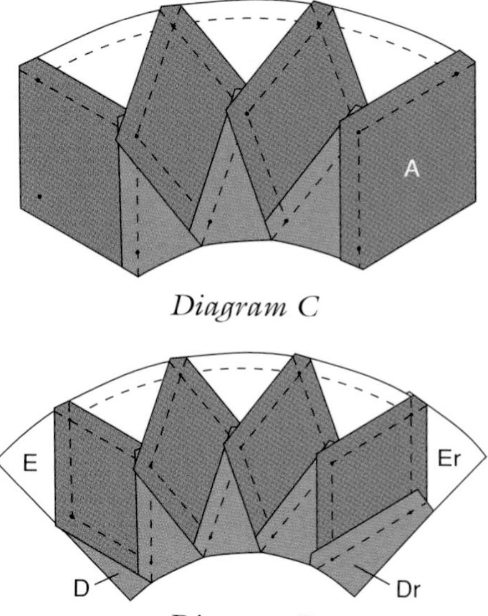

Diagram C

Diagram D

4. Join a B triangle of 1 unit to A diamond of next unit, sewing dot-to-dot *(Diagram B)*. Press seam allowance away from A. Reposition both units to align C triangle of first unit to same diamond; stitch dot-to-dot. Press this seam toward A diamond.
5. Join 3 units. Add remaining diamond *(Diagram C)*. Check to see that seam allowances are pressed as shown.
6. Sew triangles D, D reversed, E, and E reversed to ends of arc as shown *(Diagram D)*. Sew these seams edge-to-edge.
7. Before continuing, check arc against outline on Pattern G (page 53). If curve and size of arc does not match outline, assess any inconsistencies in sewing and make corrections. When satisfied with unit, stay-stitch and press outside edge of arc.
8. Make 4 arcs for each block.
9. Select 4 matching G squares for each block (muslin or dark green). Crease each square in half diagonally to mark center. Crease each arc in same manner. Place arcs on squares, matching centers and side edges. Turn under outside rounded edge of each arc and appliqué in place.
10. Select a set of 4 F pieces for each block. Turn under rounded edges of Fs and appliqué at bottom of arcs. Press.
11. For each block, lay out 4 quarter-block units, 4 sashing strips, and a sashing square *(Block Assembly Diagram)*. Use red sashing for muslin blocks and gold sashing for green blocks. Join units in rows; then join rows to complete block.
12. Make 8 blocks.

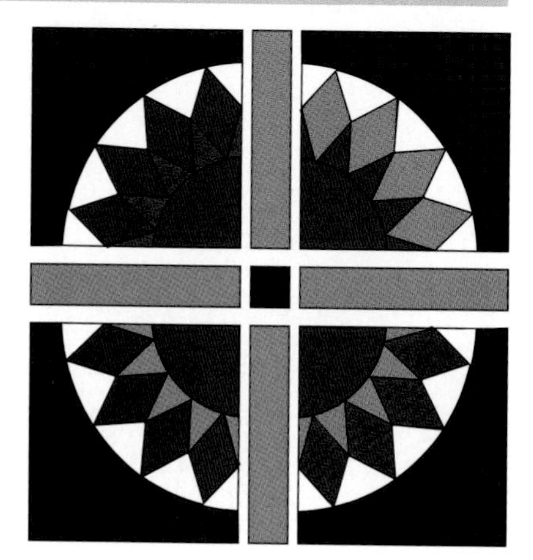
Block Assembly Diagram

❖QUILT SMART❖

Dot-to-Dot Sewing

In this block, you cannot sew across seam allowances if you want flat patchwork with sharp, accurate points and nicely inset corners. Dot-to-dot sewing replaces any idea you may have about pivoting, which simply does not give satisfactory results.

Use a ⅛"-diameter hole punch to punch small corner dots in your templates *(Diagram 1)*. If you don't have a hole punch (available at some office supply and craft stores), place your template on a sturdy board and hammer a small nail through the plastic.

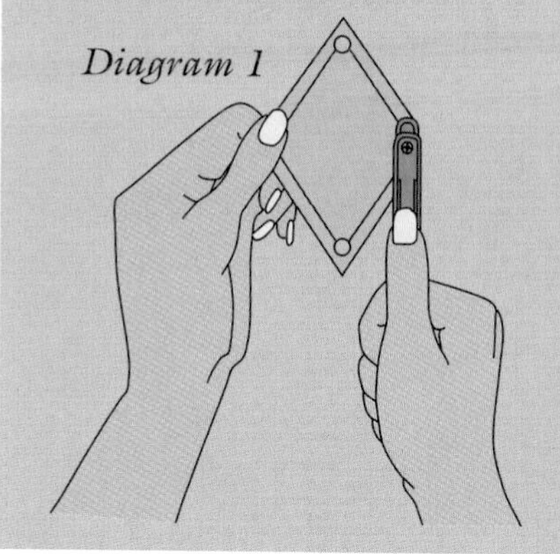
Diagram 1

Use a fine-tipped marker or pencil to mark dots on the *wrong* side of each piece.

Stitch Length

When sewing dot-to-dot, it is better to stop a tiny stitch short than to stitch too far; if stitches extend past the dot, the seam allowance cannot be pressed out of the way.

Backstitching at both ends of the seam is one way to secure it, but most people find it better to shorten the stitch length.

Start each seam by inserting the needle on the dot. With the stitch set about 20 stitches per inch, make 3 or 4 stitches away from the dot; then increase stitch length to 12 to 14 per inch. Reduce stitch length again at the seam's end. Unless the seam is very small, do not use the short stitch setting for the whole seam, as it's hard to rip out when necessary.

Center Block

1. Following steps 1–8 above, make 4 arcs for center block. To prepare arcs for appliqué, turn under seam allowance on both curved edges. (*Note:* There are no F appliqués on this block.)

2. Fold 14" background square in half diagonally and horizontally. Turn under seam allowance on long edges of 4 sashing strips. Using creases as positioning guides, pin strips on background square, aligning 1 end of each strip with edge of square.

3. Center arcs on background square, tucking sides under pinned sashing. When satisfied with placement, appliqué arcs and sashing in place. Press.

Quilt Assembly

1. Referring to photo, lay out blocks in 3 rows, with 3 blocks in each row. Alternate colors of block backgrounds as shown.

2. Join blocks in each row, matching sashing seams.

3. Join rows.

Borders

1. Measure length of quilt top through middle of pieced section. Cut 2 (1"-wide) gold border strips to match quilt length. Sew borders to quilt sides, easing to fit as needed. Press seam allowances toward borders.

2. Measure width of quilt top through middle, including side borders. Cut 2 more 1"-wide gold strips to match width. Sew borders to top and bottom edges of quilt, easing to fit.

3. From outer border fabric, cut 4 (7" x 63") lengthwise strips. See pages 141–142 for tips on making mitered borders. Sew outer border strips to quilt edges; then miter border corners.

Quilting and Finishing

1. Mark quilting designs on quilt top. Quilting design in blocks is shown on Pattern G, opposite.

2. Assemble backing. Layer backing, batting, and quilt top. Baste.

3. Quilt as marked or as desired.

4. Make 6¼ yards of straight-grain binding. Bind quilt edges.

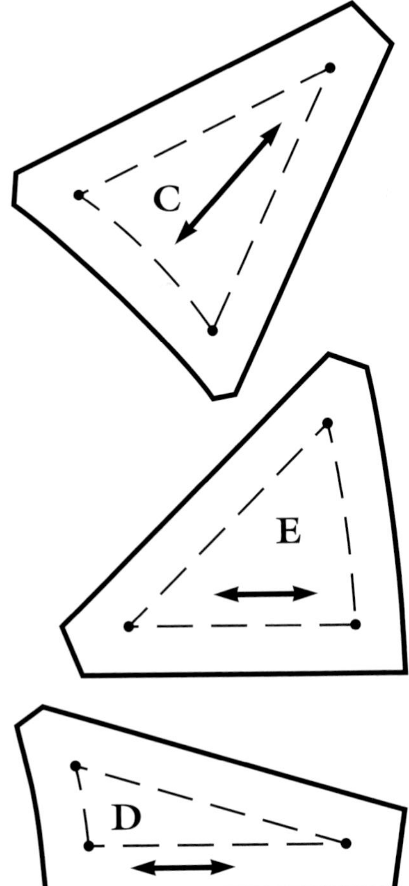

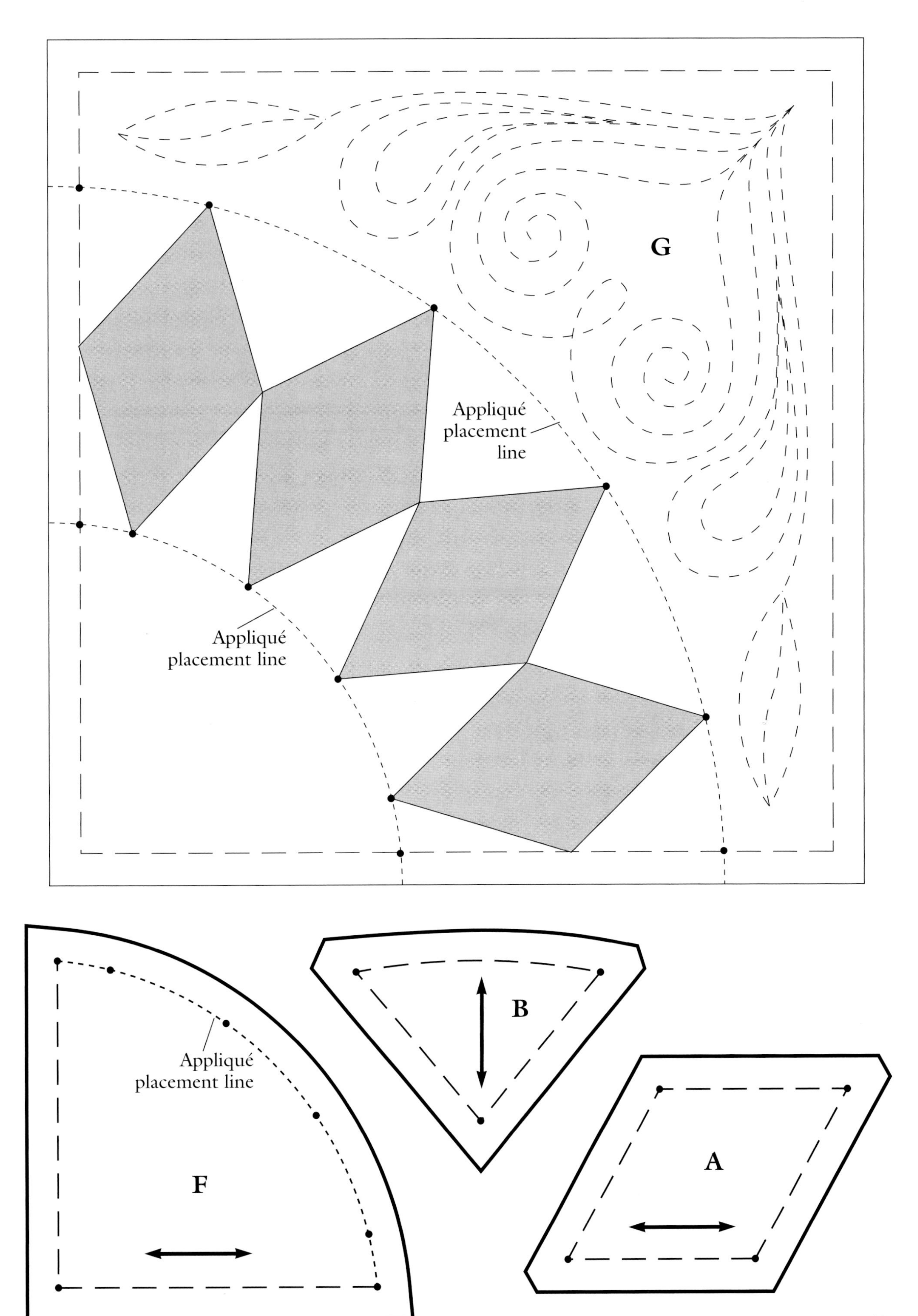
G
Appliqué placement line
Appliqué placement line
Appliqué placement line
B
A
F

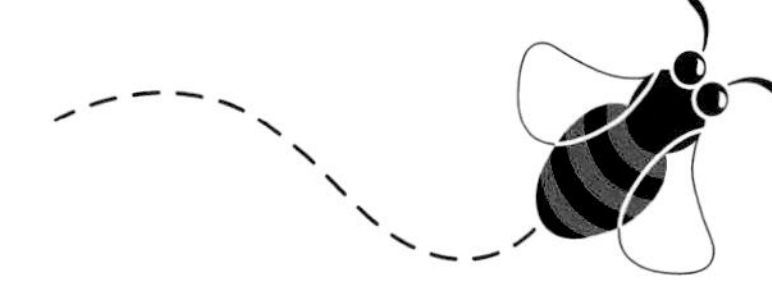

Stitch 'N' Quilt Circle

Paducah, Kentucky

Paducah is a town that knows how to celebrate quilts. The home of the American Quilter's Society (AQS) and its museum, Paducah also has the Stitch 'N' Quilt Circle. This group of 36 meets monthly to share quilts and plan community projects.

The group's activities include workshops and an annual Quilters' Day Out, when everybody in town is invited to see their quilt show and demonstrations. The Circle also makes a dogwood-themed quilt each year to raffle at the April AQS show. Proceeds from the raffle quilt are donated to Easter Seals.

Dogwood Star

1999

The annual AQS show coincides with the area Dogwood Festival, when the trees are pink and white glory and quiltmakers from around the world come to Paducah.

The Stitch 'N' Quilt Circle combines flower and quilt each year by making a raffle quilt with a dogwood theme.

Dogwood Star is the Circle's 1999 fundraiser. It combines an original appliquéd design with pieced sashing. It was won by Debra Baker Steinman of Atlanta, Georgia.

ROBERT

Dogwood Star

Finished Size
Quilt: 90½" x 102"
Blocks: 30 (10" x 10")

Materials
4 yards cream
3 yards dark red
2¾ yards rose print
2¾ yards dark green
1 yard pink for flowers and sashing squares
¾ yard green for leaves
⅛ yard yellow
8¼ yards backing fabric
Brown embroidery floss

Pieces to Cut
Instructions are for rotary cutting and quick piecing (see tips for diagonal-corners technique, page 12, and hourglass quick-piecing technique, opposite). Cut fabrics in order listed to make best use of yardage. Cut all strips cross-grain. When possible, pieces are listed in order needed, so you don't have to cut everything all at once.

Appliqué patterns A, B, and C are on page 58.

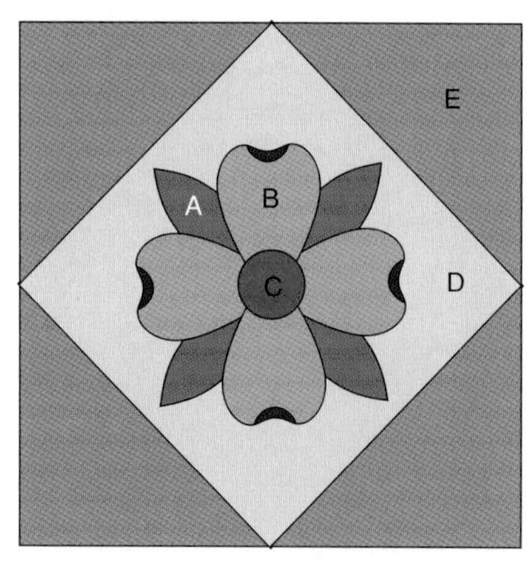

Dogwood Block—Make 30.

From cream fabric
- 6 (7½"-wide) strips. From these, cut 30 (7½") D squares.
- 7 (3¼"-wide) strips. From these, cut 84 (3¼") squares for hourglass sashing units.
- 4 (7¾"-wide) strips. From these, cut 14 (7¾" x 11") for sashing triangle-squares.
- 1 (5⅞"-wide) strip. From this, cut 2 (5⅞") squares. Cut each square in half diagonally to get 4 E triangles for corner units.
- 5 (5½"-wide) strips. From these and remainder of strip from previous cut, cut 22 (5½" x 10½") F rectangles for border units.

From dark red fabric
- 4 (5" x 99") lengthwise strips for borders.
- 4 (2½"-wide) lengthwise strips for binding.
- 14 (7¾" x 11") pieces for sashing triangle-squares.

From rose print fabric
- 9 (5⅞"-wide) strips. From these, cut 62 (5⅞") squares. Cut each square in half diagonally to get 124 E triangles for blocks and corner units.
- 6 (5½"-wide) strips. From these, cut 44 (5½") G squares for border units.

From dark green fabric
- 4 (3½" x 99") lengthwise strips for borders.
- 11 (3¼" x 29") strips. From these, cut 84 (3¼") squares for hourglass sashing units.

From pink
- 120 of Pattern B (petal).
- 3 (3"-wide) strips. From these, cut 42 (3") sashing squares.

From green
- 120 of Pattern A (leaf).

From yellow
- 30 of Pattern C (center).

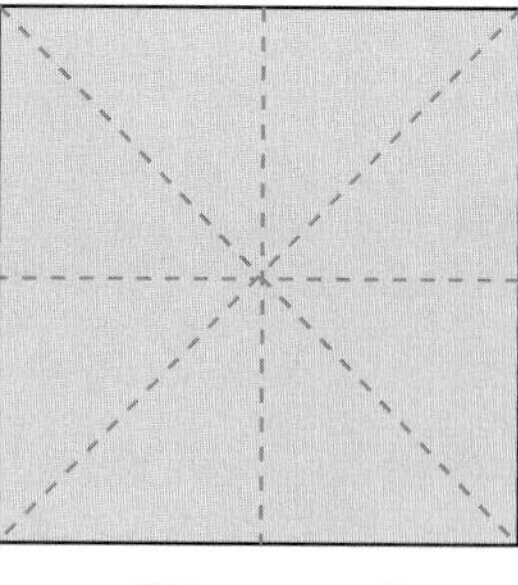

Diagram A

Block Assembly
1. Fold 1 D square diagonally, horizontally, and vertically and crease to make placement lines *(Diagram A)*. Center 4 A leaves, 4 B petals, and 1 C on square, aligning leaves and petals with creased placement lines. When satisfied with placement, appliqué pieces in place.
2. Use satin stitch or a close buttonhole stitch and 2 strands of floss to embroider notch on each petal edge. (See stitch diagram, page 58.)
3. Join rose print E triangles to opposite sides of dogwood square. Repeat on remaining sides to complete block.
4. Make 30 blocks.

Border Unit Assembly
1. Using diagonal-corners technique, sew rose G squares on F rectangle *(Diagram B)*. Make 22 border units.
2. Join rose print and cream E triangles to make a corner square *(Diagram C)*. Make 4 corner squares.

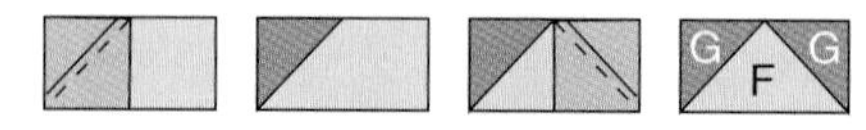

Diagram B

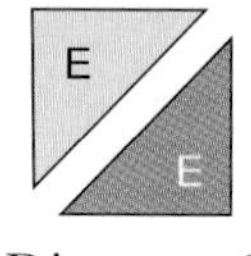

Diagram C

Sashing Assembly

1. For sashing triangle-squares, use 7¾" x 11" pieces of red and cream. On wrong side of a cream piece, draw a 2-square by 3-square grid of 3⅜" squares, leaving a 1" margin on all sides *(Diagram D)*. Draw diagonal lines through squares as shown.

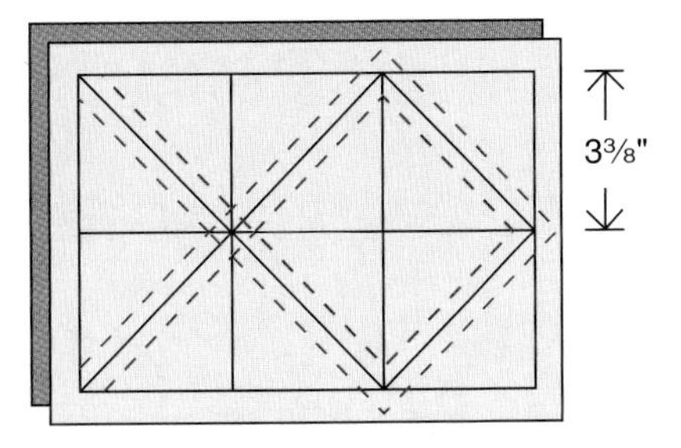

Diagram D

2. Match marked piece with a red piece, right sides facing. Sew a ¼" seam on both sides of diagonal lines as shown. Press.

3. Cut on all drawn lines to get 12 triangle-squares. Stitch 14 grids to get 168 triangle-squares. Press seam allowances toward red.

❖QUILT SMART❖

Quick-Pieced Hourglass Blocks

When you need several Hourglass units (quarter-square triangles) from the same two-fabric combination, it's faster and more accurate to quick-piece the units rather than to cut and sew individual triangles. Here's an easy method for making Hourglass units.

1. Cut a square of each fabric that is 1¼" larger than the desired *finished* size of the unit. For *Dogwood Star*, you will use 3¼" squares of cream and dark green fabrics. You will get 2 Hourglass units from each pair of matching squares.

2. On wrong side of a cream square, draw diagonal lines from corner to corner in *both* directions.

3. With right sides facing, match marked square with a green square. Stitch ¼" seam on both sides of 1 diagonal line *(Diagram 1)*.

4. Cut units apart on drawn line between stitching *(Diagram 2)*. Press units open, pressing seam allowance toward darker fabric. You will have 2 triangle-squares as shown *(Diagram 3)*.

5. On wrong side of 1 triangle-square, extend drawn line from corner of light triangle to corner of dark triangle. Then match both triangle-squares with contrasting fabrics facing and marked unit on top.

6. Stitch ¼" seam on both sides of marked line *(Diagram 4)*. Cut units apart between stitching lines as before *(Diagram 5)*.

7. Press units open to get 2 Hourglass units *(Diagram 6)*. Each unit will measure 3" square (including seam allowances). When sewn into the sashing strips, finished size of each unit will be 2½" square.

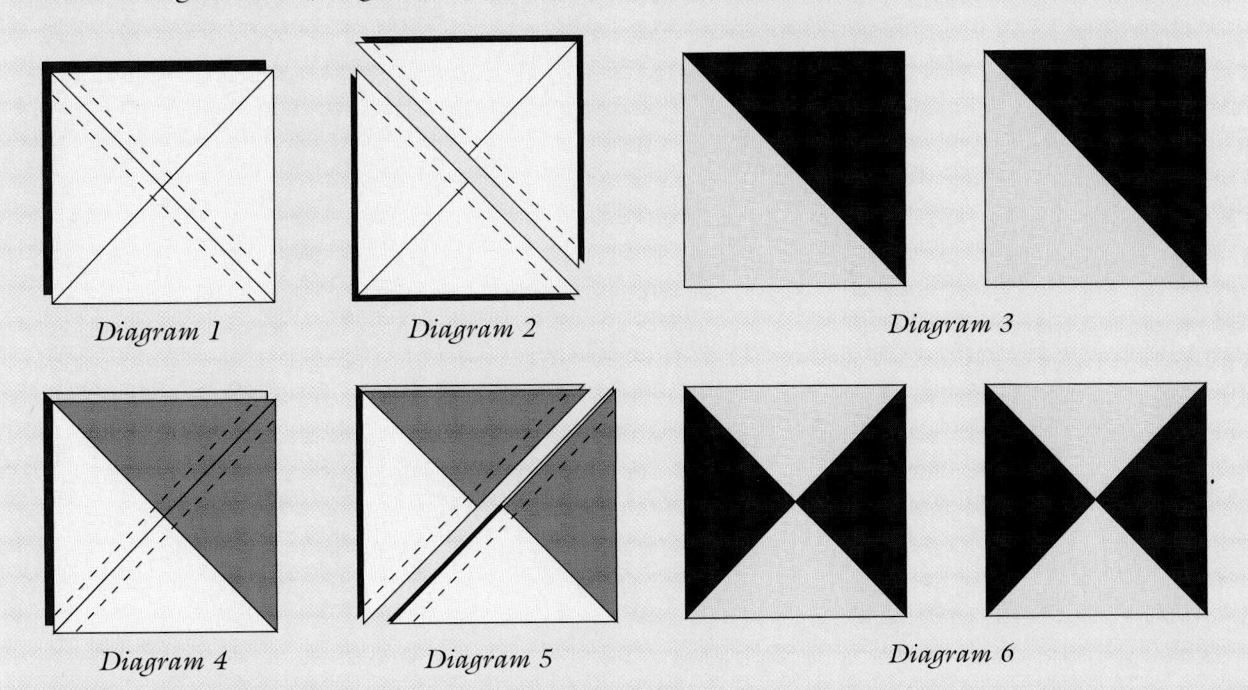

Diagram 1 *Diagram 2* *Diagram 3*

Diagram 4 *Diagram 5* *Diagram 6*

4. See instructions for hourglass quick-piecing technique (page 57). Following those directions, use cream and green 3¼" squares to make 168 Hourglass units.

5. For each sashing strip, join 2 triangle-squares and 2 hourglass units as shown *(Diagram E)*. Make 71 sashing strips.

6. For border sashing unit, join 1 triangle-square and 1 hourglass unit as shown *(Diagram F)*. Make 26 border sashing units.

Diagram E

Diagram F

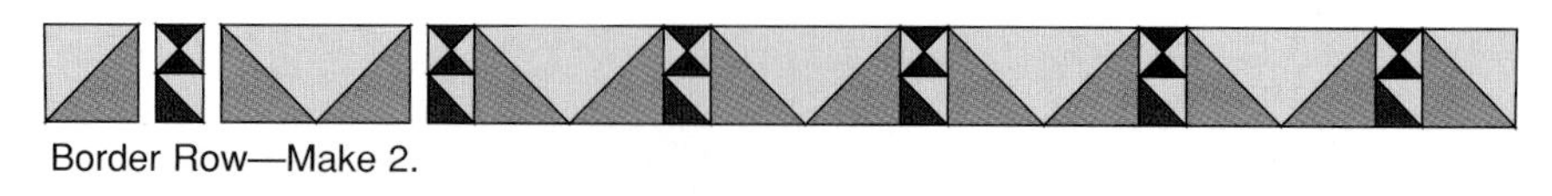

Border Row—Make 2.

Sashing Row—Make 7.

Block Row—Make 6.

Row Assembly Diagram

Quilt Assembly

Refer to *Row Assembly Diagram* and photograph throughout.

1. For Border Row, join 2 corner squares, 6 border sashing strips, and 5 border units as shown. Make 2 Border Rows.

2. For Sashing Row, join 2 border sashing units, 5 sashing strips, and 6 pink sashing squares as shown. Make 7 sashing rows.

3. For Block Row, join 2 border units, 5 Dogwood blocks, and 6 sashing strips as shown. Make 6 block rows.

4. Lay out rows as shown in photo. Starting with a Border Row, join rows.

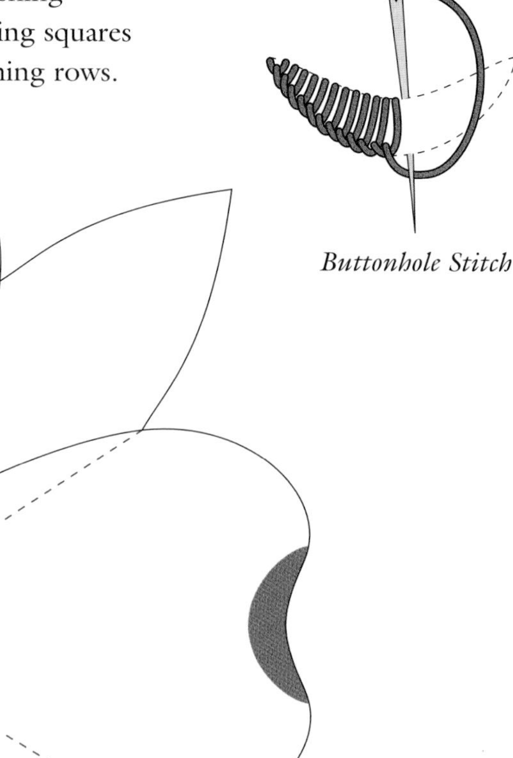

Buttonhole Stitch

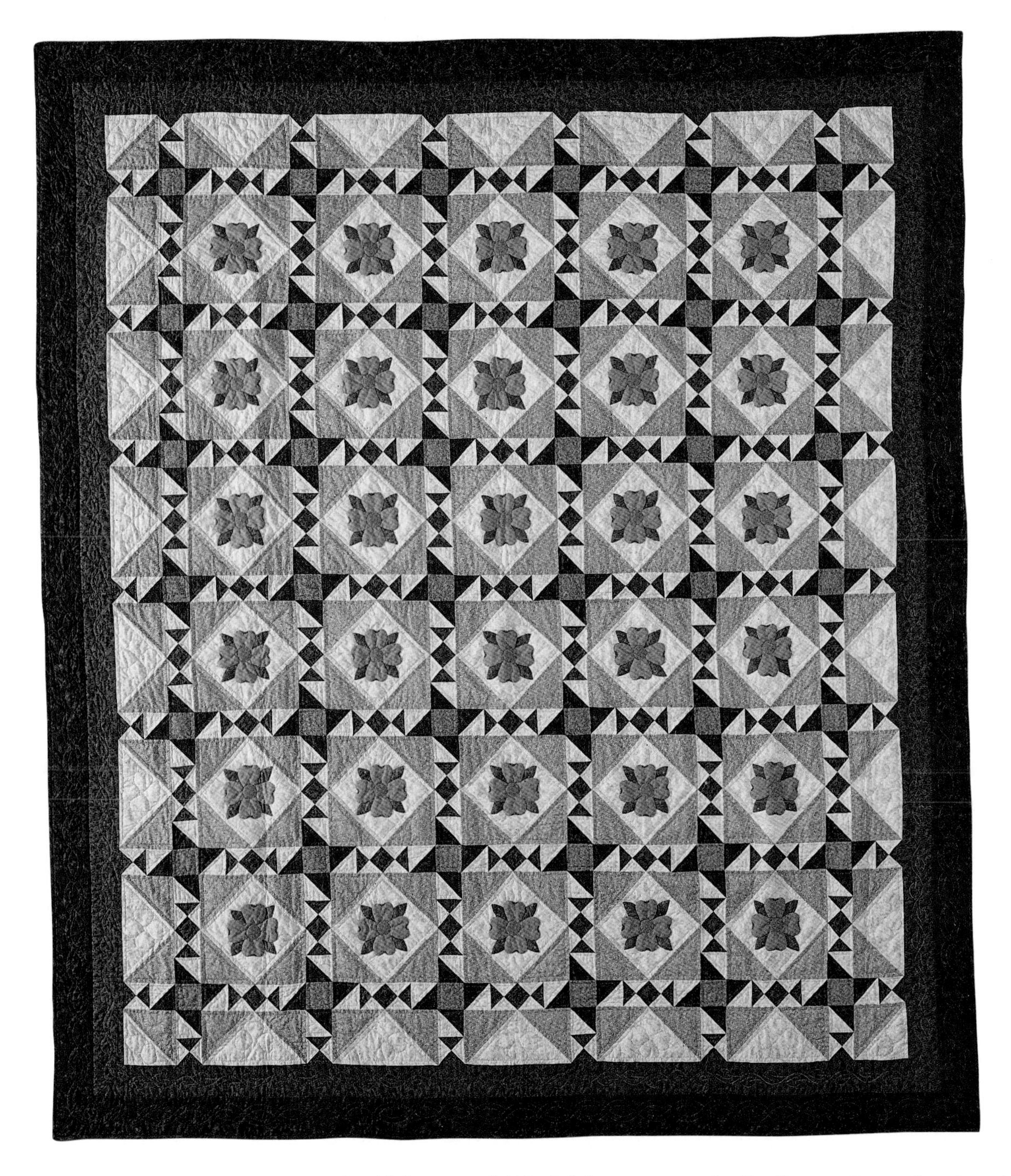

Borders

1. Join pairs of dark green and dark red border strips to get 4 two-tone border strip. Repeat to make 4 border strips.

2. Center a border strip on each side of quilt with green strip to inside. Sew borders to each side of quilt; miter border corners.

Quilting and Finishing

1. Divide backing fabric into 3 (2¾-yard) lengths. From 1 length, cut 1 (28"-wide) lengthwise panel (discard remainder of panel). Sew narrow panel between wide panels. Press seam allowances toward narrow panel.

2. Layer backing, batting, and quilt top, with backing seams parallel to top and bottom edges of quilt. Baste.

3. Outline-quilt appliqué and patchwork. Quilt shown has a dogwood quilted in outer triangles, a vine and leaf pattern quilted in green border; red border has a chain pattern.

4. Join binding strips end-to-end to get a continuous length. Bind quilt edges.

Happy Dickey
Hampden, Maine

On a cold day in 1983, four Maine women sent their children and their husbands out for a day of cross-country skiing. Then they settled in front of a blazing wood stove to create their first quilt.

Happy Dickey was one of those young women and, 17 years later she says, "I have never stopped making quilts since that day."

A wife, mother, and registered nurse, Happy is one of many in the health care professions who are creative for the sake of their own well-being. Over the years, she says, "I have never met anyone who doesn't love a quilt or have her own special quilt story."

"My quilts . . . are meant to be used and loved and passed on."

Happy's first quilts were bed size and she still prefers them to wall quilts or art quilts. "I get so much satisfaction out of creating a special quilt for someone," she says. "My quilts are machine pieced and hand quilted. They are meant to be used and loved and passed on in the family."

Happy started selling a few quilts in 1991 to pay for what she calls "my habit." She has never lacked a commission since and has sold her quilts across the United States and in Europe. She makes at least one quilt a year to raise money for a charitable cause.

Happy is a member of the Hampden Highland Quilters and the Pine Tree Quilt Guild.

Bali Snails
1999

It took Happy Dickey two years to collect the more than 80 fabrics in this quilt, all of them Bali prints by Hoffman.

A traditional Snail's Trail block usually has two contrasting fabrics. But Happy used four fabrics of similar tone in each block. "I made one block at a time, building each consecutive block on my design wall," she says. "The challenge was to balance the fabric and color throughout."

Bali Snails was Happy's graduation present for Katie Rawcliffe, who collaborated on the selection of pattern and fabrics. The quilt was shown at Maine Quilts 1999, the annual show of Maine's statewide Pine Tree Quilt Guild.

Bali Snails

Finished Size

Quilt: 89" x 100"
Blocks: 56 (11½" x 11½")

Materials

112 (12") squares assorted fabrics for blocks*
½ yard inner border fabric
2⅞ yards outer border fabric (includes binding)
3⅛ yards 104"-wide backing

* *Note:* Yardage recommendation is based on using each fabric in 2 blocks. Quilt shown has a more or less equal number of blue, pink, purple, and green fabrics with some browns, golds, and other colors mixed in. Use your own scraps and place fabrics as desired.

Plan Ahead

One Snail's Trail block doesn't seem very interesting, but multiple blocks create a striking design of interlocking pinwheels.

The block is easy to sew, but it takes planning to achieve the overall design. Use the *Planning Diagram* at right to map out your quilt so you won't have to worry about what fabric goes where once you start to sew.

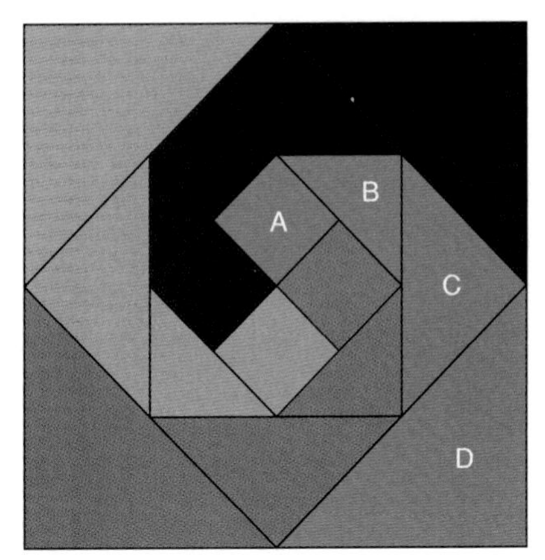

Snail's Trail Block—Make 56.

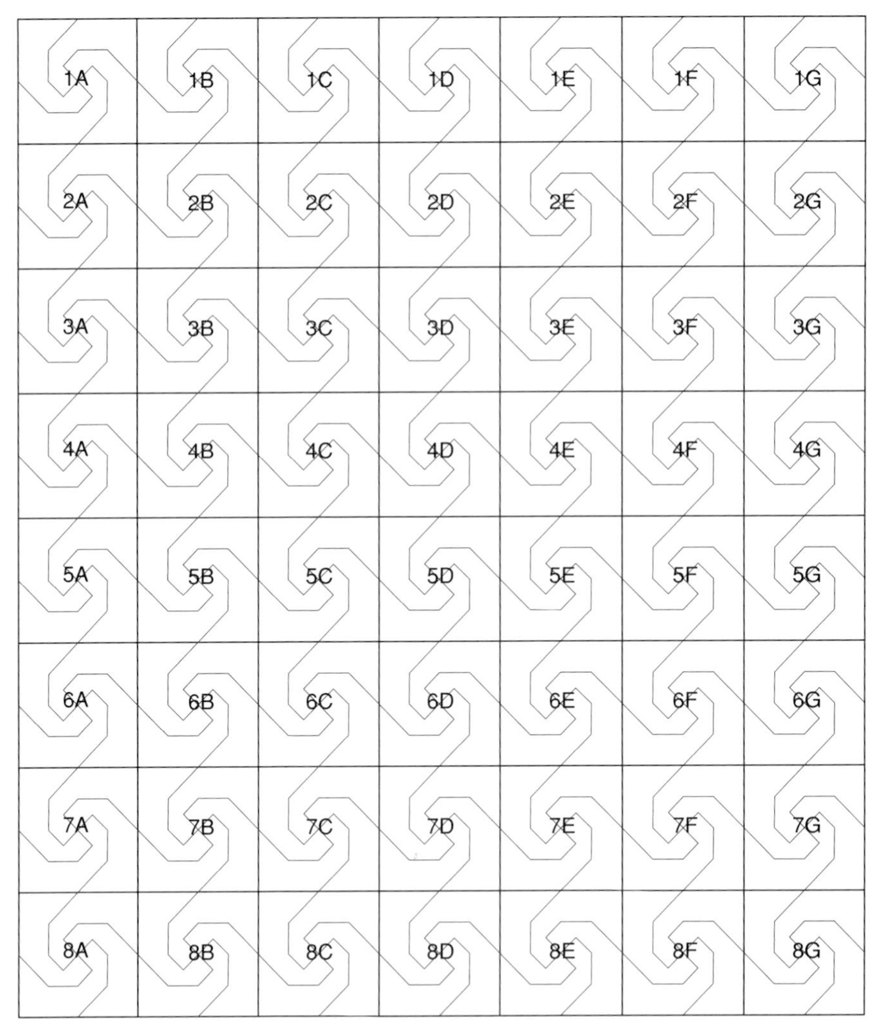

Planning Diagram

Make several photocopies to try different arrangements.

The diagram shows each block of the quilt. Each block is divided into four equal parts.

Sort your fabrics into color groups; then get a colored pencil to match each group. For example, let's say you have six green fabrics. Choose any quadrant, on any block, and color it green. Then color the *adjacent* quadrants in the *adjacent* blocks green also. Because each fabric is used twice, your six green fabrics are enough for 12 quadrants or three complete pinwheels. Repeat with each color until you've placed each fabric.

Use the diagram as a guide as you sew the blocks. It doesn't matter what fabric is where as long as adjacent quadrants are similar so the pinwheels become visible when blocks are joined.

Pieces to Cut

From each *scrap square*

- 1 (6⅝") square. Cut square in half to get 2 D triangles.
- 1 (5") square. Cut square in half to get 2 C triangles.
- 1 (3¾") square. Cut square in half to get 2 B triangles.
- 2 (2½") A squares.

Each fabric square makes 2 sets, with 1 each of pieces A, B, C, and D in each set.

From outer border fabric

- 4 (3½" x 103") lengthwise strips for outer border.
- 4 (2½" x 103") lengthwise strips for binding.

Cut 1 or more scrap squares for piecing from remaining border fabric, if desired.

Block Assembly

1. Referring to *Planning Diagram,* choose 4 fabric sets for first block (1A).

2. Use a scant ¼" seam allowance to join 4 A squares *(Diagram A).* Place fabrics to match plan for Block 1A. Press. Four-patch should be 4⅝" square, including seam allowances on outside edges. (Use a regular ¼" seam allowance for remaining seams.)

3. Sew B triangles to 2 opposite sides of four-patch, placing fabrics as shown *(Diagram B).* Press seam allowances toward triangles. Then sew B triangles to remaining 2 sides. Press.

4. Add C triangles in same manner *(Diagram C).* Then add D triangles to complete block.

5. Label block, pinning its identifying number onto it.

6. Make remaining 55 blocks in same manner. Label each completed block so you can easily place it in a quilt layout when it's time to join blocks.

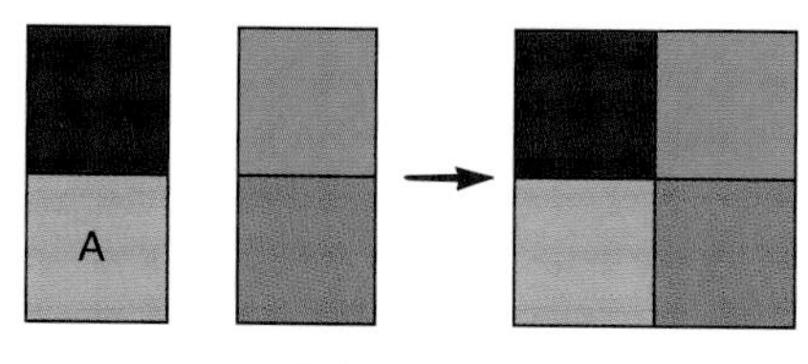

Diagram A

Quilt Assembly

1. Referring to photo and *Planning Diagram,* lay out blocks in 8 horizontal rows, with 7 blocks in each row.

2. When satisifed with placement, join blocks in each row.

3. Join rows.

Borders

1. From inner border fabric, cut 10 (1½"-wide) cross-grain strips. Join 2½ strips end-to-end for each border.

2. Join pairs of inner and outer border strips to get 4 pieced borders.

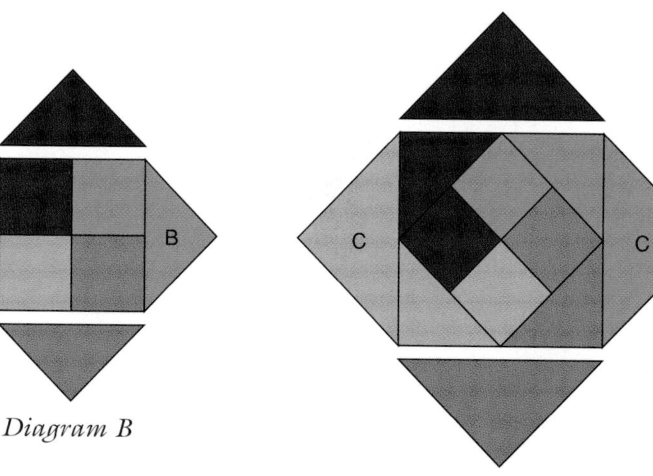

Diagram B

Diagram C

Color Variations

If you prefer a planned color scheme to a scrappy one for your Snail's Trail blocks, here are some ideas.

3. Referring to page 141, measure quilt and trim border strips to make top and bottom borders as needed. Sew borders to all sides of quilt and miter corners.

Quilting and Finishing

1. Layer backing, batting, and quilt top. Baste.
2. Outline-quilt patchwork. On quilt shown, a wave pattern is quilted in border.
3. Join reserved strips end-to-end to make 10¾ yards of straight-grain binding. Bind quilt edges.

❖QUILT SMART❖

Quilting Supplies & Resources

If you're looking for fabric, supplies, or books not available at your local shops, contact these companies for free catalogs or product information.

Connecting Threads
P.O. Box 8940
Vancouver, WA 98668-8940
1-800-574-6454

Hancock's of Paducah
3841 Hinkleville Road
Paducah, KY 42001
1-800-845-8723
www.Hancocks-Paducah.com

Keepsake Quilting™
P.O. Box 1618
Centre Harbor, NH 03226
1-800-865-9458
www.keepsakequilting.com

Oxmoor House
1-800-633-4910
www.oxmoorhouse.com

The Quilt Farm
P.O. Box 7877
Saint Paul, MN 55107
1-800-435-6201
www.quiltfarm.com

Chris Hulin
Gilman, Iowa

For a long time, Chris Hulin thought she'd never make a quilt. She loved them, but she didn't know how to sew. But in May 1991, she took a leap of faith and started teaching herself.

Her first quilt was not exactly a roaring success. A friend advised her to stick to a hobby she already knew. "But I still wanted to make quilts," Chris says, "so I just refused to be discouraged."

"I just refused to be discouraged."

Less than 10 years later, Chris's quilts are a big success. At her guild's last show, her quilts won blue ribbons and viewer's choice. Quilting has become a passion and a big part of her life.

"I love to go fabric shopping with friends," Chris says, and she admits to having a rather large collection of fabric. "Sometimes, I find I've bought the same fabric three times," Chris says. "I guess that means I *really* like it."

Chris is a member of the Jewel Box Quilt Guild.

Concertina
1999

When quilt-book author Judy Martin moved into the neighborhood a few years ago, Chris Hulin gained a new quilt buddy.

Chris now helps make quilts for Judy's books. *Concertina* is Judy's design, but Chris chose the scrappy fabrics and colors to please herself. Judy gave permission to include the quilt in *Great American Quilts 2001.* Judy's design idea, she says, was to create the look of shooting stars that were folded, like the bellows of a concertina. She and Chris accomplished this with skillful use of color and shading.

Chris used Judy's rotary cutting methods, but patterns are also given if you prefer traditional cutting. This quilt was machine-quilted by Jean Nolte.

Concertina

Finished Size

Quilt: 77⅝" x 90"

Materials

40 (3½" x 18") strips *each* assorted medium/dark fabrics for darker halves of stars

40 (3½" x 18") strips *each* assorted light/medium fabrics for lighter halves of stars

12 (3½" x 18") strips scrap fabrics for top, bottom, and side border elements

3 yards gray

3¼ yards dark gray (includes binding)

2¾ yards 104"-wide backing

Template material (optional)

Pieces to Cut

See Quilt Smart on page 71 for tips on cutting pieces A–F with a rotary cutter and acrylic ruler. For traditional cutting, make templates of patterns A–F at right and on page 70.

Cut all 45"-wide strips crossgrain, from selvage to selvage.

From each *dark star fabric*
- 2 B triangles.
- 2 D triangles.
- 1 C parallelogram.

From each *light star fabric*
- 2 B triangles.
- 2 D triangles.
- 1 C reversed parallelogram.

From scrap fabrics
- 116 D triangles.
- 18 F triangles.
- 18 F reversed triangles.

From gray fabric
- 8 (3"-wide) strips. From these, cut 80 A diamonds.
- 2 (3½"-wide) strips. From these, cut 40 B triangles.

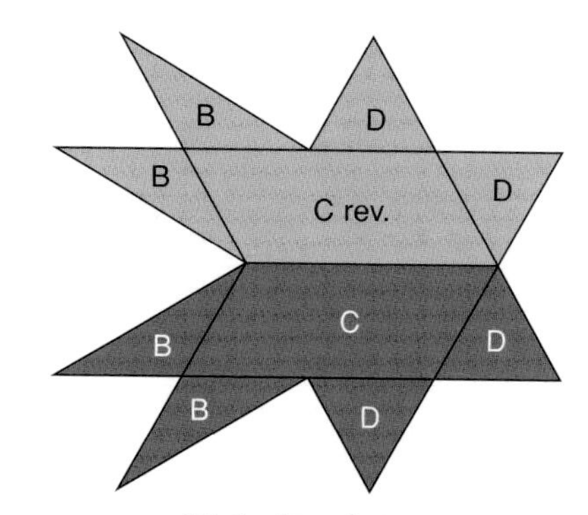

Light/Dark Star

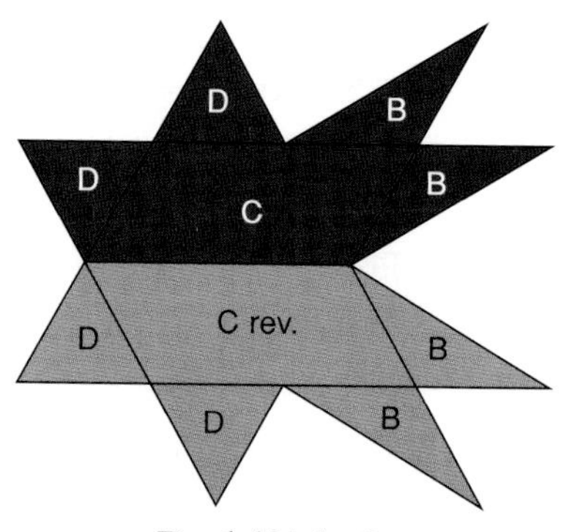

Dark/Light Star

- 6 (3"-wide) strips. From these, cut 34 C parallelograms.
- 5 (3¼"-wide) strips. From these, cut 97 D triangles.
- 3 (3⅛"-wide) strips. From these, cut 40 E triangles.
- 2 (3"-wide) strips for top border row.

From dark gray fabric
- 9 (2½"-wide) strips for straight-grain binding.
- 8 (3"-wide) strips. From these, cut 80 A diamonds.
- 2 (3½"-wide) strips. From these, cut 40 B triangles.
- 6 (3"-wide) strips. From these, cut 34 C reversed parallelograms.
- 5 (3¼"-wide) strips. From these, cut 97 D triangles.
- 3 (3⅛"-wide) strips. From these, cut 40 E reversed triangles.
- 2 (3"-wide) strips for bottom border row.

B

E

Quilt Assembly

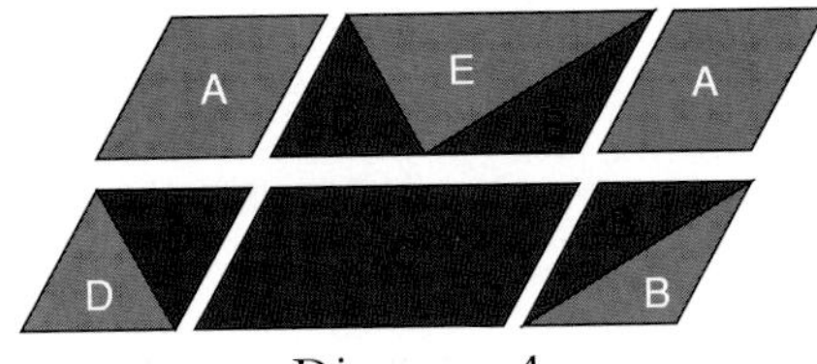

Diagram A

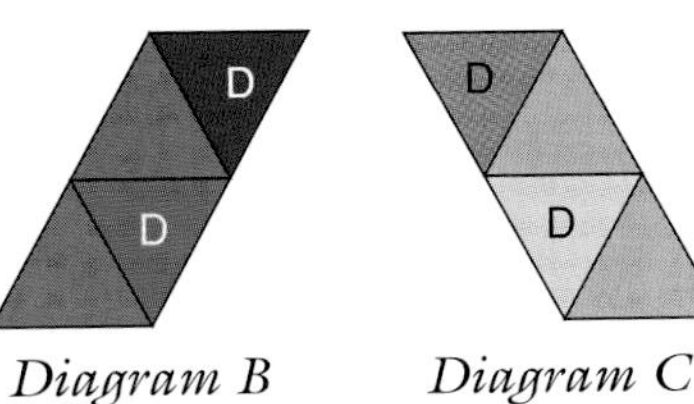

Diagram B *Diagram C*

This quilt is assembled in 18 horizontal rows. Make 1 row at a time, working from top to bottom of quilt. Make border rows last. Refer to photo and *Row Assembly Diagram* throughout.

1. Each Row 1 consists of top (dark) half of 2 stars and bottom (dark) half of 3 stars against a dark gray background. For *each* Row 1, select these pieces:

- 10 dark gray A diamonds
- 5 dark gray B triangles
- 4 dark gray C reversed parallelograms
- 9 dark gray D triangles
- 5 dark gray E triangles
- 5 sets of dark star fabrics, each set consisting of 2 B triangles, 2 D triangles, and 1 C parallelogram
- 4 scrap D triangles
- 2 scrap F reversed triangles

2. Select 1 set of star fabric. Join B, C, and D in a row *(Diagram A)*, adding dark gray B and D at ends. Sew remaining B and D to sides of an E piece. Add dark gray A diamonds on both sides of B/E/D unit. Join rows to complete star unit. Make 5 dark star units for Row 1.

3. Lay out 5 star units for Row 1, turning 3 upside down. Join units as shown below, sewing dark gray C reversed pieces between units.

4. Join 2 scrap Ds and 2 dark gray Ds *(Diagram B)*. Sew these, C reversed pieces, and F reversed triangles to ends to complete row.

5. Each Row 2 consists of top (light) half of 3 stars and bottom (light) half of 2 stars against a gray background. For *each* Row 2, select these pieces:

- 10 gray A diamonds
- 5 gray B triangles
- 4 gray C parallelograms
- 9 gray D triangles
- 5 gray E reversed triangles
- 5 sets of light star fabrics, each set consisting of 2 B triangles, 2 D triangles, and 1 C reversed parallelogram
- 4 scrap D triangles
- 2 scrap F triangles

6. Assemble star units for Row 2 in same manner as for Row 1, paying close attention to row diagram for mirror-image placement of star pieces. Join units in a row as shown, sewing gray C pieces between units.

7. Join 2 scrap Ds and 2 gray Ds *(Diagram C)*. Sew these, remaining Cs, and F triangles to row ends to complete row.

8. Make 8 of Row 1 and 8 of Row 2. Referring to photo, join rows, alternating rows 1 and 2.

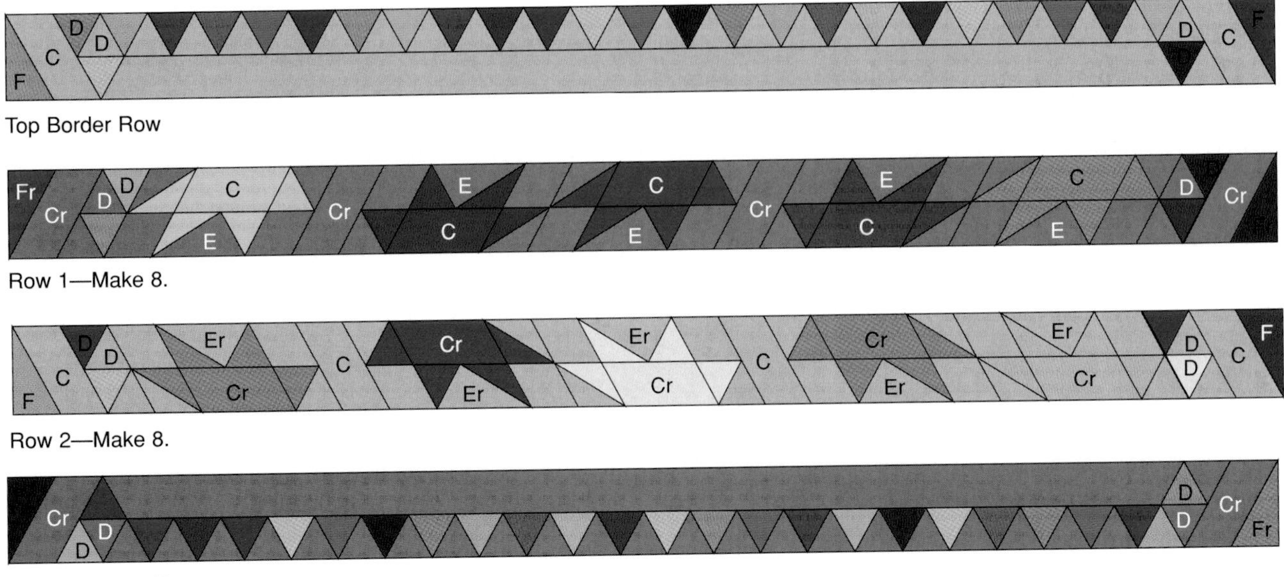

Row Assembly Diagram

Border Rows

Refer to photo and *Row Assembly Diagram* throughout.

1. For top border row, join 24 scrap D triangles and 24 gray Ds in a row.

2. Join 3"-wide gray strips end-to-end. Trim 1 end at a 60° angle. Join scrap D triangle to trimmed (left) end.

3. Match border strip to pieced D row and pin. Use a pin to mark border strip where it meets seam line of last gray D triangle. Remove border strip. Trim remaining end at a 60° angle, adding ¼" seam allowance. Add remaining scrap D and gray D to right end of gray strip. Sew gray strip to pieced D row.

4. Sew gray Cs and scrap Fs to row ends as shown to complete top border. Sew border to top edge of quilt.

5. For bottom border row, join 24 scrap D triangles and 24 dark gray Ds in a row as shown.

6. Join 3"-wide dark gray strips end-to-end and trim 1 end at a 60° angle. Join scrap D triangle to trimmed (left) end.

7. Pin gray strip to pieced D strip and measure to fit. Trim dark gray strip; then sew remaining scrap and gray D triangles in place. Sew gray strip to D strip, easing to fit as needed.

8. Sew dark gray C reversed pieces and scrap F reversed pieces to row ends to complete row. Sew border to bottom edge of quilt.

Quilting and Finishing

1. Layer backing, batting, and quilt top. Baste.

2. Outline-quilt patchwork. If desired, add echo quilting inside C pieces.

3. Make 10 yards of straight-grain binding. Bind quilt edges.

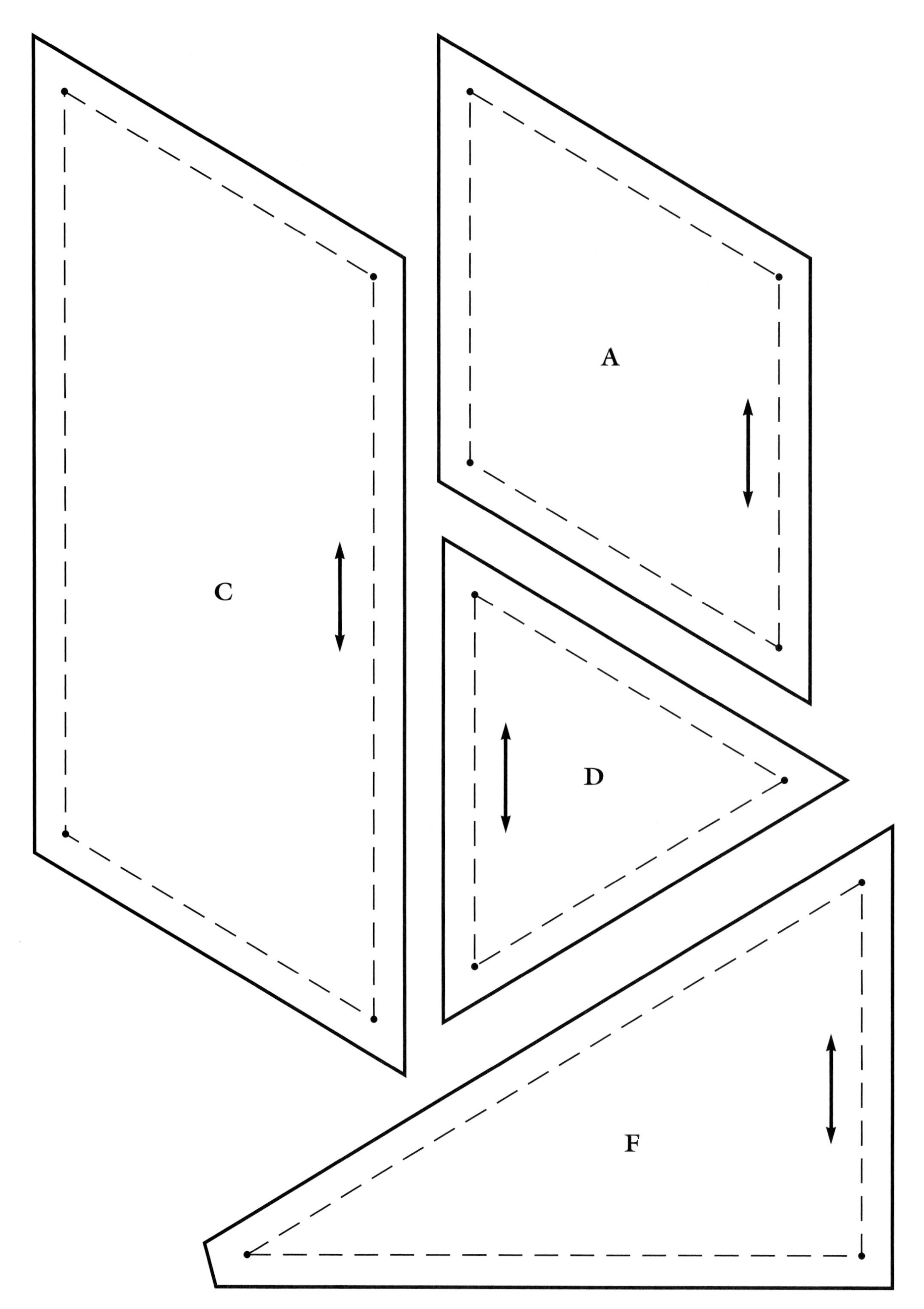
A
C
D
F

❖QUILT SMART❖

Rotary Cutting Workshop

Most quiltmakers today are very comfortable using a rotary cutter and an acrylic ruler to cut squares, rectangles, and triangles. But some are still wary about using it to cut angled shapes.

Five of the six shapes in *Concertina* are based on the 60° diamond. If you want to use your rotary cutter, try these tips.

60° Diamond (A)

1. Place a 3"-wide strip on cutting mat with selvages to your right. (*Note:* Instructions are for right-handed cutting. Lefties should reverse directions.)
2. Align one 60° line on ruler with bottom of strip *(Diagram 1)*. Trim end of strip to remove selvage and establish 60° angle.
3. Turn strip to place trimmed edge to your left. Align 60° line on ruler with bottom of strip again. Measure 3" from trimmed edge *(Diagram 2)*. Cut diamond.
4. Cut A diamonds until strip is used up *(Diagram 3)*.

Half-Diamond Triangle (B)

1. Using a strip 3½" wide, trim end at a 60° angle. Turn strip; cut 3½"-wide diamonds.
2. Cut each diamond in half to get 2 B triangles *(Diagram 4)*.

60° Parallelogram (C)

1. Trim end of a 3"-wide strip at a 60° angle. Turn strip to position trimmed edge to your left.
2. Align 60° line on ruler with bottom of strip; measure 5½" from trimmed edge *(Diagram 5)*. Cut parallelogram. Continue cutting 5½"-wide C pieces until strip is used up *(Diagram 6)*.
3. To cut C and C reversed pieces at the same time, layer 2 strips with wrong sides facing and cut through both layers.

Equilateral Triangle (D)

1. Trim end of a 3¼"-wide strip at a 60° angle. Turn strip to put trimmed edge to your left.
2. Measure and cut 3¼" diamonds *(Diagram 7)*.
3. Cut each diamond in half diagonally to get 2 D triangles *(Diagram 8)*.

Triangle (E)

1. Trim end of a 3⅛"-wide strip at a 60° angle. Turn strip to place trimmed edge to your left.
2. Align 60° line on ruler with bottom of strip; measure 6³⁄₁₆" from trimmed edge and cut parallelogram *(Diagram 9)*.
3. Cut parallelogram in half to get 2 E triangles *(Diagram 10)*.
4. To cut E and E reversed pieces at the same time, stack 2 strips with wrong sides facing.

Half-Rectangle Triangle (F)

1. Start with a strip 3⁹⁄₁₆" wide. Cut rectangles 6³⁄₁₆" long *(Diagram 11)*.
2. Cut half the rectangles in half diagonally from bottom right to top left to get 2 F triangles from each *(Diagram 12)*. Cut remaining rectangles in half from bottom left to top right as shown to get 2 F reversed triangles.

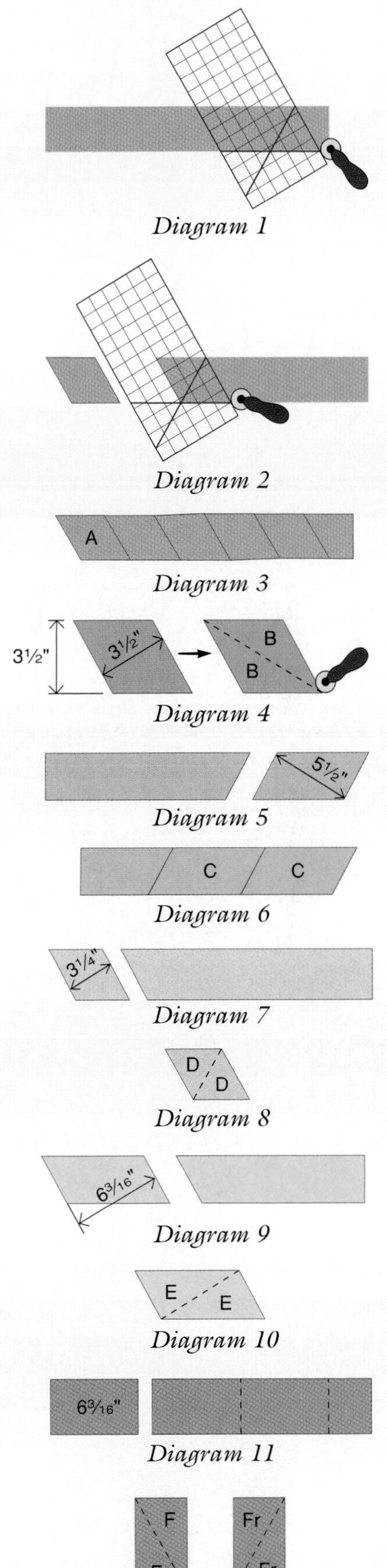

Dereck C. Lockwood

Chico, California

What started as a hobby more than 20 years ago is now a career for Dereck Lockwood.

A former clothing designer and interior decorator, Dereck's career took a detour when a spinal injury left him unemployed. "I got into quilting to kill the time," he says. Now he makes a living from machine quilting, booking tops to quilt more than eight months in advance. "I put my art on my clients' art, one complementing the other," Dereck says. "I take a top and bring it to life." He also teaches design and technique classes.

"My quilts and designs are a legacy," Dereck says. "Through them, maybe I'll be remembered by future generations."

Dereck designs quilts for competition and for publication in Seams to Be patterns. He is a member of Annies Star Quilt Guild, as well as International Quilt Association and the American Quilter's Society.

Celestial Garden

1999

Dereck Lockwood likes to combine tradition with original design to create interesting, beautiful quilts for the 21st century.

The idea for *Celestial Garden* was born when a student of Dereck's wanted to make a traditional Broken Star quilt. Always ready with a fresh idea, Dereck designed this quilt to incorporate other elements into the open areas around the star.

The quilt is made using paper-foundation piecing and strip-piecing techniques, and is embellished with Dereck's artful machine quilting.

In 2000, *Celestial Garden* was exhibited at Road to California and the American Quilter's Society show in Paducah, Kentucky.

Celestial Garden

Finished Size

Quilt: 83" x 83"
Blocks: 20 (10½" x 10½")

Materials

36 (9" x 22") assorted blue and burgundy fabrics for star (add 2" x 22" to each of 12 fabrics for pieced binding option)*
23 (8") squares pink, mauve, and lilac fabrics for lily blocks
1½ yards green
6 yards cream fabric (includes optional binding fabric)
2⅝ yards 104"-wide backing

**Note:* This is a nice quilt for friends to make side by side—since you only need half of a fat quarter, you can each buy 18 and swap halves. If you're working solo, you might choose to use some fabrics twice.

Pieces to Cut

Cut fabrics in order listed to make best use of yardage. Cut all strips cross-grain. When possible, pieces are listed in order needed, so you don't have to cut everything all at once.

From each *9" x 22" star fabric*

- 5 (1¾" x 22") strips.

From each *lily fabric*

- 3 (2¼") squares. Cut each square in half diagonally to get 6 Lily B/C triangles.
- 3 (1¾" x 5¼") Lily F strips.

From green

- 2 (2½"-wide) strips. From these, cut 34 (2½") squares. Cut each square in half diagonally to get 68 Lily G triangles.
- 5 (2"-wide) strips. From these, cut 28 (2" x 7") pieces for Leaf J and Side Unit F.

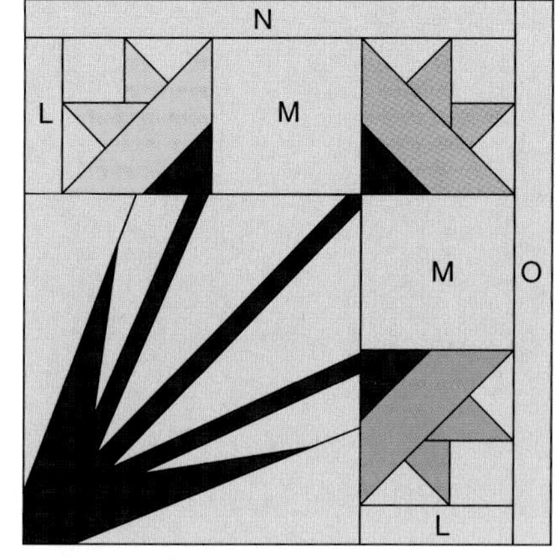

Lily Block—Make 20.

- 20 (1¾"-wide) strips. From these and scrap from previous cut, cut 20 (1¾" x 6") Leaf H pieces.
- 8 (1½"-wide) strips. From these, cut 8 (1½" x 6") Side Unit D pieces.
- 11 (1"-wide) strips. From these and scraps, cut 20 (1" x 9") Leaf D pieces, 40 (1" x 7") Leaf B/F pieces, and 8 (1" x 2½") Side Unit A pieces.

From cream

- 9 (1¾"-wide) strips. From these, cut 40 (1¾" x 6") Leaf A/G pieces and 68 (1¾") Lily A squares.
- 6 (2¾"-wide) strips. From these, cut 20 (2¾" x 7") Leaf I pieces and 34 (2¾") squares. Cut each square in quarters diagonally to get 136 Lily D/E triangles.
- 3 (9"-wide) strips. From these, cut 20 (3" x 9") Leaf C pieces and 20 (2½" x 9") Leaf E pieces.
- 2 (3"-wide) strips. From these, cut 20 (3" x 7½") Leaf K pieces.
- 8 (3½"-wide) strips. From these, cut 16 (3½" x 8") Side Unit E/G pieces, 40 (3½") M squares, and 40 (1¼" x 3½") L pieces.
- 10 (1¼"-wide) strips. From these, cut 20 (1¼" x 10¼") N strips and 20 (1¼" x 11") O strips.
- 3 (2"-wide) strips. From these, cut 16 (2" x 7") Side Unit B/C pieces.
- 8 (6" x 88") lengthwise strips for outer border.
- 4 (2" x 19") strips. From these, cut 8 each of Pattern X and Pattern X reversed for setting triangles. (Stack strips in pairs, right sides facing, to rotary-cut both at once.)
- 2 (4¾" x 19") strips. From these, cut 8 (4¾") squares. Cut each square in half diagonally to get 16 Y triangles for setting triangles.
- 6 (2½" x 60") lengthwise strips for matching straight-grain binding (optional).

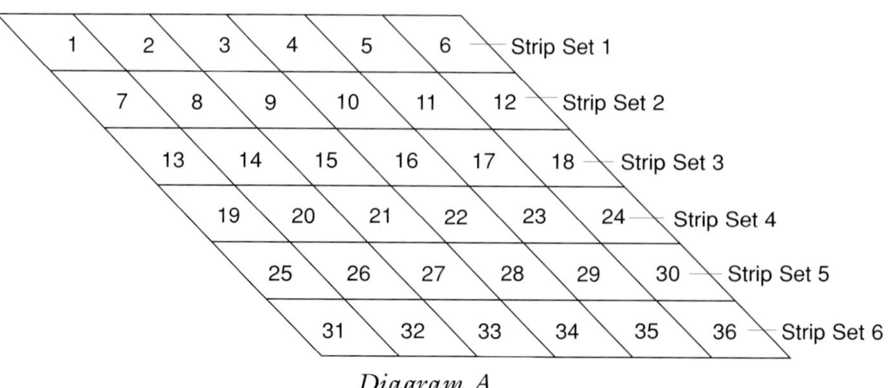

Diagram A

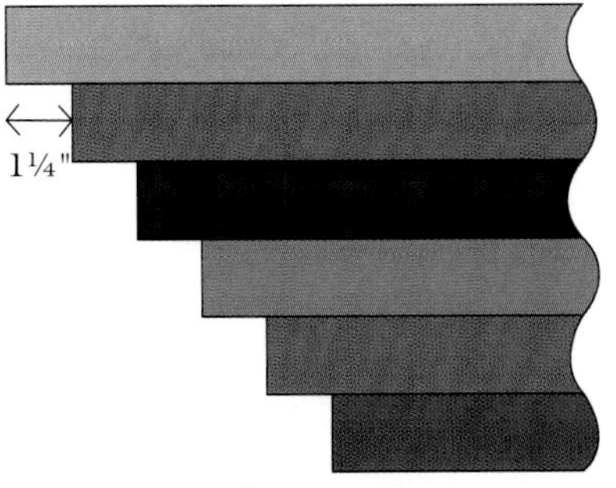

Diagram B

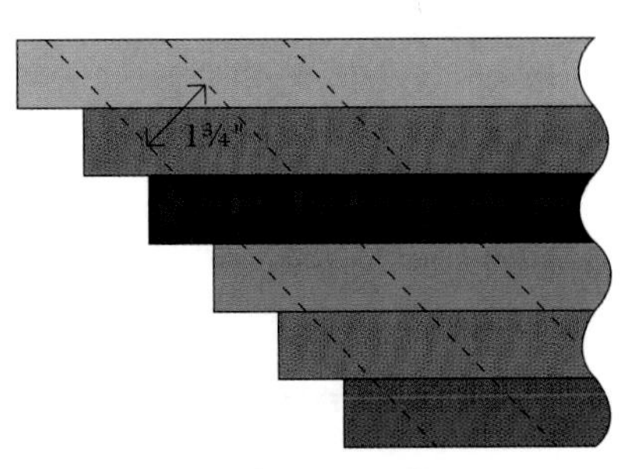

Diagram C

Star Diamonds

1. Assign each star fabric a number, 1–36 *(Diagram A)*. It's a good idea to make a photocopy enlargement so you can tape swatches in place on the diagram. Disperse fabric colors and tones throughout diamond so you don't have big splotches of a single color or value.

2. For Strip Set 1, select 1 strip each of fabrics 1–6. Join strips 1 and 2, dropping strip 2 down 1¼" from end of first strip *(Diagram B)*. Press seam allowance toward strip 2. Add strips 3–6 in same manner, dropping each strip down 1¼". Press each seam allowance toward last strip. Make 5 of Strip Set 1.

3. Use fabrics 7–12 to make Strip Set 2 in same manner. In even-numbered strip sets (2, 4, 6), press seam allowances toward first strip. For Strip Set 3, use fabric strips 13–18. In odd-numbered sets (1, 3, 5), press seams toward last strip. Use fabrics 19–24 for Strip Set 4 and fabrics 25–30 for Strip Set 5. For Strip Set 6, use fabrics 31–36. Make 5 of each strip set.

4. Lay a Strip Set 1 on cutting mat, right side up. Aligning 45° angle on ruler with bottom edge of strip set, trim uneven edges. Measuring from cut edge, cut a strip 1¾" wide *(Diagram C)*. Cut 7 segments from each strip set to get a total of 32 Strip Set 1 segments (and 3 extra). Cut strip sets 2–6 in same manner. (Set aside extras for optional pieced binding.)

5. For each diamond, select 1 segment of each strip set. Join segments in numerical order as shown *(Diagram D)*. Make 32 diamonds. In 16 diamonds, press seam allowances toward first row; in remaining 16 diamonds, press seam allowances toward last row.

6. Set diamonds aside.

Lily Block Assembly

See Quilt Smart, page 76, for tips on paper foundation piecing before beginning lily blocks.

1. Make paper foundations for 68 Lily Units and 20 Leaf Units (see patterns, pages 79 and 80).

2. Following Quilt Smart instructions, sew lily pieces A–G onto Lily Unit foundation in alphabetical order. Make 68 lily units. Trim seam allowances to ¼". Remove paper foundations.

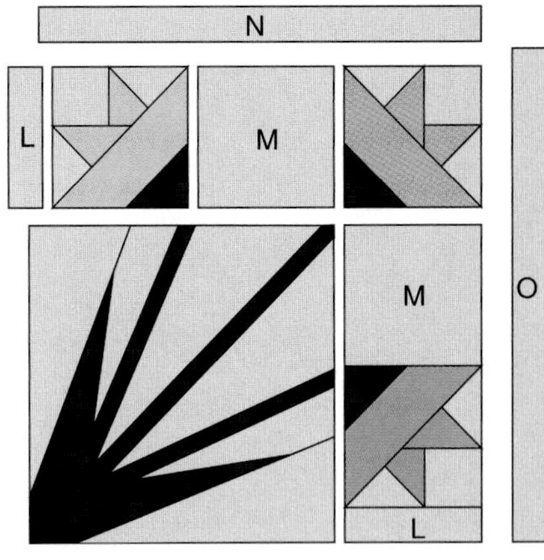

Block Assembly Diagram

3. Sew leaf pieces A–K onto each Leaf Unit foundation in alphabetical order. Trim seam allowances; then remove paper.

4. For each block, select 3 lily units of different fabrics and 1 leaf unit. You also need 2 L, 2 M, 1 N, and 1 O of cream.

5. Lay out block units in rows *(Block Assembly Diagram)*. Join L, Lily Unit, M, and Lily Unit in a row as shown. Press seam allowances away from lilies. Add N strip to top edge of this unit.

6. Sew L and M to opposite sides of remaining Lily Unit. Press seam allowances away from lily. Join this unit to 1 side of Leaf Unit. Press seam allowance away from Leaf Unit.

7. Join rows. Press. To complete block, add O strip to block edge adjacent to N.

8. Complete 20 Lily blocks. Set aside 8 remaining Lily Units for setting triangles.

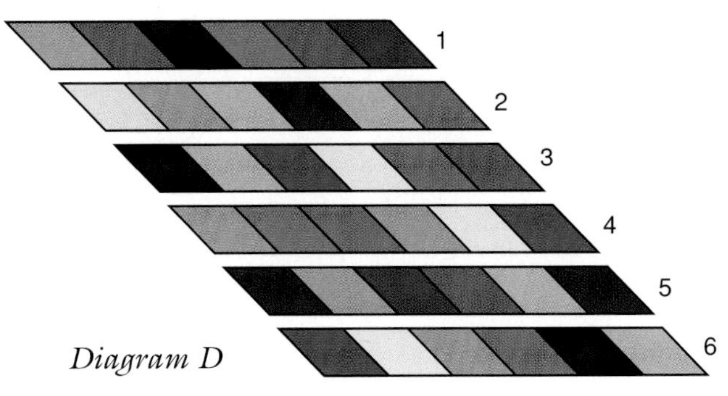

Diagram D

❖QUILT SMART❖

Paper Foundation Piecing

Small, narrow pieces can be difficult to cut and sew. Today's foundation piecing is an updated version of an old technique that can simplify this kind of patchwork. This technique is sometimes called "sew and flip."

Getting Ready

1. Photocopy design onto lightest-weight paper possible. Some copiers can copy onto tracing paper. Don't worry about distortion of the pattern in photocopying—any variation is too small to be visible.

2. Set your machine to 18–20 stitches per inch. Use neutral-colored thread so you don't have to change it while making a block.

Sew Easy

1. Pin piece A faceup on the *unmarked* side of the paper. Be sure fabric extends beyond all A seam lines *(Diagram 1)*. You may have to hold the paper up to the light to see the lines on the reverse side of the paper.

2. Pin B on top of A at joining seam line, right sides facing. (*Note:* In these instructions, as in most foundation piecing, pieces are cut slightly larger than necessary.)

3. Place block under presser foot with marked side up and fabrics underneath. Starting a few stitches before the printed seam line, stitch seam between A and B. Sew a few stitches beyond end of line *(Diagram 2)*. Clip threads and remove block from sewing machine.

4. Press fabrics in place, making sure they extend beyond seam lines for each piece *(Diagram 3)*. Trim seam allowance, being careful not to cut the paper.

5. Add C in same manner *(Diagram 4)*. Continue adding pieces in alphabetical order until block is complete.

6. Use a ruler and rotary cutter to trim block, leaving ¼" seam allowances.

7. Gently tear paper away from seams, being careful not to pull threads any more than necessary. Press block.

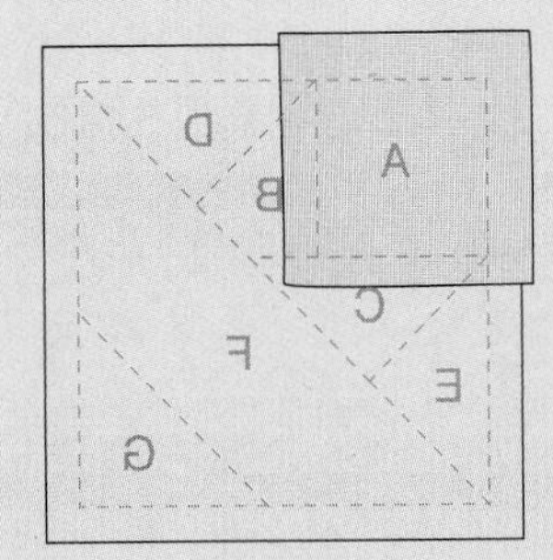

Diagram 1

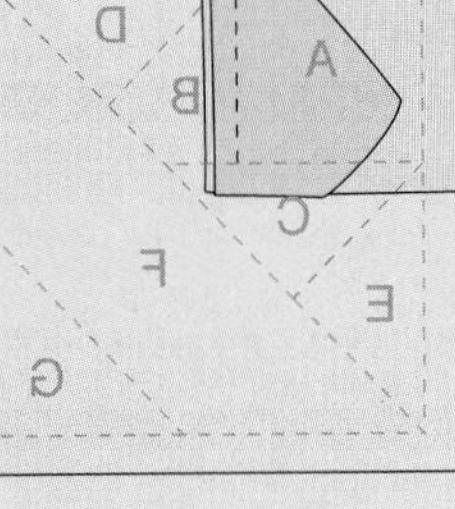

Diagram 2

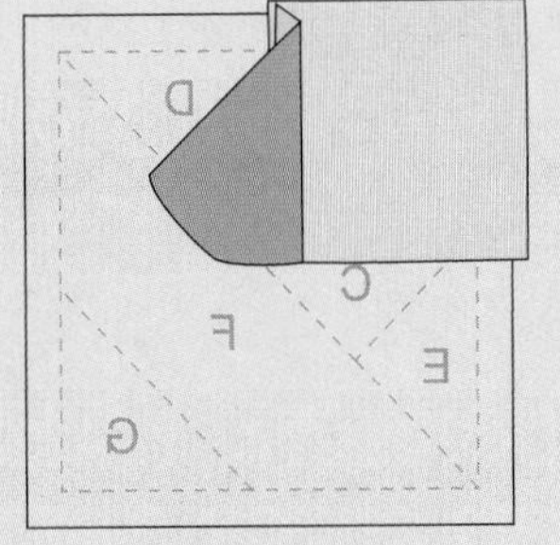
Diagram 3

Diagram 4

Setting Triangle Assembly

1. Make foundations for 8 Side Units (see pattern, page 80).

2. Sew triangle pieces A–G onto Side Unit foundations in alphabetical order. Make 8 Side Units. Trim seam allowances and clip inside corner as indicated on pattern. Remove foundations.

3. Sew 1 X and 1 X reversed to adjacent sides of each remaining Lily Unit *(Diagram E)*. Press seam allowances toward X pieces.

4. Set a Lily Unit into opening of each Side Unit. (See tips on sewing a set-in seam, page 77.)

5. Sew a Y triangle to each end of Side Unit to complete setting triangle *(Diagram F)*. Press seam allowances toward Ys.

6. Make 8 setting triangles.

X
X rev.
Diagram E

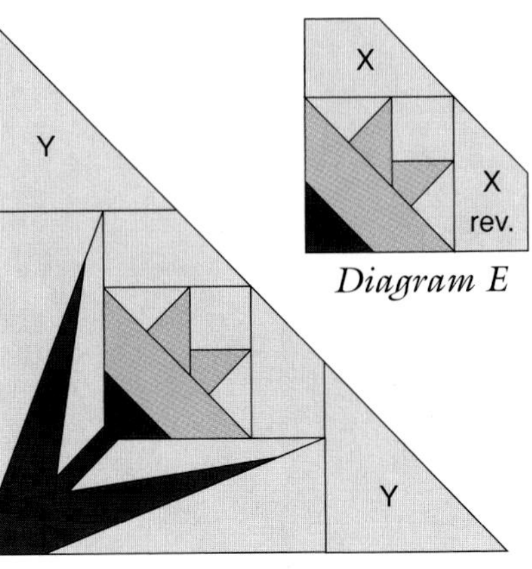

Diagram F

Quilt Assembly

1. Referring to photo on page 78, lay out 8 diamonds so that same fabric meets at center. Follow Quilt Smart instructions, at right to set blocks into Y-seam of each diamond pair and stitch seams of diamond pairs.

2. With right sides facing, place a Lily block on top of right diamond in each pair. Sew from dot to dot *(Diagram G)*. Make 4 of these units. Press seam allowances toward diamonds.

3. With right sides facing, match block of 1 unit with diamond of adjacent unit *(Diagram H)*. With block on top, stitch from outside dot to inner dot (seam shown in red).

4. Align unstitched edges of diamonds, folding adjacent block inside to keep it out of seam allowance. Pin-match diamonds. Begin at inner dot *(Diagram I)* and sew through all seams to

❖QUILT SMART❖

Machine-Stitching a Set-In Seam

When three seams come together in a Y-angle, use this technique to set the pieces together.

It's important to remember—don't stitch into the seam allowance as in most patchwork. Lightly mark the seam line on the wrong side of each piece so you won't stitch beyond that crucial matching point. (In diagrams, this point is indicated by a dot.) See page 51 for additional tips on sewing dot-to-dot. Mark seam line dots on wrong sides of each unit.

For this example, we've used the star unit that consists of two diamonds and one square or block.

1. With right sides facing, match diamond to one side of square *(Diagram 1)*. With square on top, stitch from dot to dot. Clip thread and take work out of sewing machine.

2. With right sides facing, match another diamond to adjacent side of square. With square on top, sew from dot at outside edge to inner dot *(Diagram 2)*. Reduce stitch length at dot.

3. With right sides facing, match points and edges of diamonds. Fold square out of the way. Beginning at inner dot, sew to opposite dot *(Diagram 3)*.

4. Press center seam open and square's seam allowances toward diamonds *(Diagram 4)*. Trim "ears" of diamond seam allowances even with unit edges.

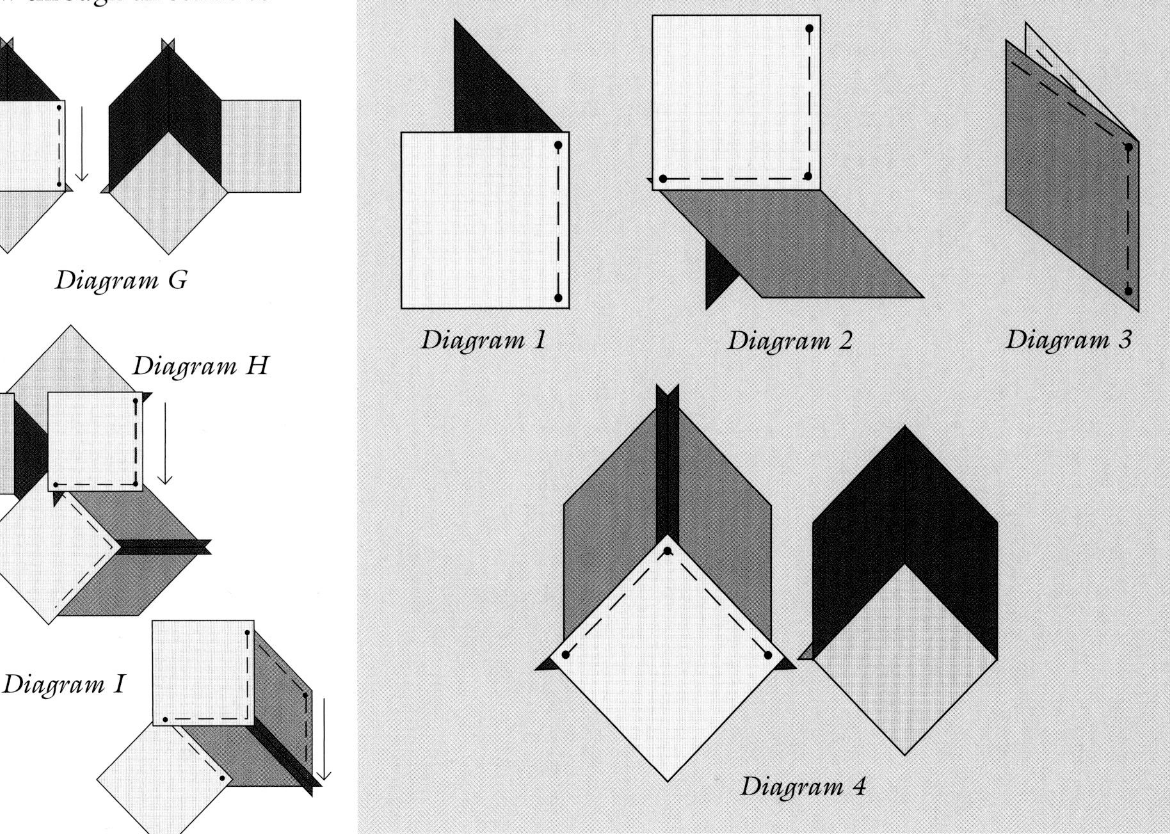

Diagram G

Diagram H

Diagram I

Diagram 1

Diagram 2

Diagram 3

Diagram 4

edge of fabric. Press diamond seam allowances open and block seams toward diamond. Assemble 2 halves of star *(Diagram J)*.

5. Join squares of each half to opposite diamond as described in Step 3.

6. Pin-match diamonds along length of center seam *(Diagram K)*. Stitch from dot through center of star, ending at opposite dot. Press seam allowance open. Press corner seam allowances toward diamonds *(Diagram L)*.

7. Join remaining diamonds in 8 groups of 3, stitching dot to dot *(Diagram M)*.

8. Set a 3-diamond unit into opening between any 2 Lily blocks. Press seam allowances toward diamonds. Working clockwise around center star, set 3-diamond units into each opening. Join adjacent diamonds.

9. Lay star on floor. Referring to photo, determine top, bottom, and sides of star. Set setting triangles into 8 middle openings, 2 on each side of quilt.

10. Lay out quilt and remaining Lily blocks. Starting at top left corner, set in bottom Lily block *(Diagram N)*. Join remaining pair of blocks; then set joined

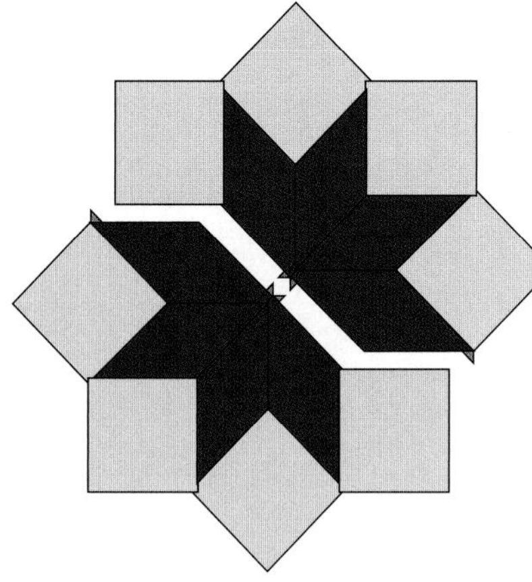

Diagram J

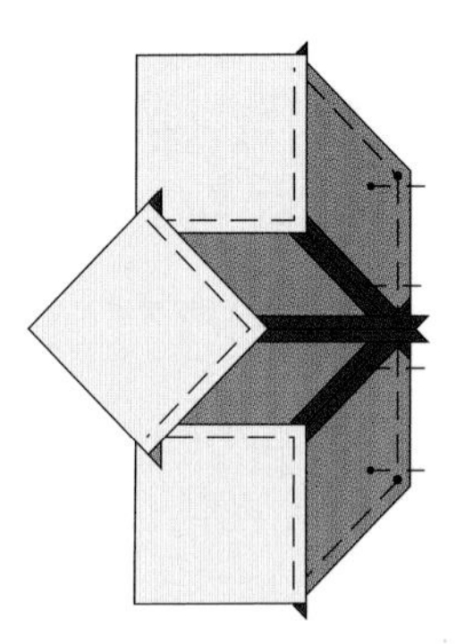

Diagram K

Diagram L

Diagram M

Diagram N

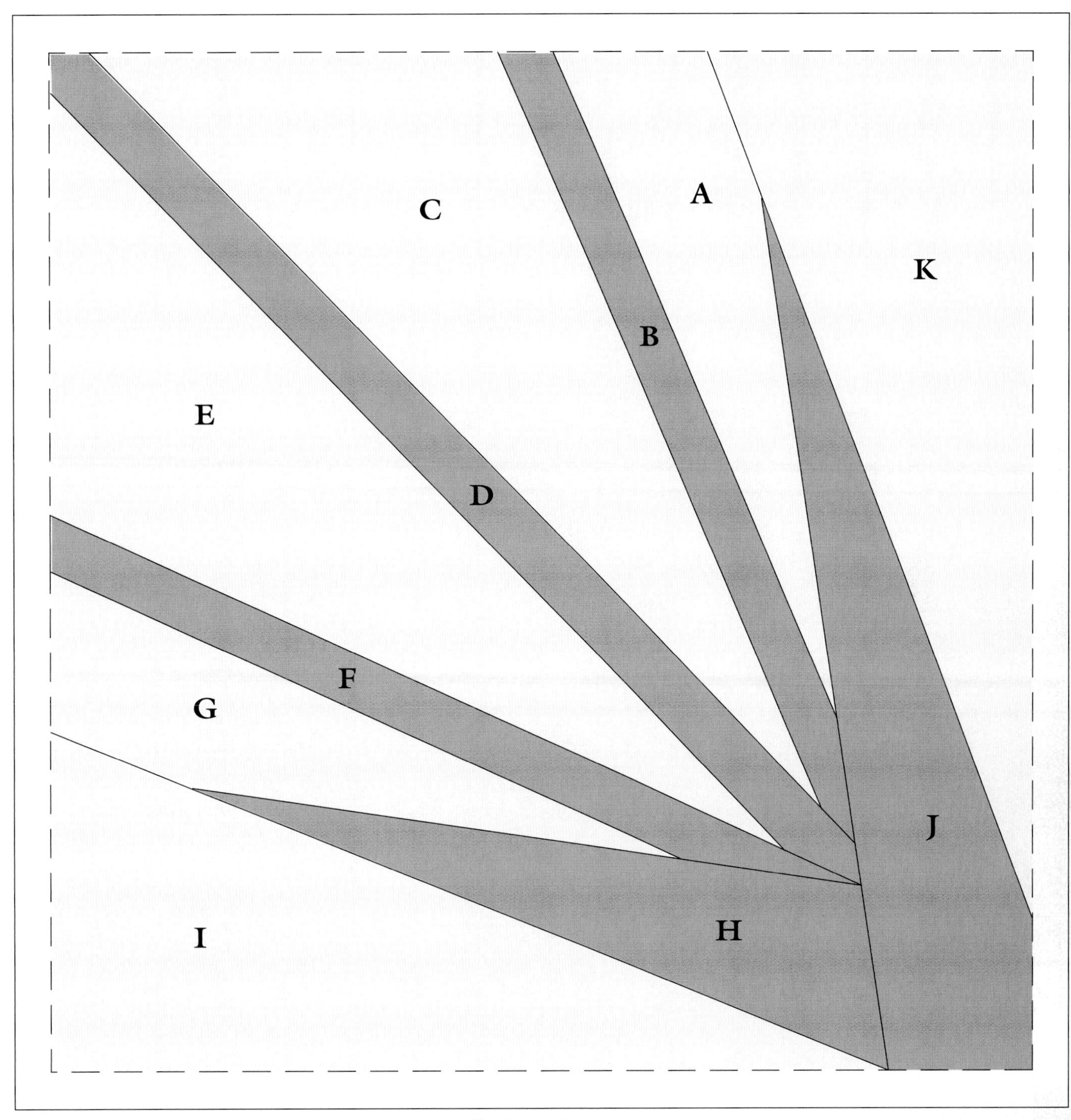

Leaf Unit Pattern

unit into opening. Repeat at remaining corners, being careful to keep blocks turned correctly.

Border

See page 141 for tips on sewing mitered border corners. Sew cream borders to all sides of quilt and miter corners.

Quilting and Finishing

1. Layer backing, batting, and quilt top. Baste.

2. Quilt as desired. Quilt shown is quilted in-the-ditch and an undulating feather vine is quilted in border. Cream background fabric is stipple-quilted. All quilting is by machine.

3. For pieced binding, you'll need to piece and cut 2 more strip sets as described for star diamonds. Add these to reserved strips. Join all strips end-to-end to make 9½ yards of narrow bias. Or use reserved cream fabric to make straight-grain binding. Bind quilt edges.

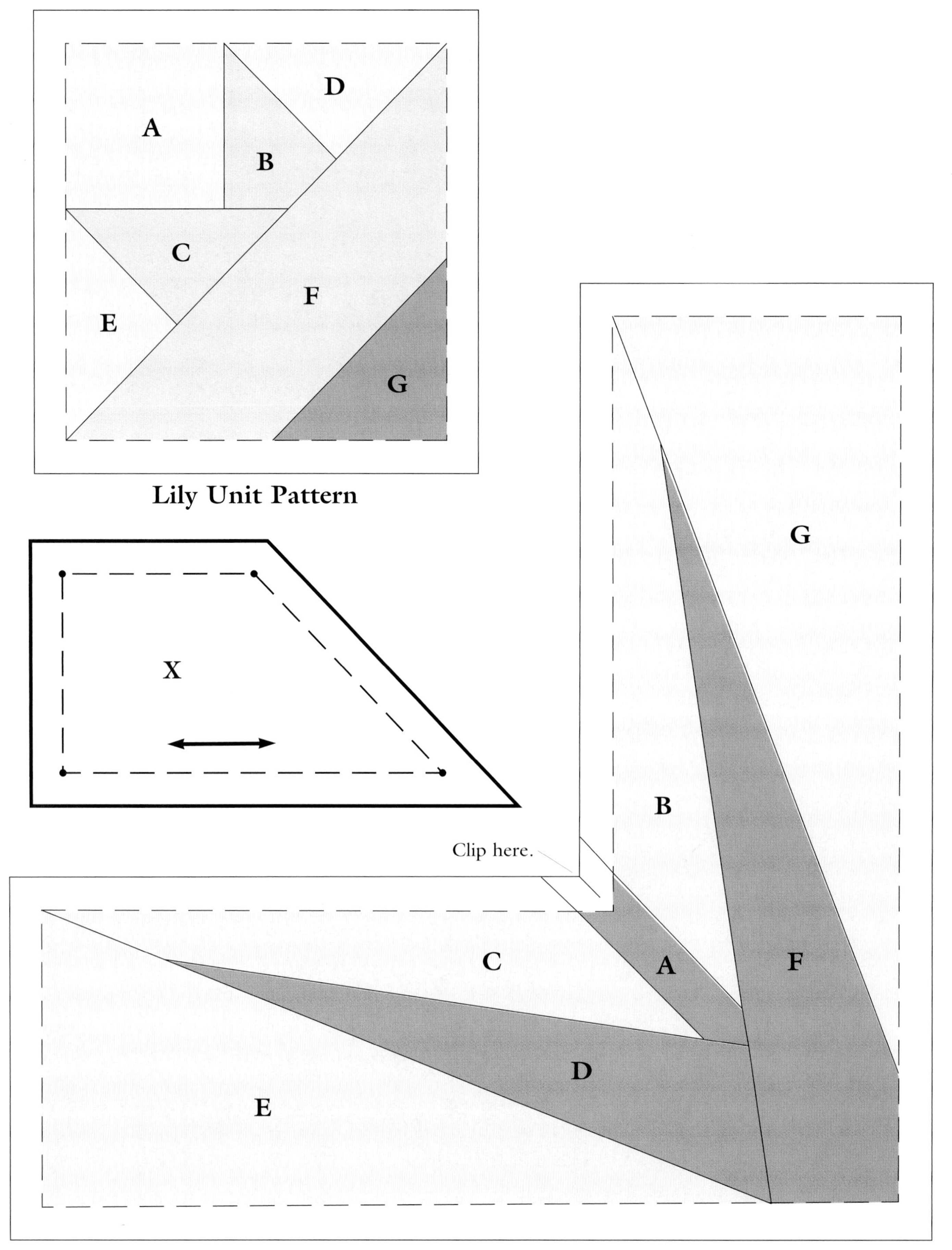

Lily Unit Pattern

Side Unit Pattern

The Monday Night Literary Society

Cape Girardeau, Missouri

Quilts, scraps, and mystery novels are just a few of the favorite things that bind these three women together in friendship.

No ordinary name would do for the quiltmaking trio of Judy Robinson, Nancy Ross, and Betty Murray. When asked if they review books, Judy replies, "Yes, quilt books!" All kidding aside, the friends swap books (who-done-its are a great favorite) almost as much as fabric and blocks. "We nearly always have one or two projects going," Judy says.

From left: Judy Robinson, Betty Murray, Nancy Ross

"We're lucky to have found each other."

But friendship is the most important ingredient in the mix. "We're lucky to have found quilting and each other," Judy says. "I have marvelous, caring friends, as well as a creative outlet that is user-friendly."

In addition to their group's activities, Betty quilts with her church group and Nancy participates in an on-line group that enjoys making mystery quilts. Judy teaches at a local quilt shop and is active in guild affairs.

All three are members of River Heritage Quilter's Guild of Cape Girardeau.

Blowin' in the Wind

1998

Nancy Ross likes to say that she didn't really become a quilter until she discovered the rotary cutter. "It changed my life," she says. That's why blocks like this quick-pieced Weathervane block are fun for Nancy to make with her friends Judy Robinson and Betty Murray.

The three made and swapped the scrappy blocks. Then Judy took a class from Sharyn Craig about nontraditional ways to set quilt blocks. Inspired by Sharyn's ideas, Judy set her blocks in a tumbling format.

Note: Sharon Craig's book *Twist 'n Turn* describes several methods for making tumbling blocks. Available at quilt shops, it is published by Chitra Publications.

Blowin' in the Wind

Block 1—Make 17.

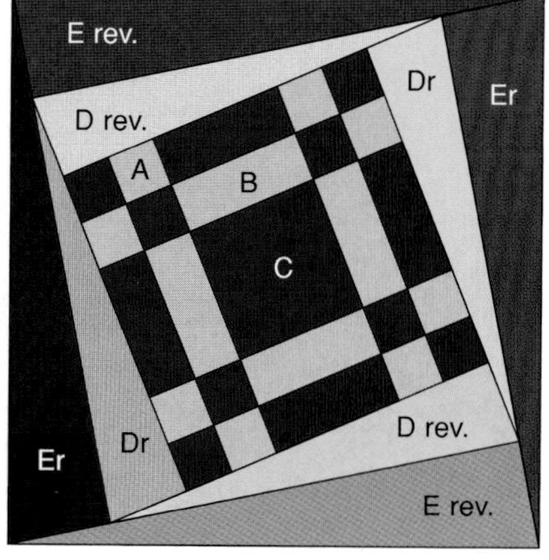

Block 2—Make 18.

Finished Size

Quilt: 61" x 84"
Blocks: 35 (11" x 11")

Materials

35 (3" x 14") light/medium prints for blocks
35 (3¼" x 18") medium/dark prints for blocks
35 (4½" x 11¼") light shirting-type prints for D triangles
59 (8" x 14") dark prints for E/F triangles, pieced binding
4 (3½") squares for corners
2 yards 104"-wide backing
Template material

Note: As in all scrap quilts, these yardages are recommendations. Use your own scraps and fabric placement as desired.

Pieces to Cut

Because of their odd angles, we recommend traditional cutting for pieces D and E. Make templates for patterns on page 84.

Cut pieces in order listed to make best use of yardage. Whenever possible, pieces are listed in order needed, so you don't have to cut all fabric at once.

From each *light/medium print*
- 2 (1½" x 14") strips.

From each *medium/dark print*
- 1 (3¼") C square.
- 2 (1½" x 14") strips.

From each *shirting print*
- 2 (2¼" x 11¼") strips. From these, cut a total of 68 D triangles for Block 1 and 72 D reversed triangles for Block 2.

From 35 dark prints
- 68 of Pattern E.
- 72 of Pattern E reversed.

From 24 dark prints
- 1 (3⅝" x 13¼") rectangle. Cut 14 rectangles in half diagonally from lower left to upper right to get 28 F border triangles. Cut remaining rectangles in half from lower right to upper left to get 20 F reversed border triangles.
- 1 (2½" x 14") strip for pieced binding.

Block Assembly

1. For each block, select 2 (1½" x 14") light strips, 2 dark strips, and a matching C square.

2. Join light and dark strips in 2 strip sets *(Diagram A)*. Press seams toward darker fabric.

3. From these strip sets, cut 8 (1½"-wide) A units and 4 (3¼"-wide) B units as shown.

4. Join A and B units in 3 rows *(Diagram B)*, adding C square in middle row as shown. Press all seam allowances toward B units. Join rows to complete center section of block.

5. For Block 1, select 4 D triangles. Sew first D to 1 edge of block with a partial seam, stopping half way along edge *(Diagram C)*. Sew second D to combined edge in a complete seam. Add Ds to remaining edges. When last D seam is sewn, complete first seam along combined edge. Press seam allowances away from Ds.

6. Add 4 Es to block in same manner, beginning with a partial seam; then add remaining Es. Complete partial seam last. Press seam allowances toward Es.

7. Make 17 of Block 1.

8. Make 18 of Block 2, using D reversed and E reversed pieces.

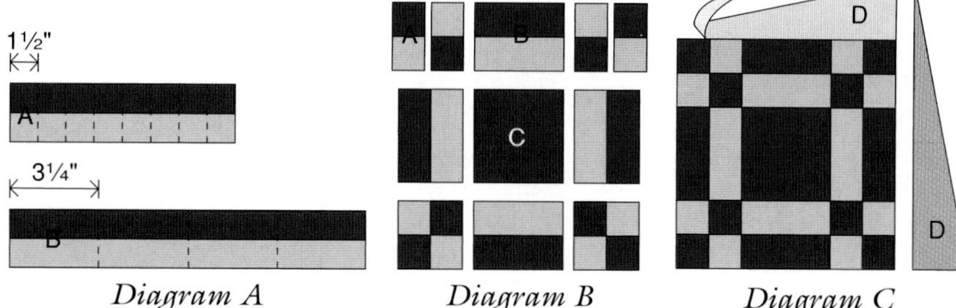

Diagram A *Diagram B* *Diagram C*

Quilt Top Assembly

1. Join 2 F triangles for each of 14 border units. Join F reversed triangles for remaining 10 units.

2. Referring to photo, lay out blocks in 7 horizontal rows with 5 alternating blocks in each row. Odd-numbered rows (1, 3, 5, 7) start and end with a Block 2. Even-numberd rows (2, 4, 6) start and end with a Block 1.

3. When satisfied with layout of blocks, join blocks in each row.

4. Referring to photo, add a border unit to ends of each row. Use F units for odd-numbered rows and F reversed units for even-numbered rows. Join rows.

5. Join remaining border units in 2 horizontal rows with 5 units in each row, alternating F and F reversed units as shown. Sew corner squares to ends of both rows.

6. Sew border rows to top and bottom edges of quilt, easing to fit as needed.

Quilting and Finishing

1. Layer backing, batting, and quilt top. Outline-quilt or quilt as desired.

2. Join reserved 2½"-wide strips to make 8¼ yards of straight-grain binding. Bind quilt edges.

E

D

Color Variations

This is a good block for the popular "I Spy" quilts, centering novelty-print motifs in the C squares. *Blowin' in the Wind* can also be fun to make in a favorite color scheme, such as jewel-tone or pastel.

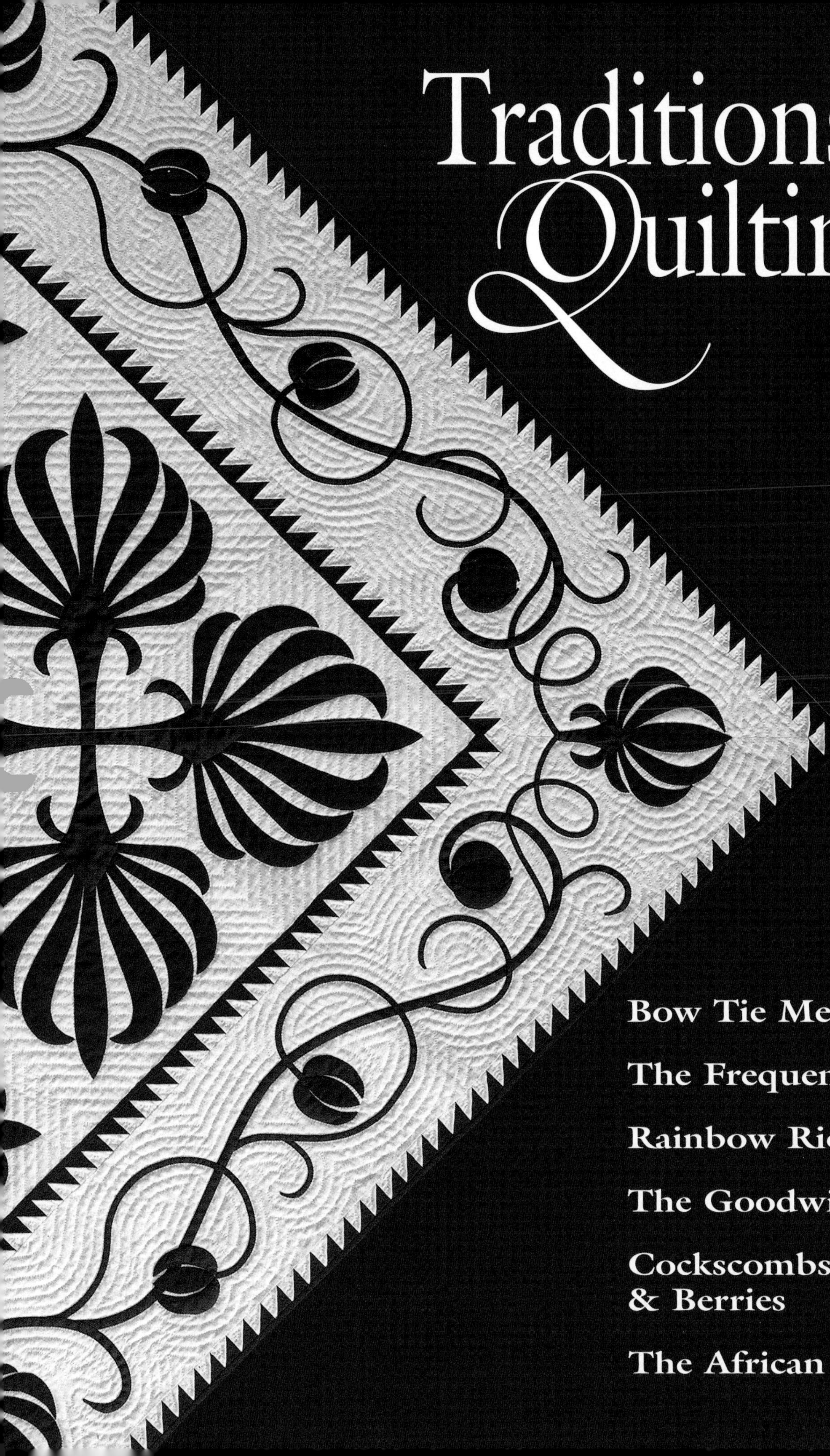

Traditions in Quilting

Bow Tie Memories

The Frequent Flyer

Rainbow Riot

The Goodwill Quilt

Cockscombs, Tulips & Berries

The African King

Laura Lorensen Franchini

Wisner, Nebraska

At the local elementary school, "Q-day" is the annual occasion when Laura Franchini brings her quilts and talks to the children about quiltmaking.

This is just one of the many civic activities Laura combines with quilting. A homemaker, Laura devotes a great deal of time toward both personal and community quilting projects. She presents trunk shows, classes, and lectures for groups in a three-state area, as well as giving presentations at local schools and nursing homes.

"I . . . started off on my own."

Always interested in handcrafts, Laura did some piecing in the early '70s, but she didn't find it interesting. A decade later, "I wanted a pieced kitchen tablecloth, so I took some quilt books out of the library and started off on my own," she says. By then, available fabrics were much more interesting and she found playing with them was "so much fun that I've worked steadily on quilts ever since." Laura likes both hand and machine methods and uses "whatever techniques best complement the work."

Laura quilts with a local church group and is also a member of the Country Piecemaker's Quilt Guild and the Nebraska State Quilt Guild.

Bow Tie Memories

1998

One of Laura Franchini's goals is to make a quilt in the same pattern or style as each of the quilts she owns that her grandmothers made.

"It's interesting to use the same patterns with the wonderful fabrics we have now," Laura says.

One of Laura's grandmother's quilts has bow tie blocks in a vertical set with fabric strips between the rows. "This was an excellent place for me to use this wonderful stripe fabric I'd been saving," Laura decided.

Laura dedicated this quilt to her parents. She used her mother's favorite colors, and the stripe fabric reminds Laura of her father's ties (that her mother probably bought for him).

To avoid set-in seams, Laura used a contemporary technique for making dimensional bow ties.

Bow Tie Memories

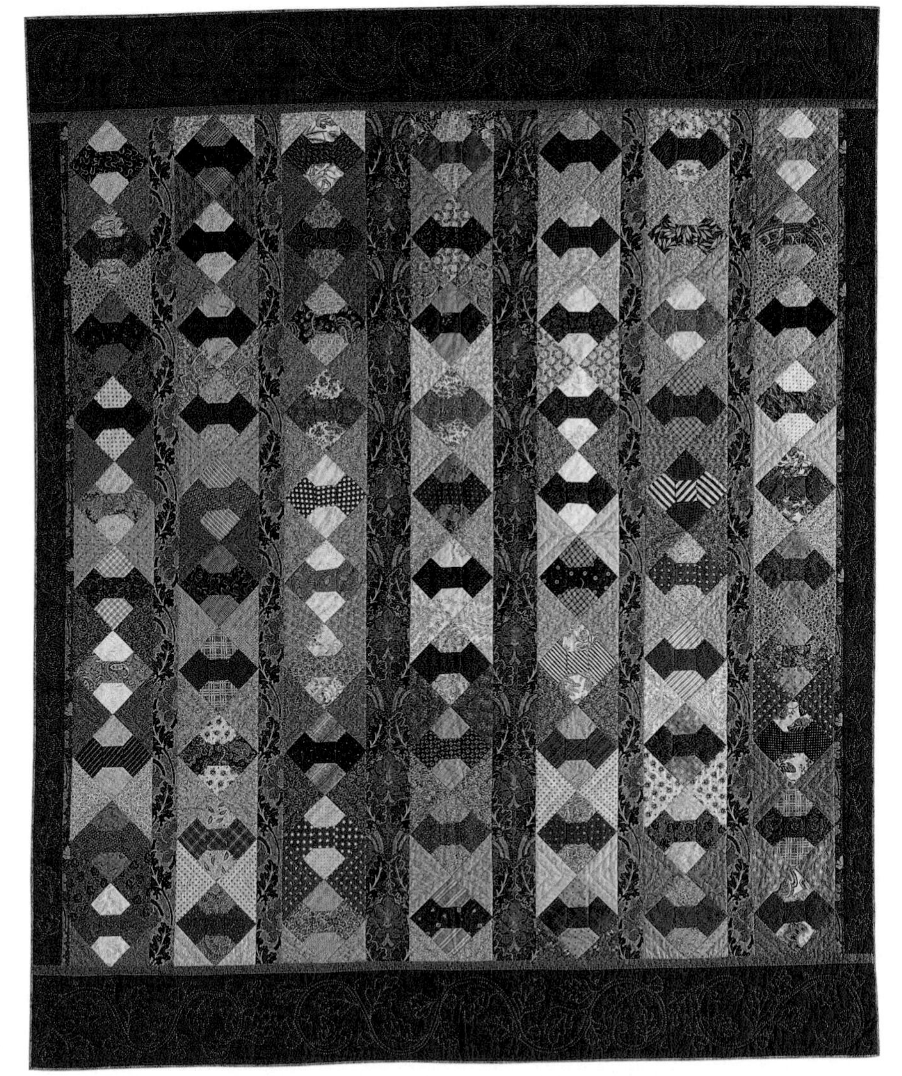

Finished Size
Quilt: 72" x 87"
Blocks: 70 (5" x 5")

Materials
70 (3" x 6") assorted light scraps for block backgrounds
70 (3" x 9") assorted dark scraps for bow ties
30 (8⅜") assorted squares for setting triangles
14 (4½") assorted squares for end triangles
2¼ yards burgundy tone-on-tone for borders*
2¼ yards theme print*
1 yard gold tone-on-tone for binding and top/bottom inner borders
5½ yards backing fabric
* *Note:* Yardage is determined by length of fabric needed, but this quilt requires only about half the width. You might want to share the fabric with a friend and make your quilts together.

Block Assembly
1. Choose 1 light scrap and 1 dark scrap for each block. Cut 2 (3") squares from light scrap and 3 (3") squares from dark.

2. With wrong sides facing, fold a dark square in half to make a rectangle.

3. Sandwich rectangle between a pair of light and dark squares, with right sides facing and raw edges aligned *(Diagram A)*. Sew squares together, catching short end of rectangle in seam.

4. Press seam allowances toward dark square. Press squares away from rectangle *(Diagram B)*.

5. Sandwich free end of rectangle between remaining squares, being careful to switch position of each fabric *(Diagram C)*. Sew across edge as before, catching short end of rectangle in seam.

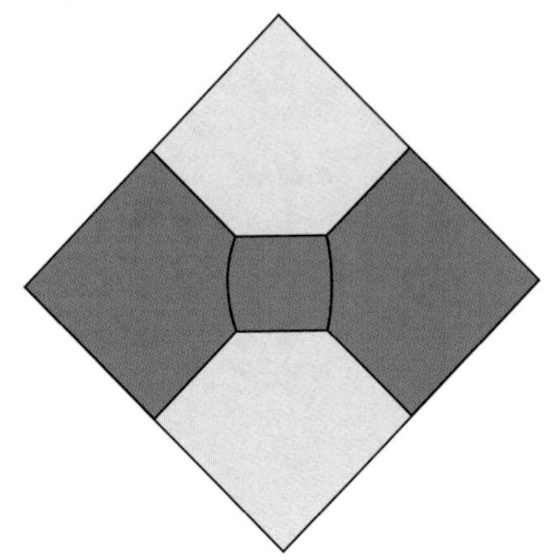

Bow Tie Block—Make 70.

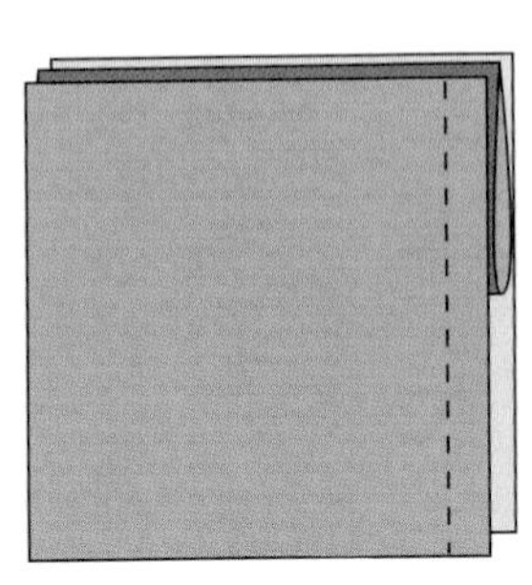

Diagram A

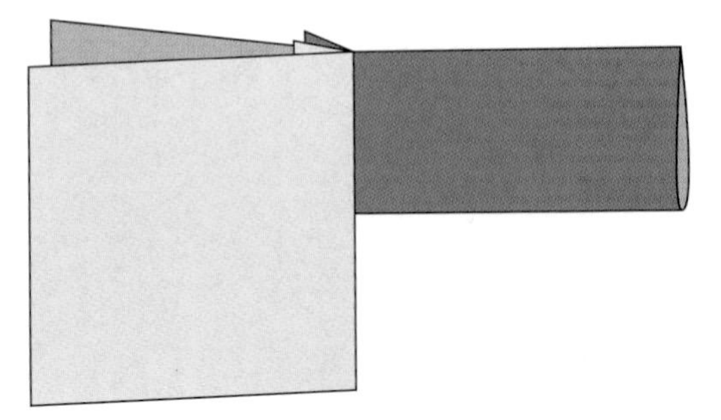

Diagram B

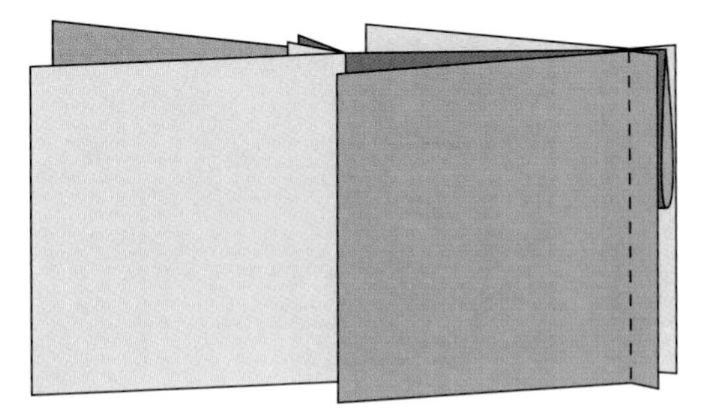

Diagram C

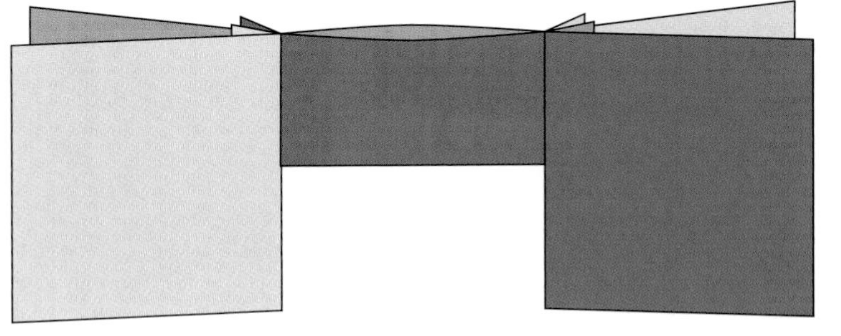

Diagram D

6. Press squares away, making rectangle a bridge between square pairs *(Diagram D).*
7. Bring square pairs together, letting rectangle refold itself between them, aligning raw edges and seam lines *(Diagram E).* Stitch joining seam *(Diagram F).*
8. Open pieces and check to see that bow tie knot lies flat. Press.
9. Make 70 Bow Tie blocks.

Quilt Top Assembly

1. From gold fabric, cut a 32" square for binding and 4 (1¼"-wide) cross-grain strips for inner borders; set aside. From remaining gold fabric, cut 2 (8⅜") squares for setting triangles.
2. Cut 32 (8⅜") squares in quarters diagonally to get 126 setting triangles (and 2 extra).
3. Referring to photo, lay out blocks in 7 vertical rows, laying a matched pair of setting triangles between blocks as shown.
4. For each pair of end triangles, cut a 4½" square in half diagonally. Add end triangles to row layouts.
5. Sew end triangles to top edges of first block in each row *(Diagram G).* Sew setting triangle to bottom left edge of first block. Sew setting triangles to opposite edges of remaining blocks as shown, ending with end triangles on bottom of last block. Press all seam allowances toward triangles.
6. Join block/triangle units to complete each row.
7. Cut 8 lengthwise strips from theme fabric: 2 (4⅛"-wide) strips, 4 (2⅝"-wide) strips, and 2 (1¼"-wide) strips. Referring to photo, alternate strips with block rows. When satisfied with placement, join block rows and sashing strips. Press seam allowances toward sashing strips.
8. Cut 2 (3¼"-wide) lengthwise strips of burgundy border fabric. Sew these to quilt sides to complete center section.

Borders

1. Measure width of quilt top through middle, including side borders. Piece gold border strips to make 2 borders to match width. Sew borders to top and bottom edges of quilt, easing to fit as needed.
2. From burgundy, cut 2 (8½"-wide) lengthwise strips. Sew these to top and bottom edges. Trim ends as needed.

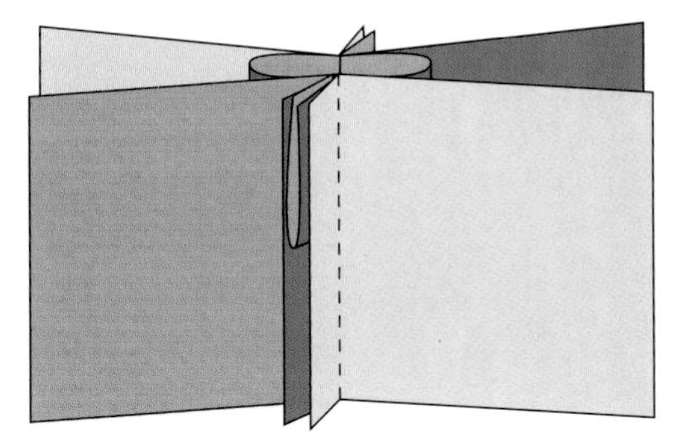

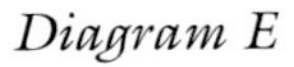

Diagram E

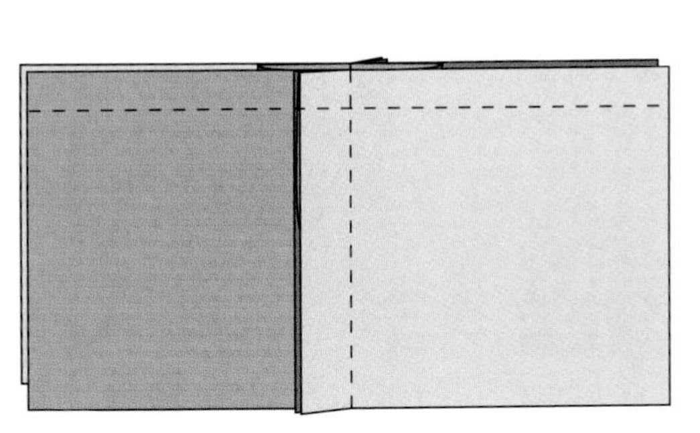

Diagram F

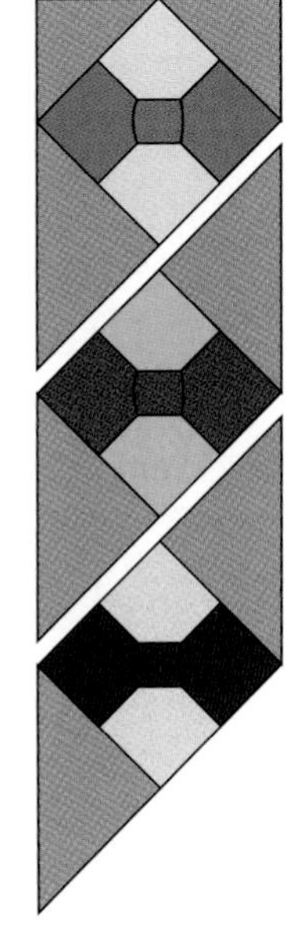

Diagram G

Color Variations

Tied up in knots about color schemes? Here are a few variations on our *Bow Tie Memories,* from little-girl pastel to black-tie formal. Pull favorites from your fabric pile to stitch up your own fashion statement.

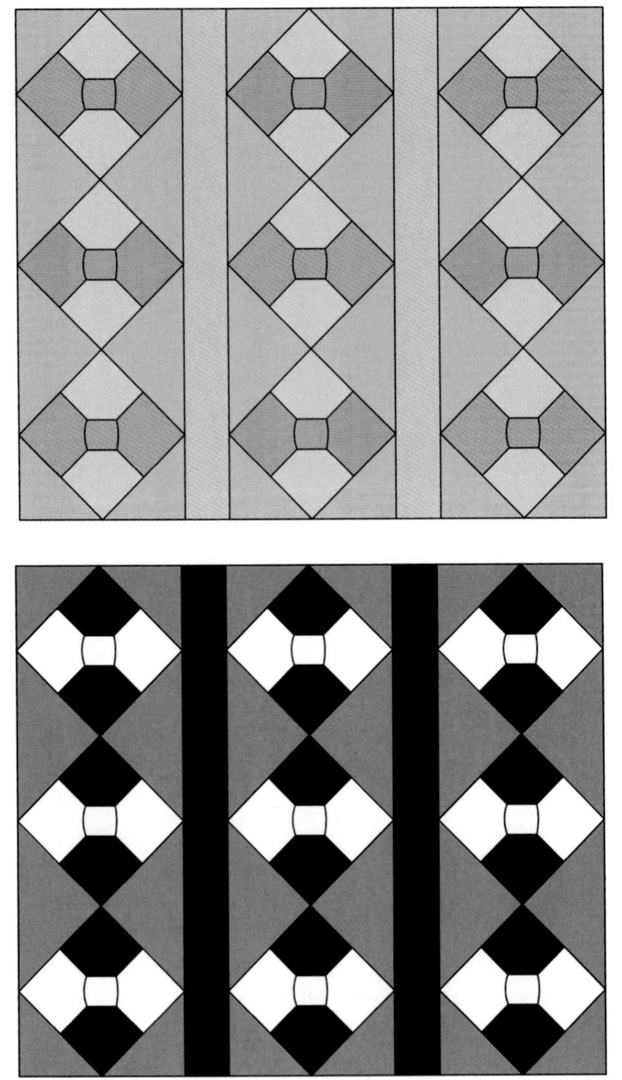

Quilting and Finishing

1. Assemble backing. Layer backing, batting, and quilt top.

2. Outline-quilt patchwork. On Laura Franchini's quilt, blocks, triangles, and narrow borders also have 2 lines of echo-quilting (spaced ¾" apart) in each triangle. A Baptist Fan design is quilted in wide sashing strips. Pattern for leaf quilted in side borders is at right. Outer borders are quilted with a ¼"-wide curving vine embellished with acorns and leaves. Laura's design was inspired by a drawing in a 1992 issue of *Quilter's Newsletter Magazine.*

3. Make 9 yards of straight-grain or bias binding from reserved square. Bind quilt edges.

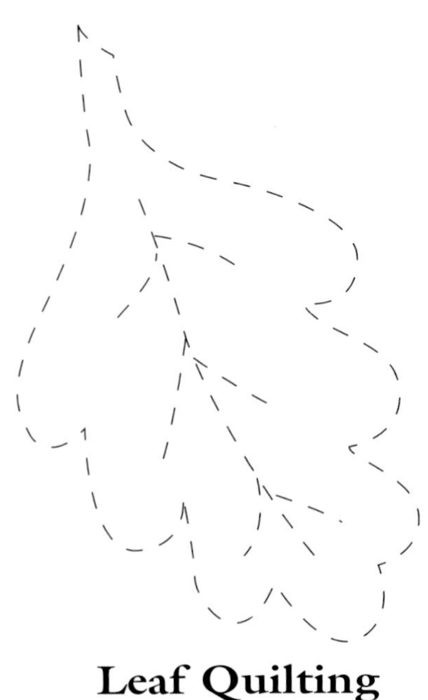

Leaf Quilting Pattern

Jennifer Patriarche

Redmond, Washington

Jennifer Patriarche is drawn to the traditions in quiltmaking. But the ones she takes most to heart are classic design and color, pride of workmanship, and the bond of friendship.

"I prefer traditional designs, interpreted for today," Jennifer says. "Today's fabrics are so beautiful; I love the interplay of color and pattern."

"I love to watch the quilt grow."

Jennifer nearly always has two pieced tops and an appliqué project underway. "I love to sew and watch the quilt grow," she says. "Anticipating the next step in the design is so fun."

Jennifer's quilting group, the Patchwork Stars, is a constant source of fellowship and support. She says, "They criticize when criticism is needed, praise when they like what I've done, and keep me quilting when a deadline looms!"

Jennifer is also a member of the Block Party Quilters of Bellevue, Washington, and she still keeps in touch with her pals in The Quilters Guild of Dallas.

The Frequent Flyer

1999

In the 1850s, Frances Johnson of Cherry Hill, North Carolina, made a quilt consisting of nine Cotton Boll blocks and three half blocks, each surrounded by flying geese. Her quilt is now the centerpiece of the collection at the North Carolina Museum of History in Raleigh.

Jennifer Patriarche bought a pattern sold by the museum (no longer available) to make a 20th-century version.

In the next 10 years, Jennifer's Cotton Boll traveled to many of the places that she did. So she named her quilt *The Frequent Flyer* to honor its adventures.

Jennifer worked on *Flyer* in fits and starts, putting it away while she worked on other projects. When the center section was finally done, Jennifer's quilting friends didn't make it easy for her. They sent her back to the drawing board at least five times before they were satisfied with her border design.

The Frequent Flyer won Best of Show at the 1999 Dallas Quilt Celebration and a first place ribbon for appliqué at the 1999 American Quilters' Society show.

The Frequent Flyer

Finished Size

Quilt: 94" x 94"
Blocks: 9 (24" x 24")

Materials

9 yards white or muslin*
8 yards red fabric
3 yards green fabric
3 yards 104"-wide backing fabric
Template material
¼"-wide and ⅜"-wide bias pressing bars

**Note:* If prewashed fabric is less than 44" wide, you may need additional fabric to cut lengthwise border strips.

Pieces to Cut

Make templates for patterns A–Q on pages 98 and 99.

Cut pieces in order listed to make best use of yardage. Whenever possible, pieces are listed in order needed, so you don't have to cut all fabric at once.

From white fabric

- Set aside 2¾ yards for borders.
- 9 (24½") squares for blocks.
- 8 (1" x 75") lengthwise strips for inner triangle-square border.
- 21 (9¼") squares for triangle-squares.
- 4 (1½") squares for inner border corners.

From red fabric

- 1 (34") square for binding.
- 21 (9¼") squares for triangle-squares.
- 36 *each* of patterns A, B, B reversed, C, C reversed, D, D reversed, E, and E reversed.

Cotton Boll Block—Make 9.

- 8 *each* of patterns H, J, J reversed, K, K reversed, L, L reversed, and O.
- 24 of Pattern P.
- 16 *each* of Pattern Q and Q reversed.

From green fabric

- 1 (29"-wide) strip and 2 (13½"-wide) strips for vines.
- 6 (3"-wide) strips. From these, cut 18 of Pattern G.
- 2 (2"-wide) strips. From these, cut 16 *each* of Pattern F and F reversed.
- 2 (2"-wide) strips. From these, cut 8 *each* of patterns M, M reversed, and N.
- 4 (2"-wide) strips. From these, cut 24 *each* of Pattern Q and Q reversed.

Block Assembly

1. Fold 1 white square in half vertically, horizontally, and diagonally and crease to make placement lines for appliqué *(Diagram A).*

2. Referring to *Block Diagram*, center 2 crisscrossed G pieces, aligning them with diagonal creases. Pin.

3. At end of each G piece, pin an A piece, also aligning it with diagonal crease. Then pin B, C, D, E, and F pieces, as well as reversed pieces.

4. When satisfied with position of each piece, appliqué pieces in alphabetical order.

5. Make 9 blocks.

Quilt Top Assembly

1. Referring to photo on page 97, lay out blocks in 3 horizontal rows with 3 blocks in each row.

2. Join blocks in each row. Then join rows to complete center section of quilt.

3. Sew 1" x 75" red strips to quilt sides, using ½" seam allowance. Press seam allowance toward red. Do not trim seam allowances. Sew remaining strips to top and bottom edges in same manner. Press. (These are the *only* seams that are ½", all other seams are standard ¼".) Joined blocks with red border should measure 72½" square.

Triangle-Square Border

1. Use 9¼" squares of white and red fabrics to make triangle-squares for borders. On wrong side of white fabric piece, lightly draw a 4-square by 4-square grid of 1⅞" squares, leaving a 1"

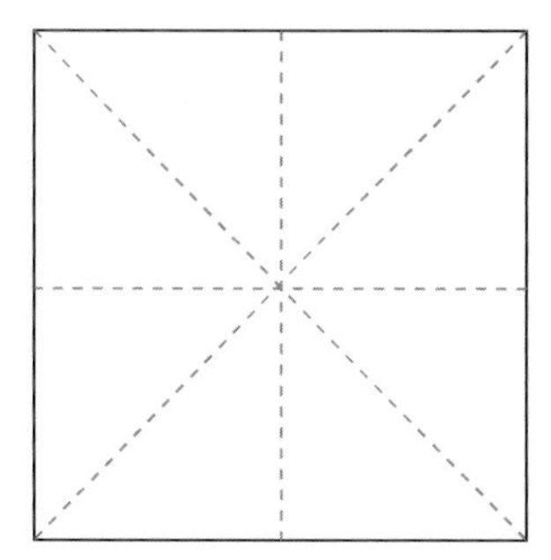

Diagram A

A CELEBRATION OF LIFE

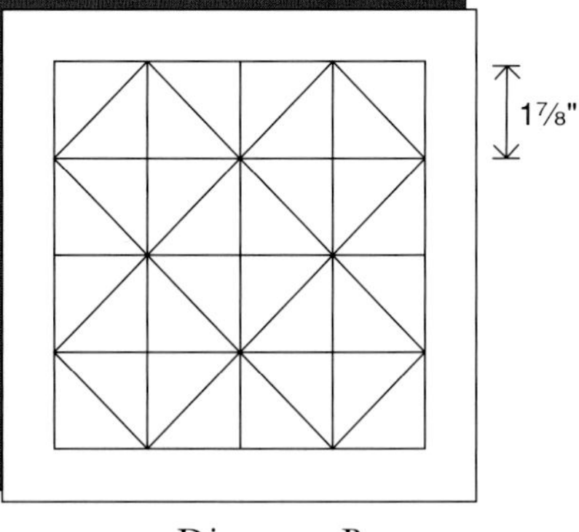

Diagram B

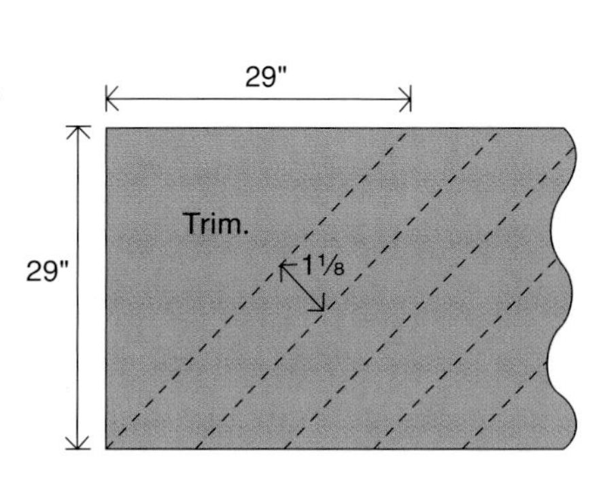

Diagram C

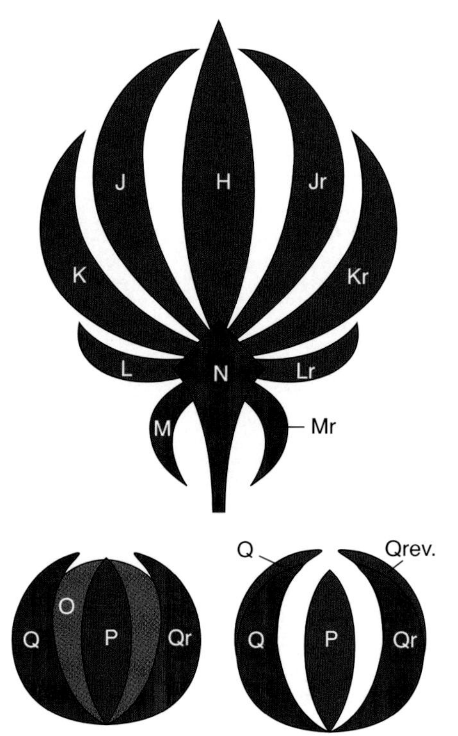

Border Flowers Diagram

margin on all sides *(Diagram B)*. Draw diagonal lines through squares as shown.

2. Match marked white piece with a red piece, right sides facing. Stitch a ¼" seam on *both* sides of diagonal lines. Press.

3. Cut on drawn lines to get 32 triangle-squares from each grid. Stitch 9 grids to get 288 triangle-squares for inner border. Press seam allowances toward red.

4. For each side border, join 72 triangle-squares in a vertical row, changing direction of squares in middle of row (see photo, page 97). Press. Sew assembled borders to quilt sides, easing to fit as needed.

5. Join 72 triangle-squares in a horizontal row for top border, changing direction of triangles in middle of row. Add 1½" white squares at row ends. Sew border to top edge of quilt, easing to fit. Assemble and join bottom border in same manner.

Preparing Bias Stems

1. On 1 long edge of 29"-wide green strip, measure 29" from corner. Trim triangle as shown *(Diagram C)*. Measuring from

Color Variations

Fly from classic to hip-hop with a change of color. Here are some ideas for some bold different looks for your own *Frequent Flyer.*

cut edge, cut 1⅛"-wide bias strips. Cut 8 strips for vines, each 41" long, and 4 (27½"-long) strips for center motifs.

2. Fold each bias strip over ⅜"-wide pressing bar, right sides out, centering raw edges on flat edge of bar. Press.

3. From 13½"-wide green strips, measure and cut a 13½" triangle. Measuring from cut edge, cut ¾"-wide bias strips. Cut 32 strips 19" long for flower stems and 16 strips 8" long for tendrils.

4. Press narrow bias strips over ¼"-wide pressing bar.

Appliquéd Border

1. From reserved fabric, cut 4 (10½" x 99") border strips. See page 141 for tips on sewing a mitered border. Stitch borders to quilt and miter corners. Press seam allowances toward border.

2. Find center of each quilt edge and place a pin 1½" above border seam line. Referring to photo, pin a 27½"-long bias strip in place on each border, tapering ends as shown.

3. Pin N stem just above each pinned vine. Pin M leaves and flower pieces H, J, J reversed, K, K reversed, L, and L reversed.

4. Referring to photo, curve vines outward from each center motif, tucking ends under pinned bias. Pin stems and tendrils; then pin P/Q/Q flower pieces and O/P/Q flower pieces in place at stem ends *(Border Flowers Diagram)*.

5. Center and pin H–L flower and M/N stem pieces on each mitered seam. Curve a narrow bias stem piece from end of stem to connect with vine as shown.

7. When satisfied with placement of all border elements, appliqué vines and flower pieces in place. Press.

Outer Border

1. Mark and stitch triangle-square grids as before. Stitch 12 grids to get 372 triangle-squares for border (and 12 extra). Press seam allowances toward red.

2. For each side border, join 92 triangle-squares in a vertical row, changing direction of squares in middle of row (see photo above). Press. Sew borders to quilt sides, easing to fit as needed.

3. Join 94 triangle-squares in a horizontal row for top border, changing direction of triangles in middle of row. Sew border to top edge of quilt, easing to fit. Assemble and join bottom border in same manner.

Quilting and Finishing

1. Layer backing, batting, and quilt top. Quilt as desired. On quilt shown, appliqué and piecing are echo-quilted.

2. Make 10¾ yards of bias or straight-grain binding. Bind quilt edges.

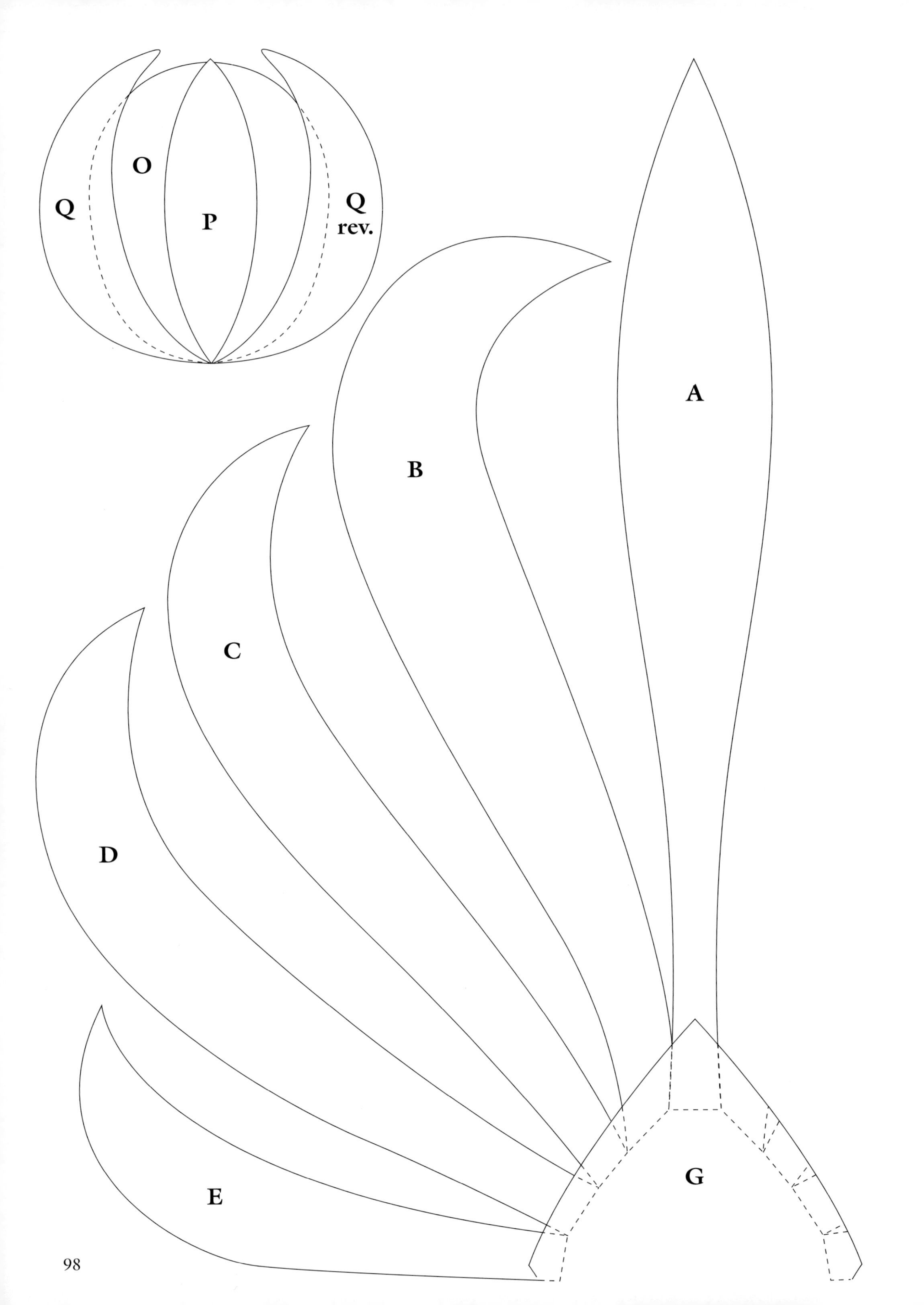
Q
O
P
Q
rev.
A
B
C
D
E
G

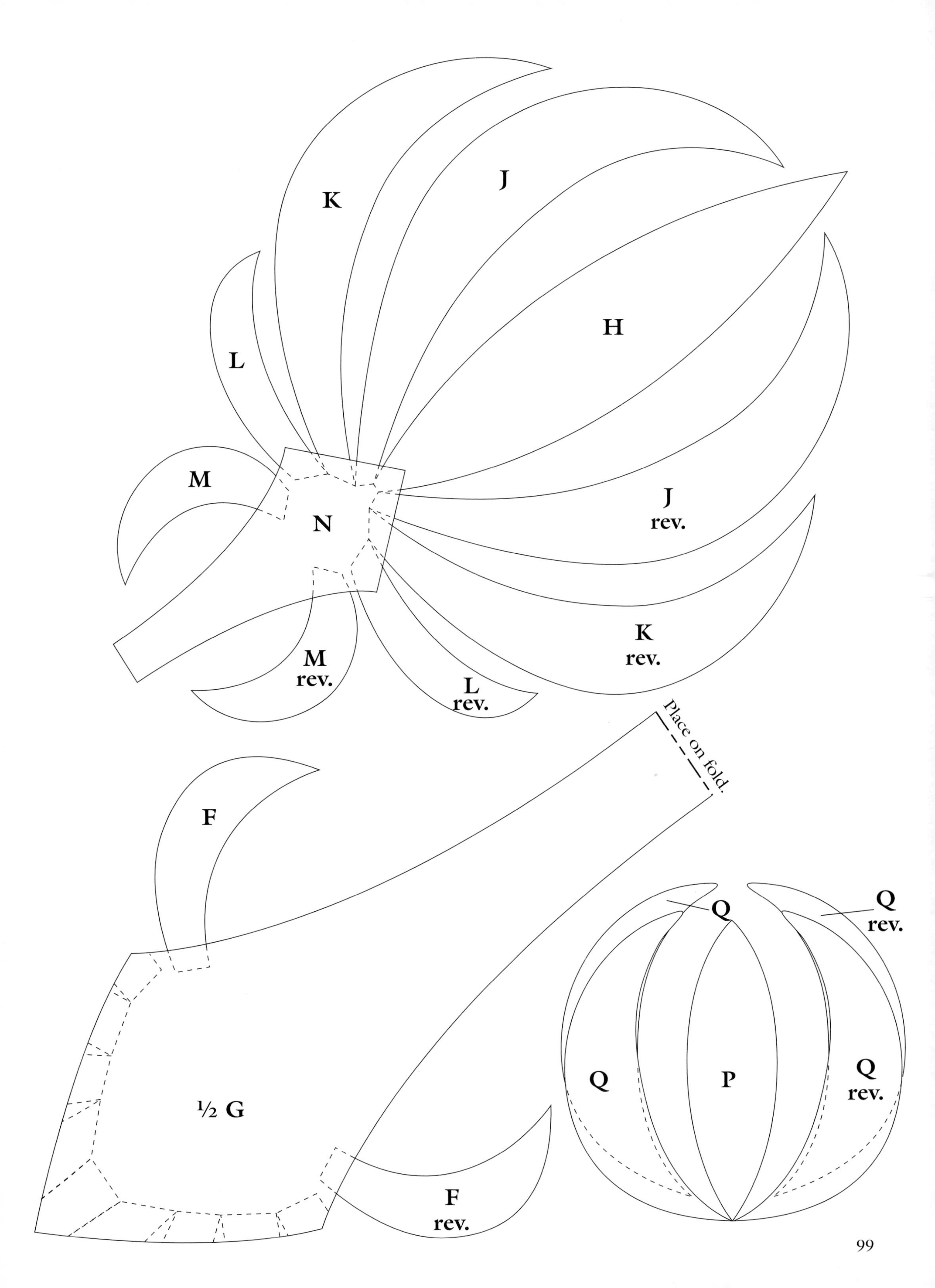
K
J
L
H
M
N
J
rev.
K
rev.
M
rev.
L
rev.
Place on fold.
F
Q
Q
rev.
Q
P
Q
rev.
½ G
F
rev.

Dorinda Evans

Laplace, Louisiana

Finding time for quilting is tough when you're as busy as Dorinda Evans. "I squeeze quilting time in whenever I can."

Dorinda's favorite thing about quilting is the creative process. "You start with the seed of an idea and watch the quilt develop," she says. She tries to use at least one fabric "that makes me uncomfortable" in each quilt. She says, "Invariably that fabric turns out to be the thing that creates movement or energy in the piece."

Dorinda's colorful scrap quilts are a far cry from the "very ugly" nine-patch that was her first childhood venture into quiltmaking. She began anew about 12 years ago under the tutelage of a friend. After that first Log Cabin quilt, she says, "I was hooked and have quilted nonstop ever since."

Rainbow Riot

1999

"I've got to make that!" Dorinda Evans said when she saw a colorful antique quilt in a magazine.

She started by drawing out the design on graph paper. Next, she selected solid fabrics for the block centers. Then she started slicing up fabric from her stash.

"I had no idea how big or how bold this quilt would be," Dorinda says. "I had no idea how a little chartreuse could perk things up."

The amazing thing about this quilt, Dorinda says, was how it gripped her once she started. The living room floor became a sea of scraps and blocks. "I wore the same housedress for three days and nights until I came to my senses," Dorinda remembers. "My family just stepped over the mess and ordered pizza."

Rainbow Riot

Finished Size

Quilt: 98" x 113"
Blocks: 168 (7½" x 7½")

Materials

⅛ yard *each* of solid yellow, orange, red, violet, blue*, and green for block centers
15 (⅛-yard) pieces yellow prints
13 (⅛-yard) pieces orange prints
6 (⅛-yard) pieces red prints
11 (⅛-yard) pieces violet prints
20 (⅛-yard) pieces blue prints
17 (⅛-yard) pieces green prints
2¼ yards outer border fabric (includes binding)
9 yards backing fabric
* *Note*: If fabric is not 44" wide, you may need more of blue.

Block Assembly

It takes 10 color variations of the Log Cabin block to make this quilt. All blocks are made in same manner. Refer to block diagrams, below, throughout.

The first color in each block name corresponds to its center square; for example, the orange-yellow block has an orange center square, while the yellow-orange block has a yellow center.

1. For orange-yellow blocks, cut 12 (2") orange solid squares for centers. For each block, choose 4 strips each of yellow prints and orange prints. Select yellowest orange fabrics, saving redder oranges for orange-red blocks.

2. From first orange strip, cut a 2" square; sew it to center square.

3. Match second orange strip to side of 2-square unit, right sides facing *(Diagram A)*. Stitch. Press seam allowance toward new log. Use rotary cutter and acrylic ruler to trim strip even with center unit as shown.

4. Turn unit so that new log is at bottom. Match first yellow strip to right side of unit, right sides facing *(Diagram B)*. Stitch. Press seam allowance toward yellow. Trim strip even with unit.

5. Continue adding logs in same manner as shown in block diagram. Always position last log at bottom and match new strip to right side of unit to sew *(Diagram C)*. Seam allowances are pressed toward each new log.

6. In this manner, make 12 orange-yellow blocks. Make additional block variations as shown in diagrams. Complete 168 Log Cabin blocks.

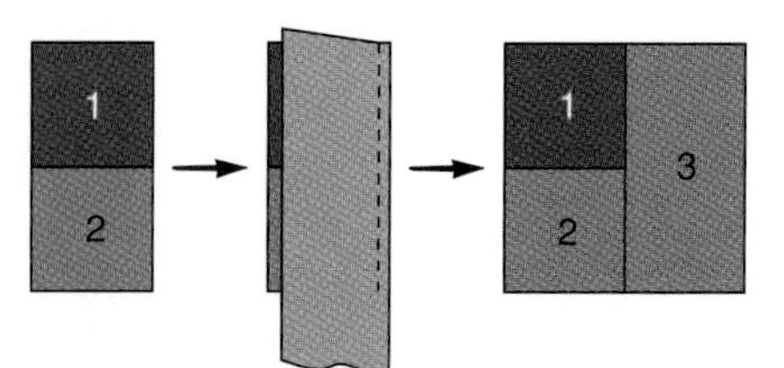

Diagram A

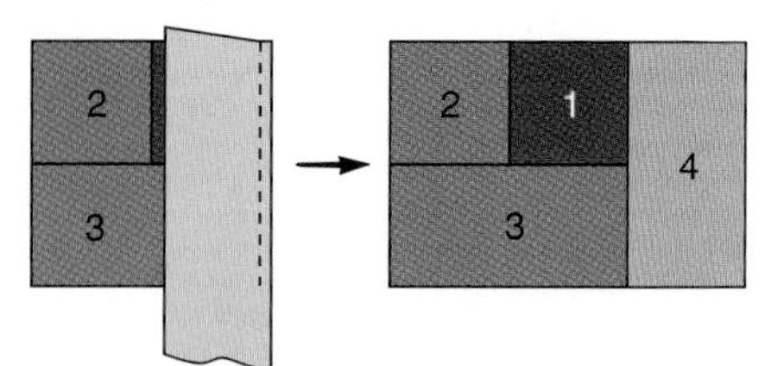

Diagram B

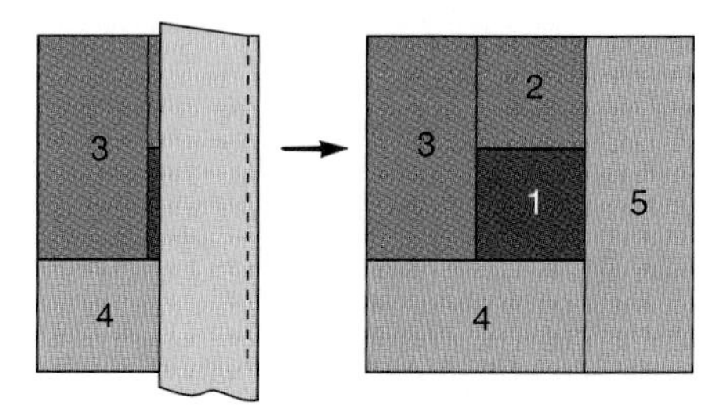

Diagram C

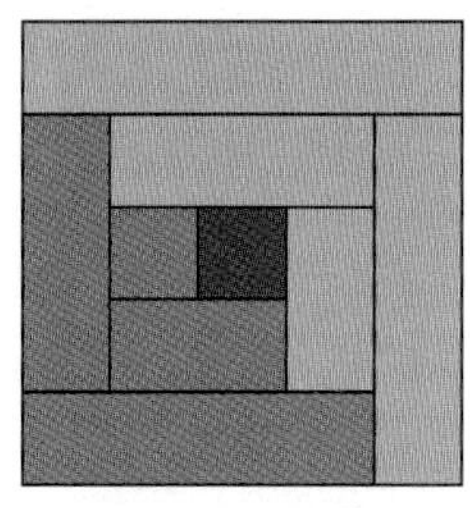
Orange-Yellow Block—Make 12.

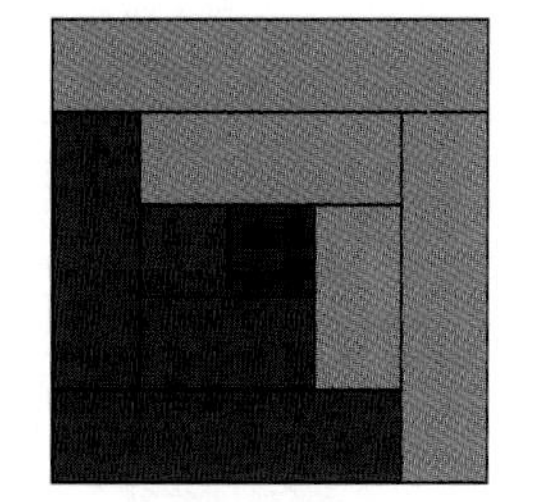
Red-Orange Block—Make 12.

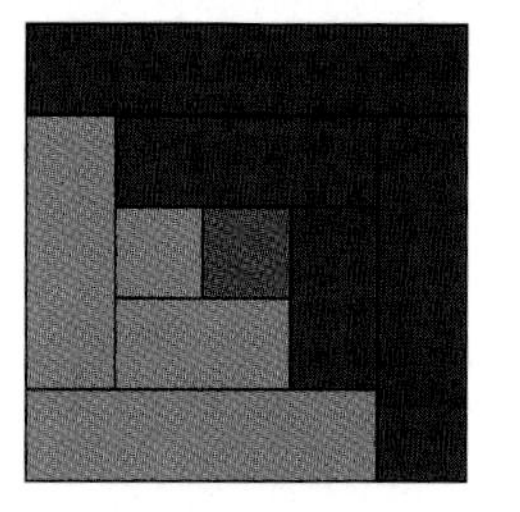
Orange-Red Block—Make 12.

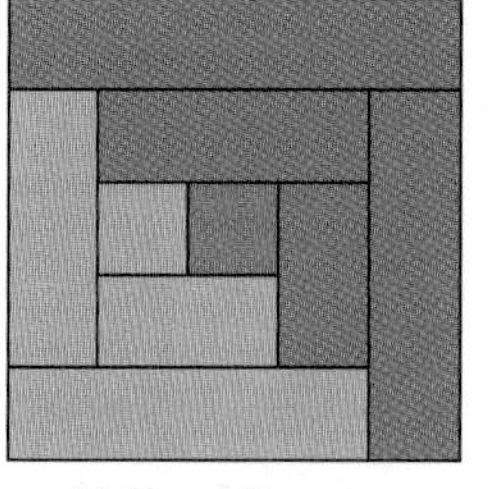
Yellow-Orange Block—Make 16.

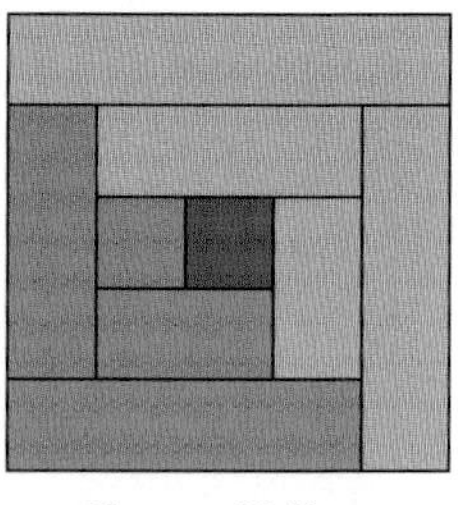
Green-Yellow Block—Make 20.

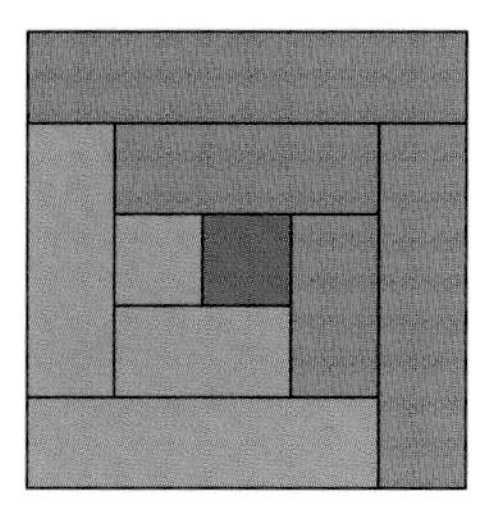
Blue-Green Block—Make 24.

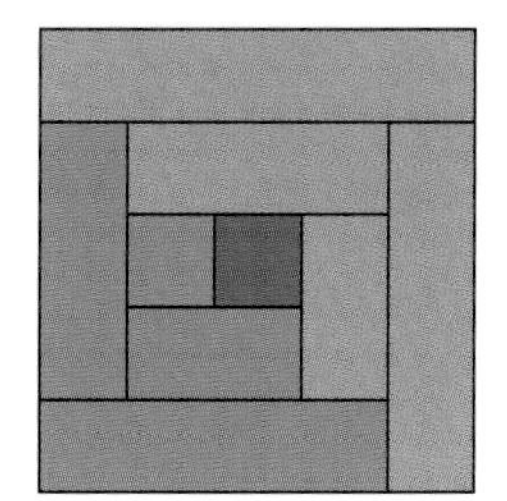
Violet-Blue Block—Make 24.

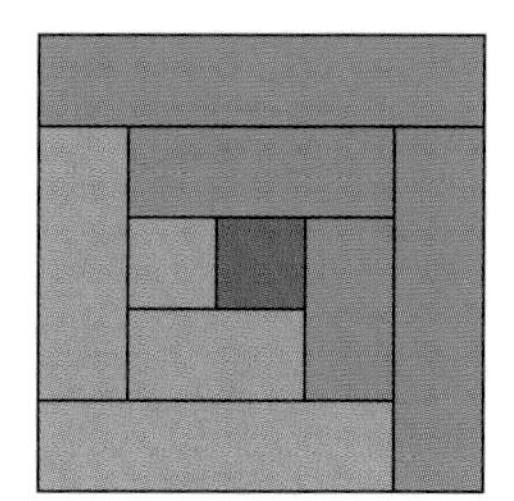
Blue-Violet Block—Make 20.

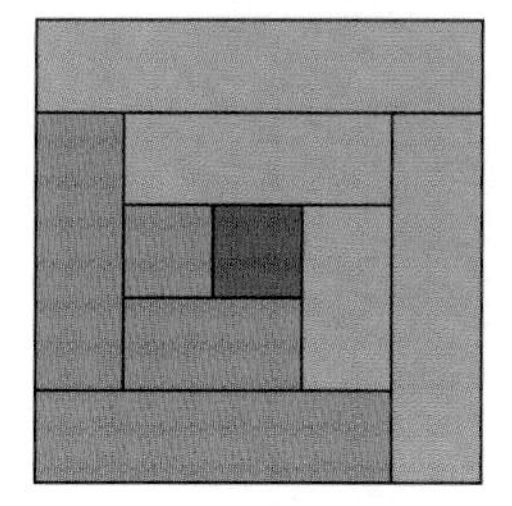
Green-Blue Block—Make 16.

Yellow-Green Block—Make 12.

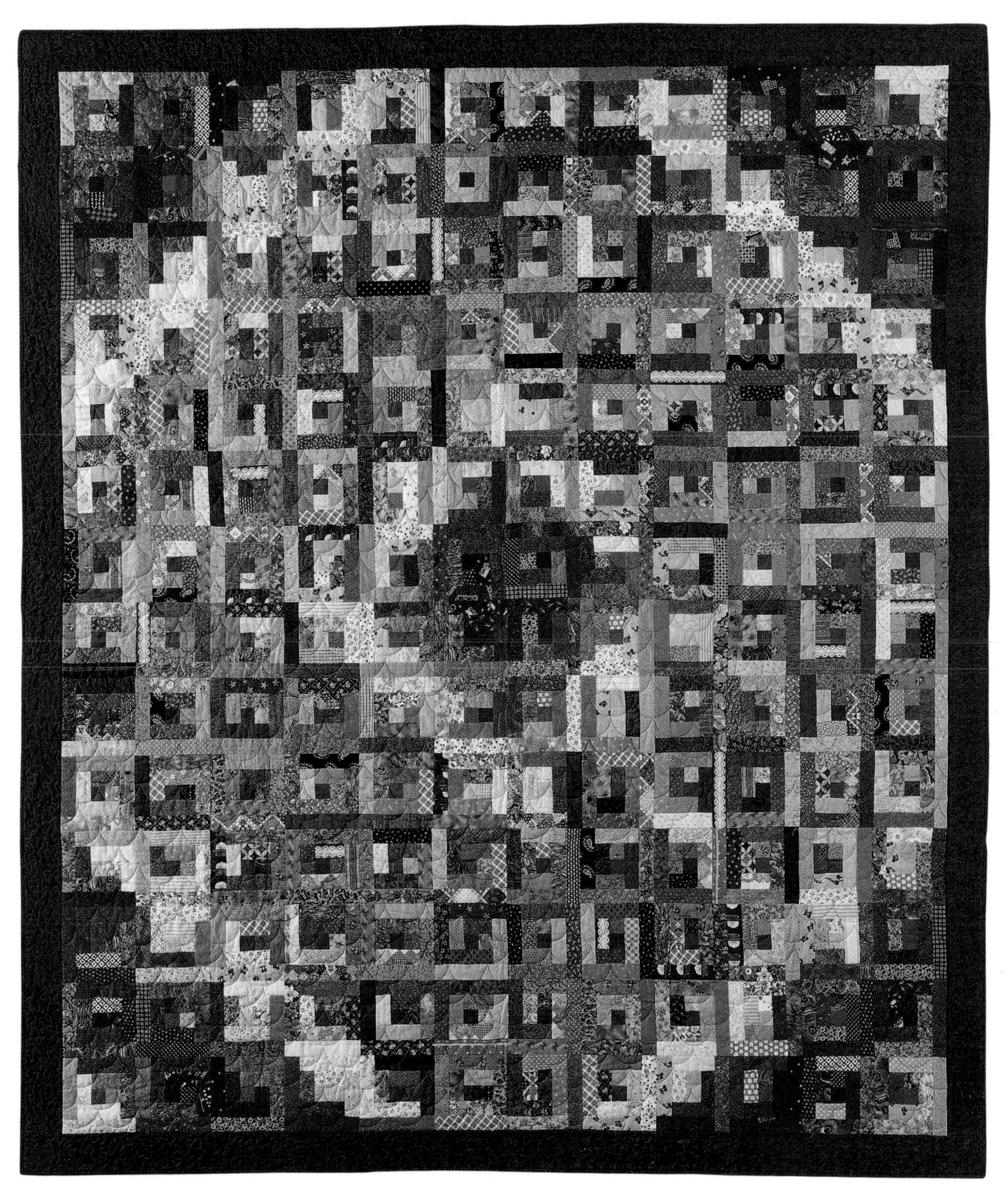

Machine-quilted by Mildred Moss of Smyrna, Georgia

Quilt Assembly Diagrams

Quilt Top Assembly

This quilt is assembled in 4 sections. For each section, you need 3 orange-yellow blocks, 3 red-orange blocks, 3 orange-red, 4 yellow-orange, 5 green-yellow, 6 blue-green, 6 violet-blue, 5 blue-violet, 4 green-blue, and 3 yellow-green. Refer to *Quilt Assembly Diagrams* throughout.

1. For Quadrant A (top left), lay out blocks in 7 horizontal rows, with 6 blocks in each row. Start at top left corner with an orange-yellow block and work across, turning all blocks to put last strip (#9) at left (indicated by arrow on diagram). Match orange to orange, red to red, and so on across each row.

2. When satisfied with layout, join blocks in each row. Press seam allowances in opposite directions from row to row. Join rows to complete Quadrant A.

3. Lay out blocks for Quadrant B (top right) in rows. Start at top left corner of quadrant with a blue-green block and work across, turning all blocks to put last strip (#9) at top. Match green to green, yellow to yellow, and so on across each row. When satisfied with layout of blocks, join blocks in each row. Press. Join rows to complete quadrant.

4. Join quadrants A and B to complete top half of quilt.

5. Repeat steps 1–4 to complete second half of quilt. Turn this half upside down and join halves.

Borders

1. Cut 12 (4¼"-wide) cross-grain strips of border fabric. Sew 3 strips end-to-end for each border.

2. Measure length of quilt top through middle of quilt. Trim 2 border strips to match length. Sew borders to quilt sides, easing to fit as needed.

3. Measure width of quilt top through middle, including side borders. Trim remaining strips to match width. Sew borders to top and bottom edges of quilt.

Quilting and Finishing

1. Assemble backing. Layer backing, batting, and quilt top. (Backing seams will be parallel to top and bottom edges.) Baste.

2. Quilt as desired. Quilt shown is machine-quilted in an allover clamshell pattern; borders are quilted in a large stipple pattern.

3. Use remaining border fabric to make 12 yards of straight-grain binding. Bind quilt edges.

Orange County Quilters Guild
Orange, California

To paraphrase an old saying, quilters love company. The Orange County Quilters Guild has more than enough company—within a year of its beginning in 1981, its membership outstripped any available meeting facility. Since then, active membership has been limited to 400.

For personal support, small quilting bees work outside the guild. "There's no way of knowing how many friendship groups there are," says guild member Beverly Packard. She jokes, "There are groups of ladies in hiding for fear they may be asked to take on a project." Some groups produce lots of quilts, while others produce very few. But all the groups play an important role in the life of Orange County quiltmakers. Guild activities include workshops, a biannual show, and an annual retreat jokingly called "Camp Watch-A-Patcher."

The Goodwill Quilt
1999

In January 1996, Memory Russell found scraps of a quilt in a bin at Goodwill Industries.

The scraps didn't include a whole block, but there was enough for Memory's friend Beverly Packard to figure out the pattern. And the fabrics—19th century shirtings, sassafras browns, and double pinks—were almost exactly duplicated by the current crop of reproduction fabrics.

Meanwhile, the Orange County guild needed someone to handle the group's next raffle quilt. Beverly had done that job before and knew it took more time than she could spare. But when she'd finished a scrap quilt based on the one from the Goodwill bin, a volunteer was still needed. So Beverly agreed to lead the effort, and it was decided that the guild would make yet another version of the Goodwill quilt.

Thirty-four volunteers got the hand-piecing done in no time; then the group took turns at quilting. Everything was done to make the new quilt as much as possible like the original.

"The quiltmaker's name has been lost, along with the name of the pattern," Beverly says. So the guild members named their work *The Goodwill Quilt,* with permission from Goodwill Industries for use of their name in conjunction with this quilt.

The Goodwill Quilt

Finished Size

Quilt: 84" x 84"
Blocks: 36 (9" x 9")

Materials

36 (6" x 18") brown prints or 11 fat quarters*
36 (8" x 18") white/cream shirting prints or 15 fat quarters*
36 (6") squares red prints or 4 fat quarters*
3 yards brown/red floral print
1¼ yards red print for border and binding
5 yards backing fabric or 2½ yards 90"-wide backing
* Fat quarters = 18" x 22"

Pieces to Cut

Instructions are for rotary cutting and quick piecing. For traditional piecing, use patterns A, B, and C on page 108.

From each brown print

- 5 (3½") A squares.
- 8 (2") B squares.

From each white print

- 8 (2" x 3½") C pieces.
- 20 (2") B squares.

From each red print

- 8 (2") B squares.

From brown/red floral print

- 4 (3" x 90") lengthwise strips for outer border.
- 25 (9½") setting squares.
- 5 (14") squares. Cut each square in quarters diagonally to get 20 setting triangles.
- 2 (7¼") squares. Cut each square in half diagonally to get 4 corner triangles.

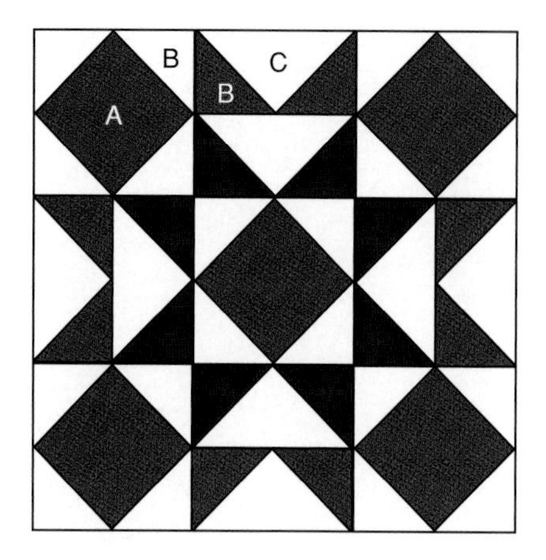

The Goodwill Block—Make 36.

Block Assembly Diagram

From red border print

- 8 (1½"-wide) cross-grain strips for inner border.
- 1 (32") square for binding.

Block Assembly

1. For each block, select 5 brown A squares, 8 brown B squares, 8 red Bs, 20 white Bs, and 8 white Cs. Choose sets of 1 fabric or mix up prints as desired.

2. See Quilt Smart on page 12 for step-by-step instructions for diagonal-corner quick-piecing technique. Following those directions, sew a white B square to corners of each A square as shown *(Diagram A).*

3. In same manner, sew brown and red B squares to corners of each white C piece as shown *(Diagram B).*

4. Lay out units in 3 horizontal rows *(Block Assembly Diagram).* Join red and brown B/C units; then join units in each row. Join rows to complete block.

5. Make 36 blocks.

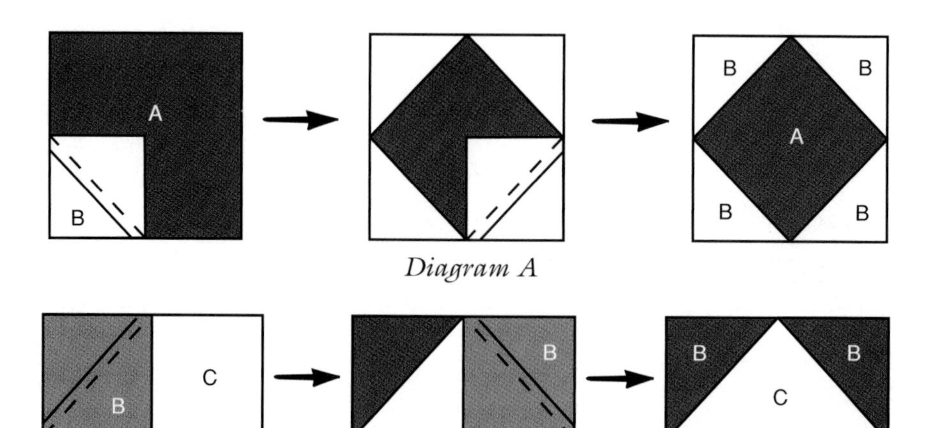

Diagram A

Diagram B

Quilt Top Assembly

1. Lay out blocks, setting triangles, and setting squares in 11 diagonal rows *(Quilt Assembly Diagram)*. When satisifed with placement, join units in each row. Add corner triangles as shown. Press all seam allowances toward setting pieces.

2. Join rows.

Borders

1. Join 2 red strips end-to-end for each inner border.

2. Measure length of quilt top through middle of pieced section. Trim 2 inner border strips to match length. Sew borders to quilt sides, easing to fit as needed. Press seam allowances toward borders.

3. Measure width of quilt through middle of quilt top, including side borders. Trim remaining borders to match width. Stitch borders to top and bottom edges of quilt, easing to fit as needed.

4. Join brown/red floral borders to each quilt side. Miter border corners.

Quilting and Finishing

1. Layer backing, batting, and quilt top. Baste.

2. Outline-quilt patchwork. Add lines of quilting, about ¾" apart, in setting triangles and border.

3. Make 9½ yards of bias or straight-grain binding. Bind quilt edges.

Quilt Assembly Diagram

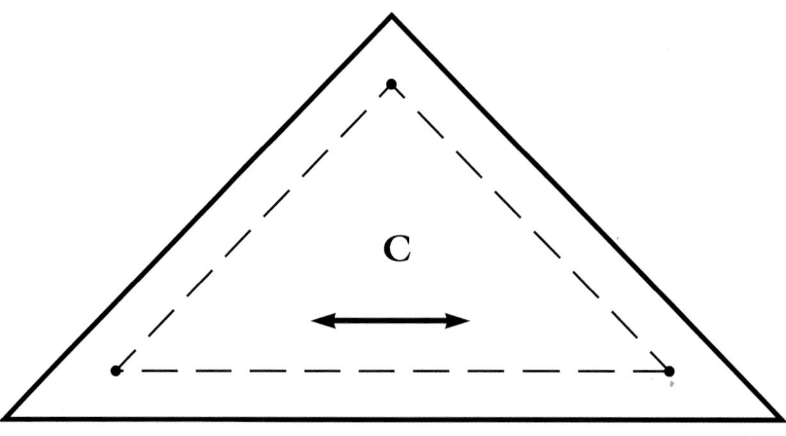

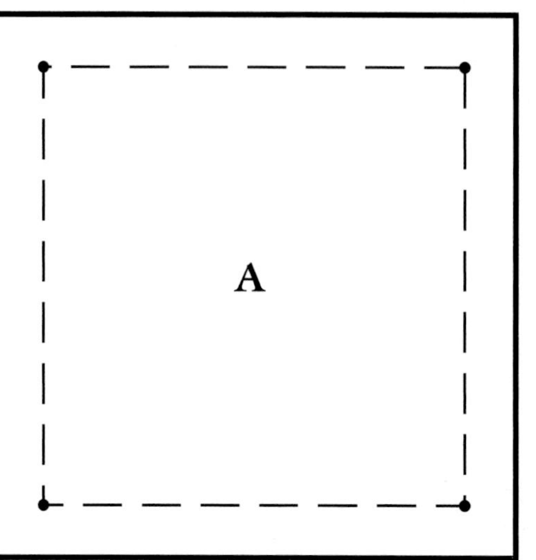

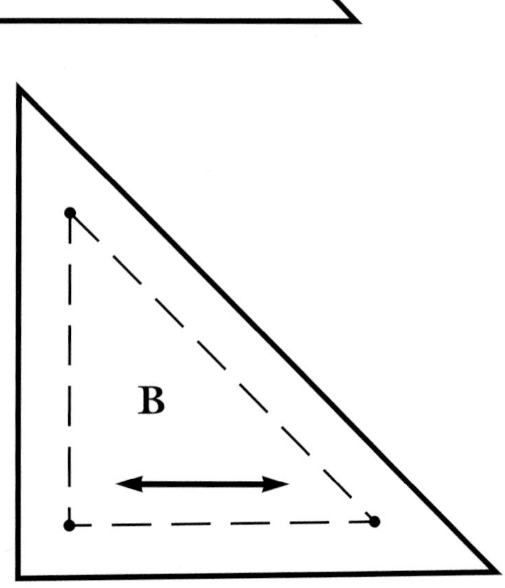

Color Variations

Make a personal statement with your favorite colors and fabrics. Here are some of our suggestions for different interpretations of this classic quilt.

Susan Horn

Sea Cliff, New York

Matthew Horn recently told his mother, Susan, how lucky he feels to sleep under a quilt that she made just for him, while all his 12-year-old friends sleep under store-bought blankets. Susan immediately promised to make him another quilt.

There are quilts in every room of the Horns' Long Island home, products of Susan's nine years of quilting. She started with a library book and a kit ordered from a magazine. "After a month of sewing, I'd completed a twin-size nine-patch quilt," Susan remembers. Says the busy homemaker, "It was wonderful to finish something that stayed finished."

"There seems to be no limit to what can be created in cloth."

The fabric, color, and geometry of quiltmaking fuels Susan's creative spirit. She says, "I've learned to trust my instincts, to take a break when a solution to a problem is not readily apparent, knowing that as I do other things, the way to go will make itself known."

Susan sees each quilt as a bridge between past and future that carries the traditions of quilters past into a new century. "As the quilting world continues to expand," says Susan, "there seems to be no limit to what can be created in cloth."

Susan, who says she makes each quilt in her own time and for her own pleasure, is a member of the Long Island Quilter's Society.

Cockscombs, Tulips & Berries

1999

At a recent quilters' retreat, Gwen Marston taught a class on classic 19th century four-block quilts and folk art. Susan Horn got home from the retreat and applied what she'd learned to make this folk art-style version of a cockscomb in a basket.

"I like the traditional four-block format," Susan says. She drafted her own design, inspired by the strong graphic imagery of a quilt of Gwen's.

Susan drew her design freehand on paper and then cut out the paper pattern, adding seam allowance. "It's all very free," Susan says.

In 1999, *Cockscombs, Tulips & Berries* was shown at Quilters Heritage Celebration in Lancaster, Pennsylvania, and was juried into the American Quilters' Society show in Paducah, Kentucky.

Cockscombs, Tulips & Berries

Finished Size

Quilt: 68" x 76"
Blocks: 4 (28" x 28")

Materials

5 yards tone-on-tone cream background fabric
3 yards red print
1 yard green fabric
½ yard variegated blue fabric (or yardage required to cut cockscombs from desired sections of fabric)
¼ yard royal blue fabric
¼ yard black fabric
⅛ yard rust fabric for berries
4" x 22" strip red or hot pink for cockscomb inserts
5" x 12" scrap red or hot pink for basket inserts
5" x 10" scrap peach fabric
4¼ yards backing fabric
½"-wide bias pressing bar
Freezer paper

Pieces to Cut

When possible, pieces are listed in order needed, so you don't have to cut everything all at once. Appliqué patterns are on pages 114–117. See Block Assembly for tips on freezer-paper appliqué before cutting appliqué pieces.

From cream fabric

- 4 (28½") squares.
- 1 (8½" x 58") vine strip.
- 20 (7" x 15½") pieces for triangle-square quick piecing or 198 (2⅞") squares for traditional piecing. Cut 2⅞" squares in half diagonally to get 396 triangles for border.

Cockscombs Block—Make 4.

From red fabric

- 32" square for binding.
- 20 (7" x 15½") pieces for triangle-square quick piecing or 198 (2⅞") squares for traditional piecing. Cut 2⅞" squares in half diagonally to get 396 triangles for border.
- 8 of Pattern C.
- 8 of Pattern E.
- 5 of Pattern X.
- 28 berries.

From green fabric

- 2 (13½" x 42") strips for bias appliqué. From these, cut a 13½" square for vine. Set aside remainder for stems.
- 8 of Pattern G.
- 8 of Pattern H.
- 5 of Pattern Z.
- 12 berries.

From variegated blue fabric

- 4 of Pattern A.
- 5 of Pattern Y.

From royal blue fabric

- 8 of Pattern D.
- 126 berries.

From black fabric

- 4 of Pattern B.

From rust fabric

- 62 berries.

From peach fabric

- 4 of Pattern F.

Preparing Bias Stems

1. On 1 long edge of each 13½"-wide strip, measure 13½" from corner. Trim triangle *(Diagram A)*. Measuring from cut edge, cut 1⅜"-wide bias strips. Cut a total of 24 bias strips for stems, each about 19" long.

2. Fold each bias stem over pressing bar, right sides out, and centering raw edges on flat side of bar. Press each stem.

Block Assembly

1. Trace first part of Pattern A (page 116) onto dull side of freezer paper, including placement lines for center reverse appliqué. Turn paper and match dots to trace second part of Pattern A. Do not add seam allowances. Cut out complete template on drawn line.

2. Make freezer-paper templates of all remaining patterns.

3. Press shiny side of each template onto right side of fabric. Cut out appliqués for 1 block, adding a 3⁄16" seam allowance around each template. Leave templates in place on cut pieces.

4. Using small, sharp scissors or a rotary cutter, carefully slit fabric to make openings for reverse appliqué in cockscomb (A) and basket (B).

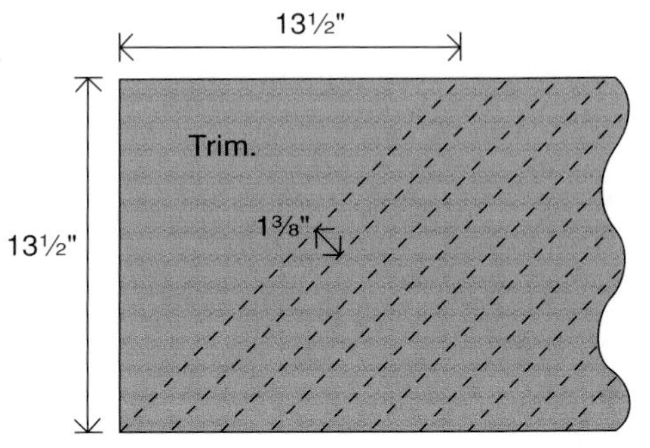

Diagram A

5. Fold 1 cream square in half lengthwise. Crease fold to make placement guide for appliqué.
6. Place basket on background square, matching center with fold. Pin basket in place with bottom edge of basket template about 2" from edge of square.
7. Center cockscomb on square with bottom edge under basket. Tip of cockscomb template should be 2½" from top edge of square. Cut a 2"x 11" scrap of red or pink fabric and slide it under cockscomb. Appliqué cockscomb, using paper template as a guide to needle-turn edges. Leave bottom edge flat where it is covered by basket. Needle-turn edges of center slit to expose fabric underneath and appliqué. Remove template when appliqué is complete.
8. Tuck end of a berry stem under basket, about ¼" from each basket corner, placing raw edges of stem against background fabric. Referring to photo, curve stem over to place end about 1¼" from bottom of background square and 2¼" from side edge. Appliqué stem in place.
9. Position C flower stems and E flower stems; then pin flowers in place. (Trim stems as needed; C flower should be 1¾" from top and side edges of background square; E/F flower is also about 1¾" from side edge.) Pin D in center of each C flower and F under E as shown. Pin G and H leaves on each C flower stem. When satisfied with placement of pieces, appliqué flowers, leaves, and stems in place.
10. Appliqué basket edges, sliding a 2½" x 6" scrap of pink or red under top edge. Needle-turn slit's edges to expose scrap fabric.

11. Select 46 berries—28 royal blue, 11 rust, 2 green, and 5 red. Appliqué 3 blue berries on basket and 2 blue berries at ends of berry stems. Scatter remaining berries on both sides of berry stems and appliqué.
12. Re-use freezer-paper templates to appliqué 3 more blocks.

Vine Appliqué

1. Referring to tips on page 144, use reserved 13½" green square to cut 62" of 1⅜"-wide continuous bias. Fold and press bias to ½" wide.
2. Referring to photo, pin vine on 8½"-wide cream strip as desired.
3. From green scraps, cut 6 bias strips 1⅜"-wide and 2½" to 5" long. Press twigs over bias bar; then pin prepared twigs in place.
4. Position X and Z leaves. Pin Y leaves on top of Xs. Arrange remaining berries on vine as desired. When satisfied with placement of all pieces, appliqué pieces in place.

Quilt Top Assembly

1. Referring to photo, make 2 rows, with 2 blocks in each row. Then join rows.
2. Match vine strip to bottom of blocks, matching center of vine strip to center seam. Stitch strip to blocks. Press seam allowance toward vine strip.

Borders

1. On wrong side of each 7" x 15½" cream piece, draw a 2-square by 5-square grid of 10 (2⅞") squares, leaving a ½" margin around grid *(Quick Piecing Diagram)*. Draw diagonal lines through squares as shown. Match marked fabric with a red piece, right sides facing.
2. Machine-stitch on both sides of all diagonal lines. Press. Cut apart on drawn lines to get 20 triangle-squares. Stitch and cut 20 grids to get 198 triangle-squares (and 2 extra) for border.
3. Join 32 triangle-squares in a vertical row for side borders. Make 6 rows. Join 3 rows for each border. Sew a border to each side of quilt, easing to fit.
4. Join 6 horizontal rows of 34 triangle-squares. Join 3 rows for top border and 3 rows for bottom. Sew borders to top and bottom edges of quilt. Press seam allowances away from borders.

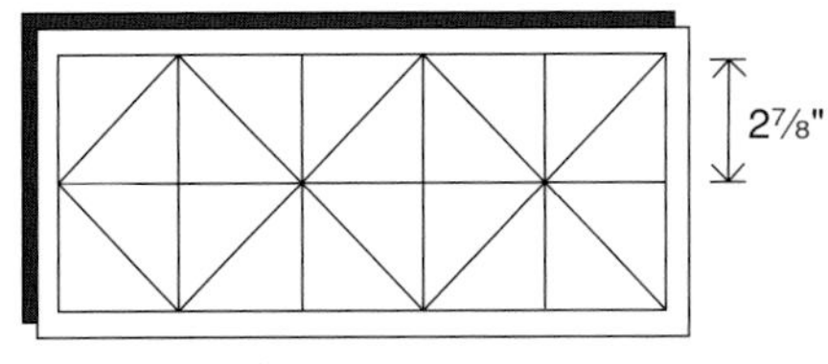

Quick-Piecing Diagram

Quilting and Finishing

1. Assemble backing. Layer backing, batting, and quilt top. Baste.
2. Outline-quilt appliqué. Quilt shown has diagonal lines quilted in triangle-squares and cross-hatching quilted in background.
3. Make 8¼ yards of straight-grain or bias binding. Bind edges.

Color Variations

Since this is a fantasy folk art design, your *Cockscombs* color schemes can take a walk on the wild side. Here are a few ideas to get you started.

D

C

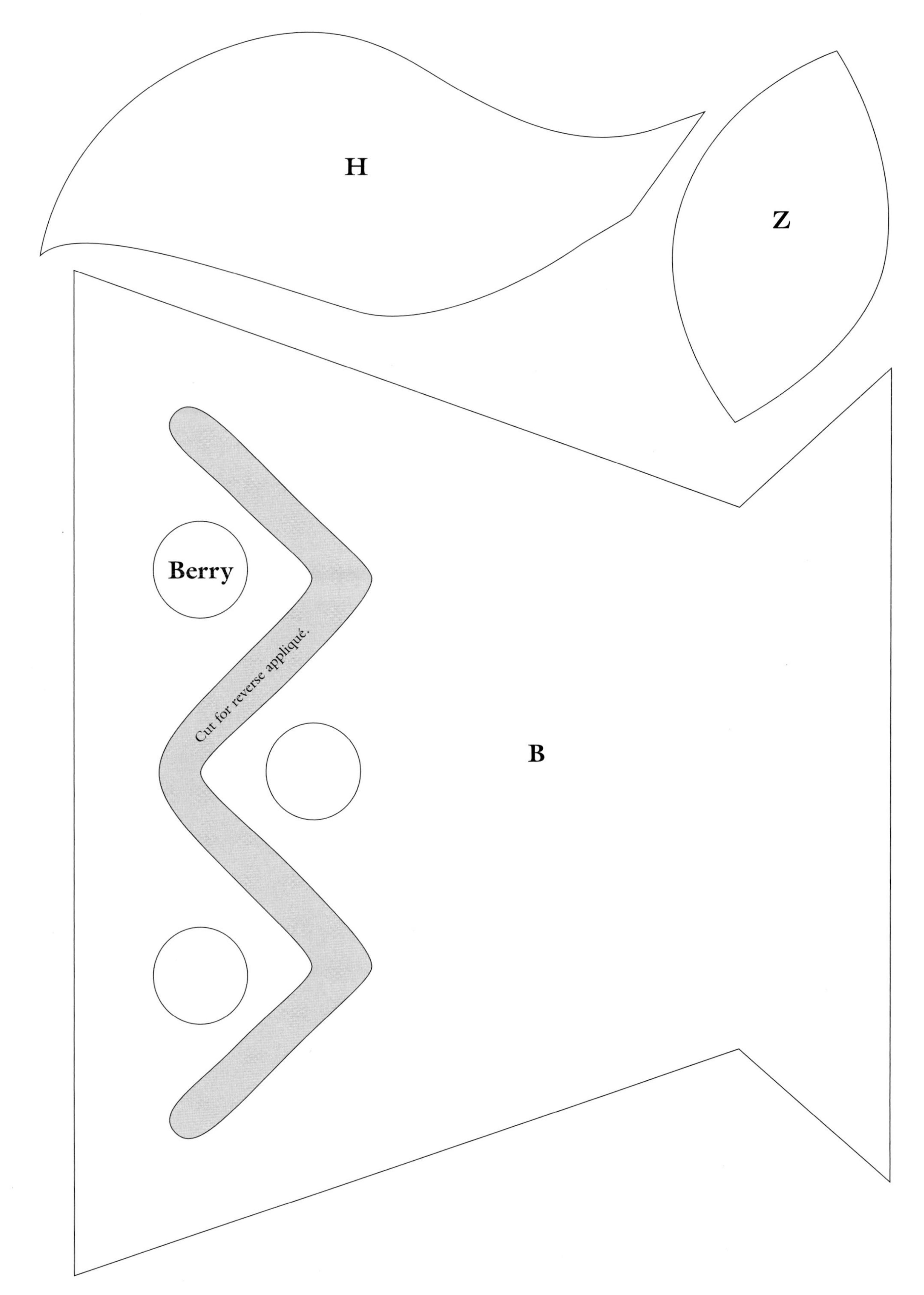
H
Z
Berry
Cut for reverse appliqué.
B

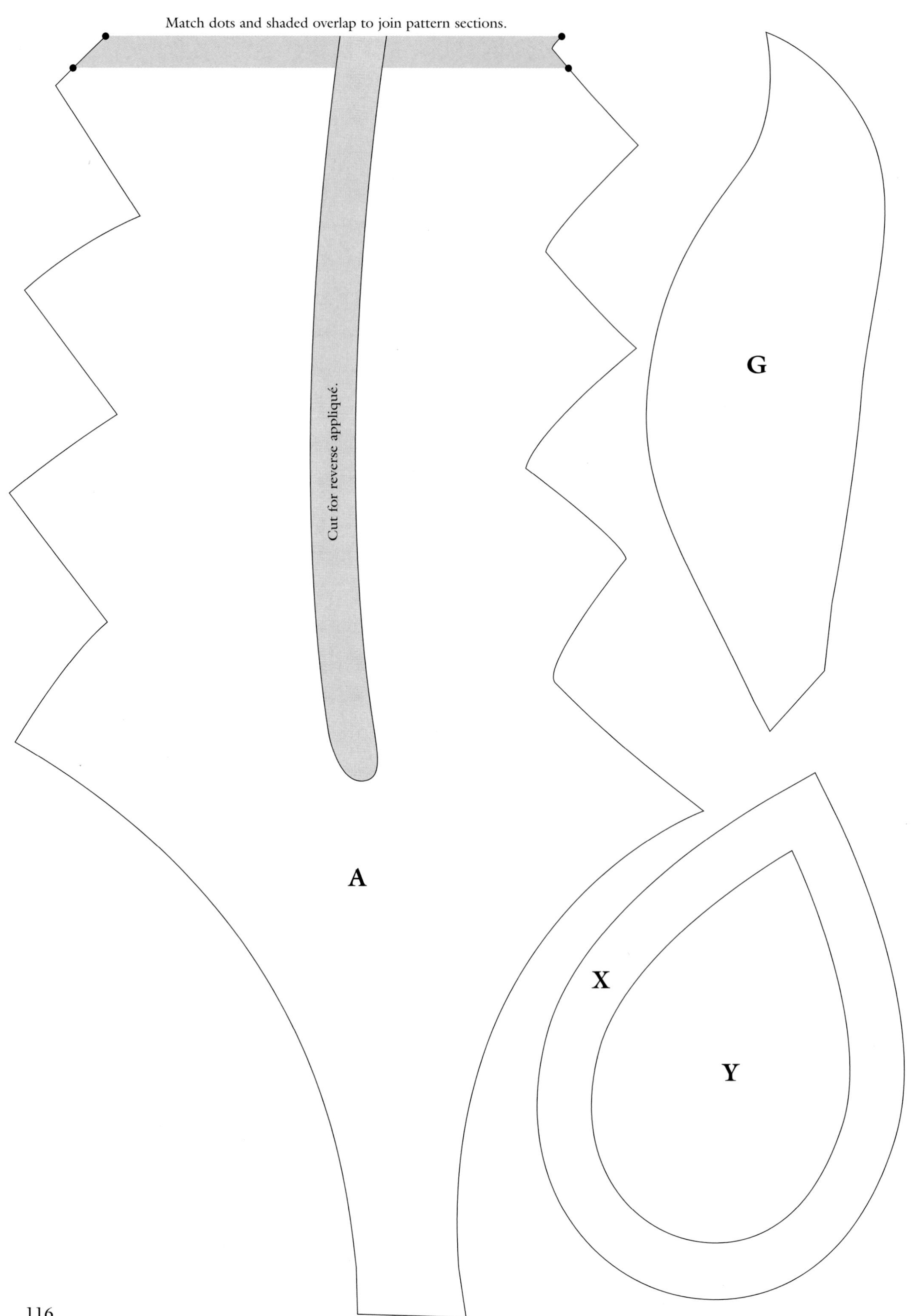
Match dots and shaded overlap to join pattern sections.
Cut for reverse appliqué.
A
G
X
Y

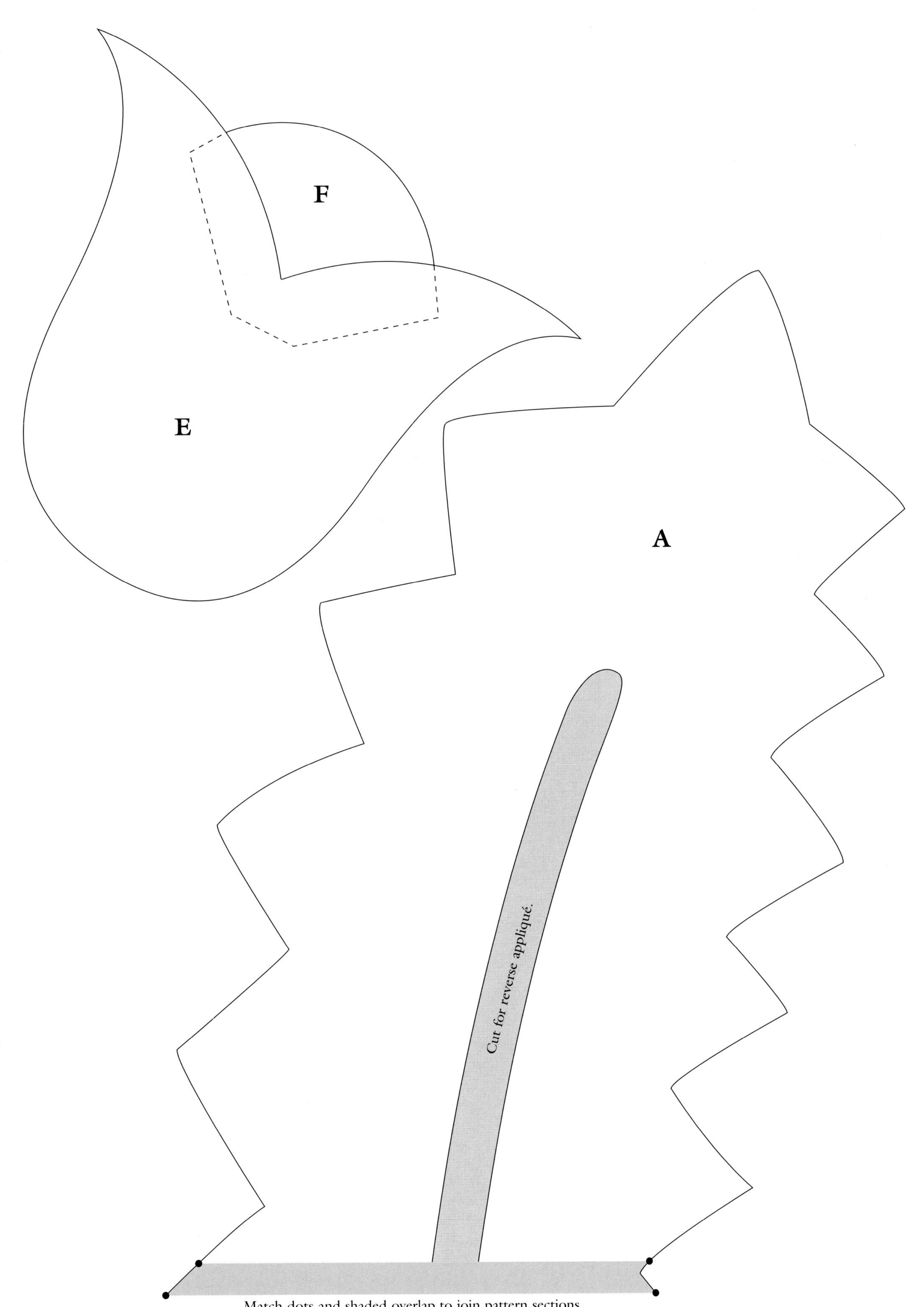

Match dots and shaded overlap to join pattern sections.

Elayne D. Vognild

Crossville, Tennessee

Now that her husband is retired, Elayne Vognild expects quilting will become a bigger part of her life than ever before.

Before retirement, the Vognilds lived in Alabama, where Elayne shared her love of quilting with members of the Birmingham Quilters Guild. Her enthusiasm for quilting knows no limit. "Shopping for fabric, designing quilts on the computer, piecing, appliqué, and hand quilting—I love it all," she says.

In 1983, Elayne was introduced to quilting by a neighbor who shared a pattern for a pieced vest. The next project was a baby quilt that Elayne quilted without using a thimble. That painful lesson learned, Elayne has been quilting, with thimble, ever since.

"I learned each technique by taking a class or workshop," she says, "I'll make a small quilt and give it as a gift and keep for myself the new information."

The African King

1998

Elayne Vognild's fabric collecting is a cross-country affair. The fabrics in *The African King* come from shops coast to coast—from Louisiana, Oregon, Texas, Colorado, Alabama, Georgia, Tennessee, and California.

A quilt pictured in a magazine inspired Elayne to try her hand at a traditional design using nontraditional fabrics. She selected the classic Kaleidoscope or Spider Web block and interpreted it in African-style fabrics.

The African King won a blue ribbon and a judge's choice ribbon at Birmingham Quiltfest '98 and was juried into the American Quilters' Society's 1999 show.

The African King

Finished Size

Quilt: 93" x 108"
Blocks: 42 (12" x 12")

Materials

168 (2" x 30") strips assorted gold, black, orange, and rust fabrics for blocks
42 (4⅜" x 8¾") red and gold prints for block corners
32 (3½" x 43") strips assorted black prints and stripes for sashing strips and borders
34 (3½") squares red and gold prints for sashing squares
1 yard black binding fabric
3¼ yards 104"-wide backing
Template material

* *Note:* As in all scrap quilts, these yardages are recommendations. Use your own scraps and fabric placement as desired.

Block Assembly

1. Choose 1 (2"-wide) strip each of a light, a medium, and a dark value; then choose any fourth strip. Join strips in any order *(Diagram A)*. Press all seam allowances in same direction.

2. Make a template of Pattern X (page 121). Mark seam lines on template as shown on pattern.

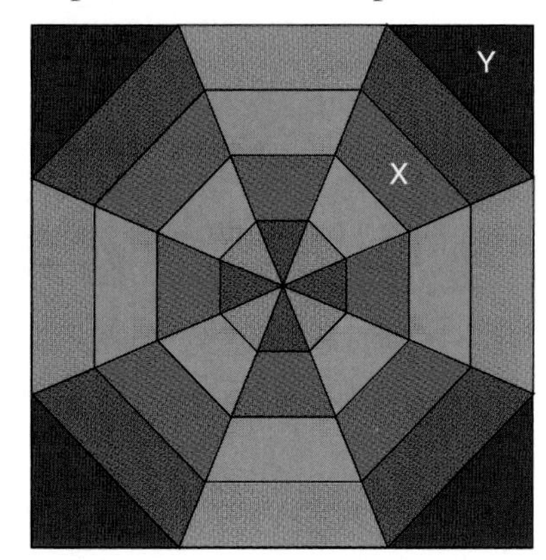

Kaleidoscope Block—Make 42.

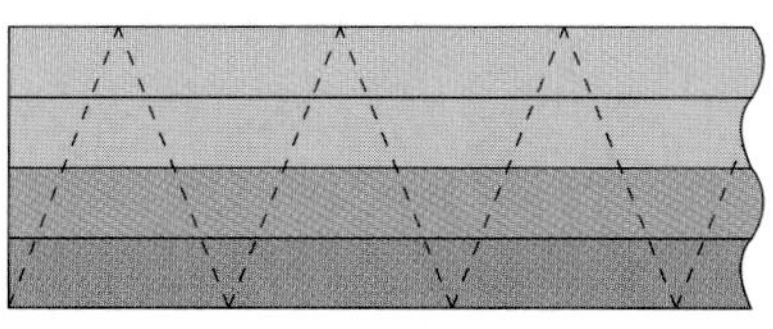

Diagram A

3. Place template on strip set, matching bottom of template with 1 edge of strip set. Cut 1 X triangle. Turn template upside down, aligning its bottom edge with opposite edge of strip set, and cut another X triangle. In this manner, cut 8 X triangles.

4. Join alternating triangles in 4 pairs as shown *(Block Assembly Diagram)*. Join pairs; then join halves. Press all seam allowances in same direction.

5. Cut 1 (4⅜" x 8¾") piece into 2 (4⅜") squares. Cut each square in half diagonally to get 4 Y triangles. Sew a triangle to each corner of block. Press seam allowances toward X triangles.

6. Make 42 blocks.

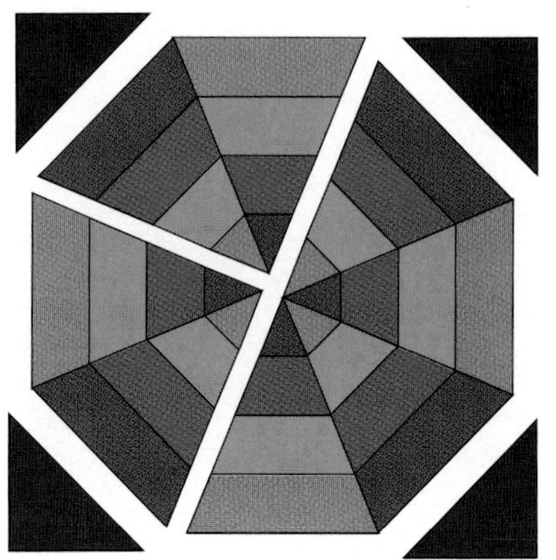

Block Assembly Diagram

Quilt Assembly

1. Cut a 36" square of binding fabric; set aside. Add remaining fabric to 3½"-wide strips for sashing. From these, cut 71 (3½" x 12½") sashing strips.

2. Referring to photo, lay out blocks in 6 vertical rows, with 7 blocks in each row. Lay sashing strips between blocks. Lay out remaining sashing strips in vertical rows between block rows, adding squares between strips as shown. (Set aside 4 red squares for border corners.)

3. Join units in each row. Assemble sashing rows in same manner. Press seam allowances in all rows toward sashing strips. Join rows.

Borders

1. Measure width of quilt top. Piece varied lengths of remaining 3½"-wide strips to make 2 borders to match quilt width. Then measure length of quilt top. Join remaining strips to make 2 side borders to match width.

2. Sew top and bottom borders to quilt edges, easing to fit as needed. Press seam allowances toward borders.

3. Add red squares to ends of each side border; press seam allowances toward borders. Sew borders to quilt sides.

Quilting and Finishing

1. Layer backing, batting, and quilt top. Baste.

2. Quilt as desired.

3. Use reserved square to make 11½ yards of straight-grain or bias binding. Bind quilt edges.

Color Variations

There are many ways to spin this traditional Kaleidoscope block. Try a monochromatic color scheme that depends on light and dark to create a design. Or consider a version of pastel batiks.

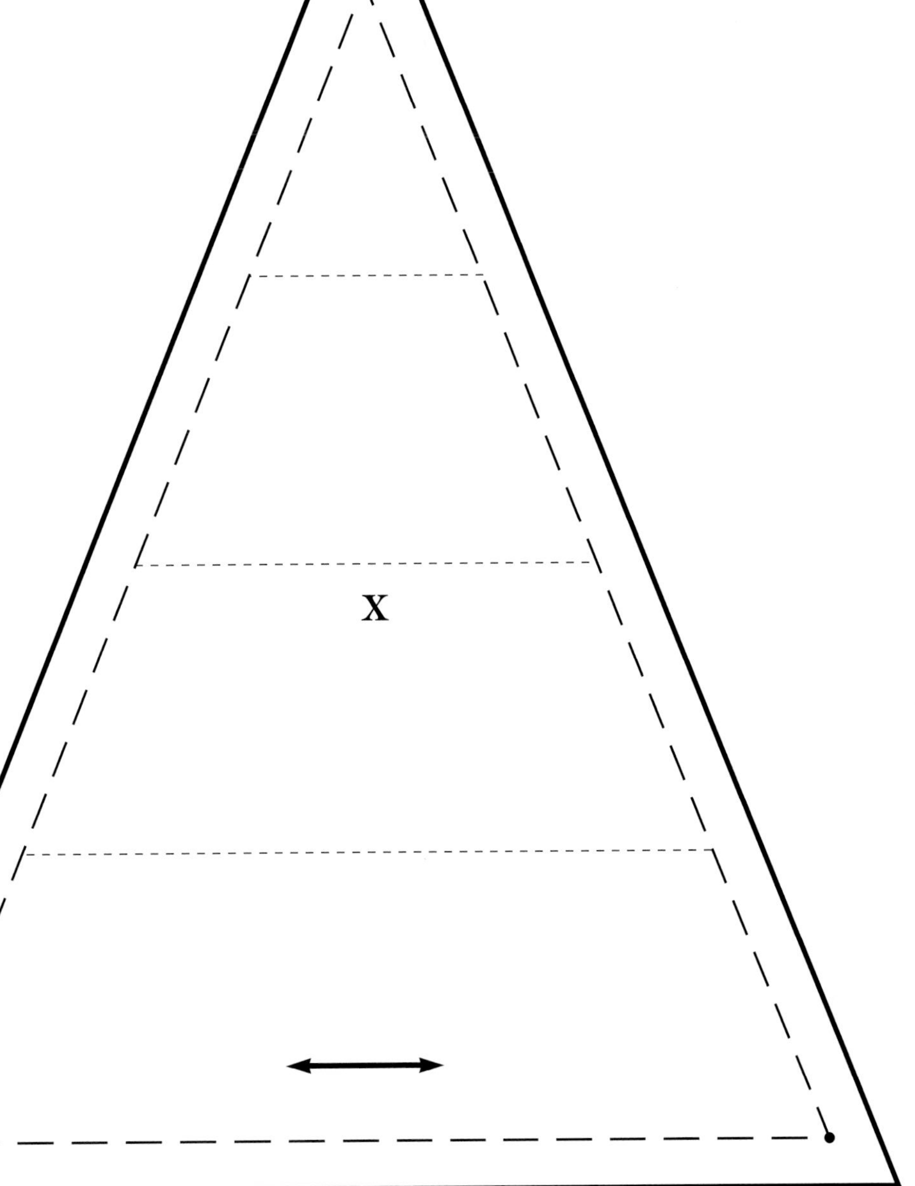

Designer Gallery

Kahalu'u Bay
Dancing in the Rain
Just Plane Fun
Perennials
Moon Dance
Serendipity Sparkles
Ginger Jar of Fun
Greasy Grass
Prairie Thunder
All Dogs Are Good

Valorie Plesha

Thornton, Colorado

Valorie Plesha isn't the first (or the last) quilter to underestimate the challenge of her first quilting project. In 1990, Valorie's husband gave her a how-to quilting book for Christmas and her mother-in-law gave her instructions for a project.

"How hard can it be?" Valorie mused. After all, she was a life-long sewer and this project was just lots of little pieces sewn in straight seams. And quilting was just a basic running stitch, right? Hah! "I was surprised by how much work it turned out to be," Valorie remembers, "but I started another quilt immediately after finishing the first, and have had at least one quilting project underway ever since."

"I rarely go anywhere without a project and my hoop."

Valorie fell in love with Hawaiian quilts in a quilt shop on Kauai. A newcomer to appliqué, she started small. Her first pillow was completed in a week, and she was permanently hooked on Hawaiian appliqué.

A computer programmer, Valorie enjoys the creativity and handwork of quiltmaking. Appliqué and hand quilting are favorites—in the words of a friend, "slow and satisfying." And the work is portable. "I rarely go anywhere without a project, my hoop, and a sewing kit," she says.

Valorie is a member of the Haole Connection. The group members were originally students of Deborah Kakalia, who taught Hawaiian quilting in the Denver area years ago. Valorie was invited to her first meeting in 1992 and, she says, "I have enjoyed the company and quilts and encouragement of these ladies ever since." She also enjoys helping the older of her two daughters piece doll quilts.

Kahalu'u Bay

1998, 83" x 82"

After Valorie Plesha spent a lovely day swimming with fish in a little Hawaiian bay, she enshrined the experience forever in this quilt that she named for that idyllic place.

A long-time devotee of Hawaiian quilts, Valorie studied other Hawaiian quilts for ideas and combined them with what she'd seen in Hawaii. First she made paper cutouts of motifs she wanted to use—fish, snails, shells—and then, "I added and removed and repositioned and redrafted and resized until I was satisfied," she says.

Originally intended to be a crib quilt for the baby Valorie was expecting at the time, the design demanded a larger scale and *Kahalu'u Bay* became the first bed-size quilt she ever made.

Valorie used fabrics from the Pointillist Palette line to capture the undulating colors of an underwater scene.

Kahalu'u Bay won first place for amateur appliqué at the 1999 American Quilter's Society show in Paducah.

Margaret Dunsmore

Ottawa, Ontario

Margaret Dunsmore's quiltmaking started off on a fairly routine path—she made crib quilts for friends and wall hangings for her home. Then her quilting career was interrupted for several years by increasingly long work days and other concerns. But when she took it up again, her quilts took flight.

"I resolved that when I did start again, I would do a series of birds on the wing," Margaret says.

Now that she no longer works outside the home, Margaret spends several days a week quilting in her home studio. The series, entitled *Quilts Take Wing,* includes six quilts so far. After exhibiting the work in Vancouver, Paducah, and Houston, among other places, Margaret's first one-woman show opened at the Mississippi Valley Textile Museum in Almonte, Ontario, in August 1999.

"The images draw the viewer into the bird's world."

Each quilt in the series features a bird against a stylized geometric background. "The images draw the viewer into the bird's world," Margaret says. One of her quilts features Elisha, a wayward flamingo who escaped from its Connecticut home and was recaptured in Canada.

In addition to the bird quilts, Margaret enjoys collaborative projects such as round-robins and mixed media. She worked with Maggie Glossop, a felt maker, to create a mixed media triptych of stained glass window images representing the devotions of Matins (sunrise), Meridies (mid-day), and Vespers (sunset).

Margaret is a member of Ottawa Valley Quilters Guild, the Canadian Quilters' Association, American Quilter's Society, and the International Quilt Association.

Dancing in the Rain

1998, 69" x 51"

Bird enthusiast Margaret Dunsmore wondered if the Great Blue Heron performs a ritual courtship dance similar to that of the Japanese crane. When she found that it did, she made this quilt to share her discovery.

In a poem enscribed on the quilt's backing, Margaret describes the male heron lifting his wings and spreading his tail feathers to entice a prospective mate. The female joins the dance, stretching, shrieking, and splashing in the shallow water before an audience of frogs and snakes.

The piece combines hand appliqué, machine piecing, and trapunto. Some feathers are dimensional, others are formed from silk, wool, and acrylic yarns, couched over lines of machine quilting.

Dancing in the Rain won a Canadian Quilters' Association Best of Show rosette at the 1999 Ottawa Valley Quilters Guild's Festival of

Quilts and an honorable mention at the 1999 American Quilter's Society show in Paducah, Kentucky. The quilt has also been shown at the Canadian Museum of Nature.

Andi Parejda

Arroyo Grande, California

It's not often that one can look back and identify a definite turning point in life. But Andi Parejda knows her life as a quiltmaker changed forever in 1993 when she joined the Thursday Night Friendship Group.

"These women are a major influence on me as a designer," Andi says. "We bounce ideas off one another and charge up one another's creative juices when they're low." Andi also credits classes and shows with giving her confidence and inspiration.

"We charge up one another's creative juices."

A devotee of various types of needlework, Andi saw women quilting around a frame for the first time when she was a graduate student in St. Louis. Years later, a new mother looking for a personal outlet, she took a class at a local shop. The Thursday night quilters came into her life two years later.

Andi is also a member of the South (San Luis Obispo) County Quilters Guild and the Santa Maria Valley Quilt Guild.

Just Plane Fun

1998, 52" x 58"

A red and white quilt, circa 1910, is among the 100 best quilts of the 20th century chosen recently by a team of experts. A few years ago, Andi Parejda was inspired to recreate this engineering marvel of a quilt, using contemporary strip piecing and rotary cutting methods.

Once Andi created her vortex circle, reduced in scale, it took her months to think up this setting for it. She used Pointillist Palette fabrics to create shadows under each circle and added assorted black and white fabrics.

Just Plane Fun was shown at the National Quilters Association's Omaha show in 1999 and Road to California in January 2000.

Perennials

1999, 64" x 72"

Sometimes inspiration and luck go hand in hand to create something wonderful.

Andi found inspiration in the late Paul Pilgrim, who made an art of combining old and new elements in his quilts.

Her luck was finding a treasure trove of 1930s Dresden Plate fragments and 1950s-era six-pointed stars.

Andi used these vintage pieces in a new setting, adding modern plaids and an African batik. The stars fill in the plates' empty centers, creating a double flower.

Andi says the flowerpot, as well as the mix of period fabrics, suggests the continuation of past in present and the cycle of life and renewal.

In 1999, *Perennials* was exhibited at the National Quilters Association's Omaha show and the International Quilt Association show in Houston. It was juried into the American Quilter's Association Nashville show in August 2000.

Anne C. Morrell-Robinson

Windsor, New York

Anne Morrell-Robinson is the kind of person who needs to stay busy. And if she can fill her time with warmth, beauty, and personal expression, then so much the better.

"It is a great joy to take needle, thread, and fabric and combine them into something of value," Anne says. She shares these feelings with others by teaching and exhibiting her work.

Quiltmaking may be in Anne's genes. Her great-great-grandmother was a prolific quiltmaker who passed her skills down through succeeding generations. Anne became a serious quilter in the early 1970s. Since then she has produced more than 330 quilts, many of them commissioned works.

"I use color and fabric to reflect the richness and balance of nature."

Anne's one-of-a-kind quilts "are an extension of my rural lifestyle," she says. She thinks of them as "hybrid vigor," blending ancient symbols, traditional techniques, and contemporary design. "I use color and fabric to reflect the richness and balance of nature in all its moods," Anne says.

In addition to teaching, Anne designs and sells patterns for dolls and quilts for her pattern company, Pincushion Productions. It all helps to pay for more supplies and fabric, she says with a laugh. "It also allows me to meet wonderful people and travel to places I otherwise would never see."

Anne is a member of Common Threads Quilt Guild of Vestal, New York, and the Mayflower Quilters' Society of Halifax, Nova Scotia.

Appliqué and signature patch from back of Moon Dance

Moon Dance

1998, 94" x 94"

Nature has many secrets that humans rarely see. Anne Morrell-Robinson was lucky to spy a gathering of dancing rabbits one moonlit night.

Taking cues from historic designs, Anne translated those midnight gambols into this pieced and appliquéd quilt. On the border, embroidered rabbits race across the face of each bright moon.

Moon Dance won first place for traditional appliqué/large quilts at the 1999 Quilts=Arts=Quilts show in Auburn, New York. It also won second place at the New York State Fair and a third place at Quilters' Heritage Celebration in Lancaster, Pennsylvania. *Moon Dance* was Viewers' Choice at shows in Troy and McLean, New York.

Laura Lorensen Franchini

Wisner, Nebraska

Now that there are so many wonderful fabrics available for quiltmakers, it's hard for some of us to remember way, way back when the selection was less than thrilling.

But Laura Franchini remembers the first quilt blocks she hand-pieced back in 1972. They just weren't very interesting. So she put them away and forgot about them. By the time her interest in patchwork returned in the mid-1980s, the fabric world had changed.

"This was about the time Jinny Beyer came out with her first fabric line," Laura remembers. "I found them so wonderful, I was hooked." Arranging and rearranging fabrics and blocks proved to be so much fun that Laura has been quilting ever since.

Laura's quilts reflect her love of fabric and color. And the more fabrics, the better. "I include many, many fabrics in my quilts," Laura says, "and people have always found that interesting."

"I found (the fabric) so wonderful, I was hooked."

A homemaker for nearly 19 years, Laura is devoted to numerous personal and community quilting projects. She brings lectures and trunk shows of quilts to schools, church groups, and nursing homes in a three-state area. She also volunteers at the International Quilt Study Center in Lincoln, Nebraska.

Laura quilts with a local church group and is also a member of the Country Piecemaker's Quilt Guild and the Nebraska State Quilt Guild.

Serendipity Sparkles

1998, 72" x 72"

Making leftovers into something interesting is every homemaker's challenge. Laura Franchini does it with fabric.

Her *Serendipity Sparkles* started with leftovers. Laura took ends of strip-pieced units and made them into 16-patches. Very dark and very light scraps read as solids, which Laura sees as sparkles. Adding large four-patches and setting triangles of blending medium tones finished off the main section of the quilt.

Nothing about the quilt was planned. "It was made to use up leftovers," Laura says. "Each step was spontaneous."

Laura used many colors of rayon thread for free-motion machine quilting. She quilted four trees in the center section, each rooted in a corner. The border is quilted in leaves of many colors.

Serendipity Sparkles was shown at the 1999 National Quilters Association show in Omaha and the Nebraska State Fair. It won a blue ribbon at the 1999 Cuming County Fair.

Mary Lou Weidman

Spokane, Washington

When Mary Lou Weidman started making folk art-style quilts about 10 years ago, her friends thought the quilts were "gaudy and weird." She says they "thought I was having a breakdown." But Mary Lou stuck to her own style. She wanted her quilts to tell stories, because she knows how important they can be.

Mary Lou became a serious quiltmaker in 1975 as she stitched away the hours of her son's hospital treatments. Her work attracted the interest of nurses and other parents, and she soon had many of them stitching. As they sewed, the quilters told tales of love and pain and family. "In the hospital, I met people with wonderful stories," Mary Lou says. "I wanted to put them in my quilts and share their experiences."

"Everything in life is a quilt waiting to happen."

It was a struggle to learn to do this effectively. Despite an art background, Mary Lou admits that, at first, "I had a lot of hideous quilts." When she made a quilt that featured a friend's dog, the friend asked, "which of these blobs is supposed to be my dog?" Mary Lou persevered, saying "if you're not making mistakes, you're not learning anything."

Today, Mary Lou incorporates people and things she loves in each quilt. She says, "Everything in life is a quilt waiting to happen." Using scraps of a dress or bits of jewelry as embellishment adds something of the person whose story is told. Buttons are a basic ingredient in her recipe.

Mary Lou is a nationally known quiltmaker, author, teacher, and fabric designer who encourages quilters to shed their inhibitions. She says, "Give yourself permission to let go and tell your own best story." Her pattern line, Mary Lou & Company, offers patterns for some of her quilts, but she prefers that each quilt tell a tale of its own.

Ginger Jar of Fun

1997, 44" x 57"

One of Mary Lou Weidman's favorite quilt themes is containers. "I love making quilts with vases, bowls, and baskets," she says. The idea is to fill the container with "things from the heart."

For this quilt, Mary Lou used bright-colored fabrics and buttons from grandma's jar to make a wall hanging full of whimsy. A floral fabric defines the large bowl, which erupts with appliqués of vibrant fantasy flowers, a whale-topped bird house, an owl, and a bird of a different feather. Machine quilting in variegated thread adds even more flowers, framed with a cheerful patchwork border.

Carol Ann Sinnreich

Lawton, Oklahoma

When Carol Ann Sinnreich and her husband retired in 1990, this native of New York's apple country settled in Oklahoma. There she became passionate about the history of the American West. Carol Ann put that together with a renewed commitment to quiltmaking and found a theme for a series of works in innovative pictorial appliqué.

"I never met a fabric that I didn't like."

Carol Ann considers quiltmaking a full-time occupation. She spends most days sketching, doing research, preparing workshops, or working with fabric in her studio.

"I became intrigued with the idea of combining traditional patchwork patterns with pictorial appliqué," Carol Ann says. She deftly incorporates familiar patches into each work. But it's painting pictures with fabrics that is her real niche. For Carol Ann, a fine arts graduate, drawing the images on paper is easy. The challenge is to find the right fabrics to bring the picture to life. She means it when she says, "I never met a fabric that I didn't like."

Carol Ann is a member of Central Oklahoma Quilt Guild, Wichita Mountains Quilt Guild, Oklahoma Quilters' State Organization, Studio Art Quilt Associates, and several national quilting organizations.

Greasy Grass

1997, 81½" x 63½"

On June 25, 1876, Sioux and Cheyenne warriors surrounded and annihilated five companies of the 7th U.S. Cavalry. History books call it the Battle of Little Bighorn. But the Indians call the place Greasy Grass.

Carol Ann selected Burgoyne Surrounded for a patchwork background to this story. A 1913 painting by William Herbert Dunton inspired the design of the warriors in the foreground.

Prairie Thunder

1999, 67" x 54"

Carol Ann designed this quilt in homage to the massive herds that once darkened the Great Plains. She imagined a thundering stampede, a storm of dust in its wake.

She included prairie dogs in the scene, since they were just as numerous as buffalo in the 19th century. These little figures also help the viewer appreciate the need to get out of the way!

Carol Ann was able to photograph a bison herd that roams free on the Wichita Mountains Wildlife Refuge in southwest Oklahoma.

The buffalo was a source of spirituality for native Americans, as well as food. On the back of this quilt, Carol Ann appliquéd a stylized version of a Navajo petroglyph, shown at right. Typical of ancient images, it shows the animal's heartline from mouth to heart, with an arrow through its heart.

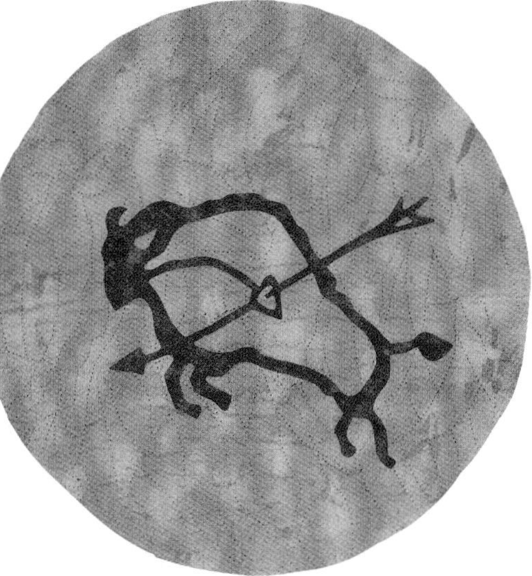

Prairie Thunder was seen at the International Quilt Association show in Houston, Texas, in October 1999.

Becky Triplett
Omaha, Nebraska

Like countless American women, Becky Triplett learned to quilt at her grandmother's knee. When Becky was 5, her grandmother allowed her to do a little quilting. "I'm sure she took it out, though," Becky says.

Becky became a die-hard quilter by taking a class at a local quilt shop in 1982. Since then, quilts have filled her mind with creative ideas. "I probably spend more time thinking and dreaming about quilts than actually making them," she says. "Someday I'll have time to make all the quilts I dream about."

"Someday I'll have time to make all the quilts I dream about."

A favorite aspect of quilting is making new friends through quilts. "I really enjoy being around people who are so creative and enthusiastic," she says.

Becky is a member of the Omaha Quilt Guild and the Nebraska State Quilt Guild.

All Dogs Are Good

1998, 62" x 82"

Like most quilters, Becky Triplett finds inspiration in all aspects of life. Hers just happens to have a wet nose.

Some years ago, Becky found a 1932 edition of *The Book of the Scottish Terrier.* According to this book, a William Haynes wrote, "All dogs are good; any terrier is better; a Scottish terrier is best." Becky's sentiments, exactly, and an idea for a quilt if ever there was one.

Armed with the image of Murphy, her own much-loved Scottie, Becky drafted the dog blocks on a computer and printed them in several sizes for paper-piecing.

All Dogs Are Good won a blue ribbon at the 1998 Omaha Quilt Guild show as well as an honorable mention for Becky's hand quilting. The quilt also won a judge's ribbon at the 1999 show of the American Quilter's Society in Paducah, Kentucky.

Quilt Smart Workshop

A Guide to Quiltmaking

❖

Preparing Fabric

Before cutting any pieces, be sure to wash and dry your fabric to preshrink it. All-cotton fabrics may need pressing before cutting. Trim selvages from the fabric before you cut pieces.

Making Templates

Before you can make one of the quilts in this book, you must make templates from the printed patterns given. (Not all pieces require patterns—some pieces are meant to be cut with a rotary cutter and ruler.) Quilters have used many materials to make templates, including cardboard and sandpaper. Transparent template plastic, available at craft supply and quilt shops, is durable, see-through, and easy to use.

To make a plastic template, place the plastic sheet on the printed page and use a laundry marker or permanent fine-tip marking pen to trace each pattern. For machine piecing, trace on the outside solid (cutting) line. For hand piecing, trace on the inside broken (stitching) line. Cut out the template on the traced line. Label each template with the pattern name, letter, grain line arrow, and match points (corner dots).

Marking and Cutting Fabric for Piecing

Place the template facedown on the wrong side of the fabric and mark around it with a sharp pencil.

If you will be piecing by machine, the pencil lines represent cutting lines. Cut on each marked line.

For hand piecing, the pencil lines are seam lines. Leave at least ¾" between marked lines for seam allowances. Add ¼" seam allowance around each piece as you cut. Mark match points (corner dots) on each piece.

You can do without templates if you use a rotary cutter and ruler to cut straight strips and geometric shapes such as squares and triangles. Rotary cutting is always paired with machine piecing, and pieces are cut with seam allowances included.

Hand Piecing

To hand piece, place two fabric pieces together with right sides facing. Insert a pin in each match point of the top piece. Stick the pin through both pieces and check to be sure that it pierces the match point on the bottom piece (*Figure 1*). Adjust the pieces as necessary to align the match points. (The raw edges of the two pieces may not align exactly.) Pin the pieces securely together.

Sew with a running stitch of 8 to 10 stitches per inch. Sew from match point to match point, checking the stitching as you go to be sure you are sewing in the seam line of both pieces.

To make sharp corners, begin and end the stitching exactly at the match point; do not stitch into the seam allowances. When joining units where several seams come together, do not sew over seam allowances; sew through them at the point where all seam lines meet (*Figure 2*).

Always press both seam allowances to one side. Pressing the seam open, as in dressmaking, can leave gaps between stitches through which the batting may beard. Press seam allowances toward the darker fabric whenever you can, but it is sometimes more important to reduce bulk by avoiding overlapping seam allowances. When four or more seams meet at one point, such as at the corner of a block, press all the seams in a "swirl" in the same direction to reduce bulk (*Figure 3*).

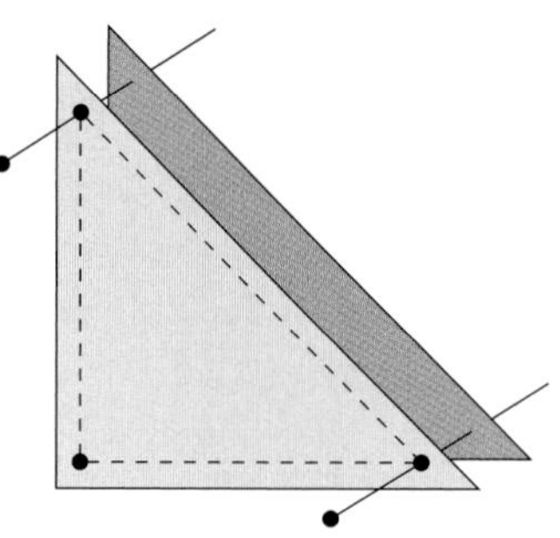

Figure 1–Aligning Match Points

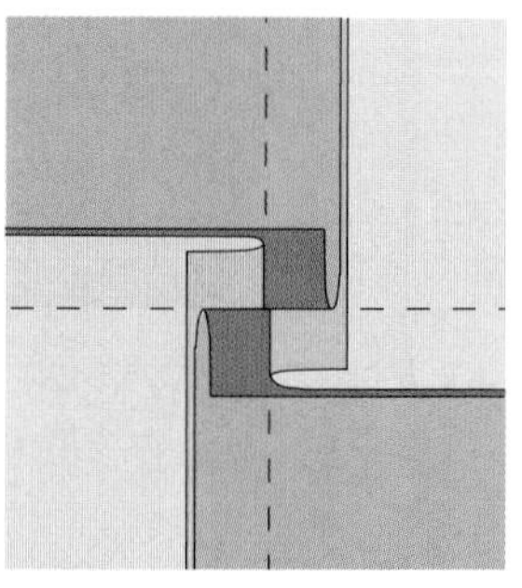

Figure 3–Pressing Intersecting Seams

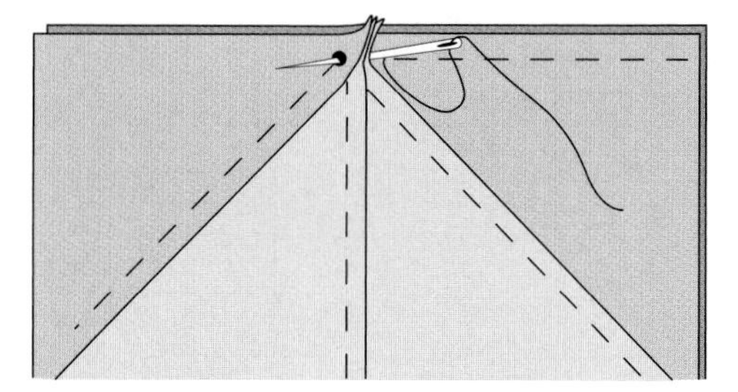

Figure 2–Joining Units

Machine Piecing

To machine piece, place two fabric pieces together with right sides facing. Align match points as described under "Hand Piecing" and pin the pieces together securely.

Set the stitch length at 12 to 15 stitches per inch. At this setting, you do not need to backstitch to lock seam beginnings and ends. Use a presser foot that gives a perfect ¼" seam allowance, or measure ¼" from the needle and mark that point on the presser foot with nail polish or masking tape.

Chain piecing, stitching edge to edge, saves time when sewing similar sets of pieces (*Figure 4*). Join the first two pieces as usual. At the end of the seam, do not backstitch, cut the thread, or lift the presser foot. Instead, sew a few stitches off the fabric. Place the next two pieces and continue stitching. Keep sewing until all the sets are joined. Then cut the sets apart.

Press seam allowances toward the darker fabric whenever possible. When you join blocks or rows, press the seam allowances of the top row in one direction and the seam allowances of the bottom row in the opposite direction to help ensure that the seams will lie flat (*Figure 5*).

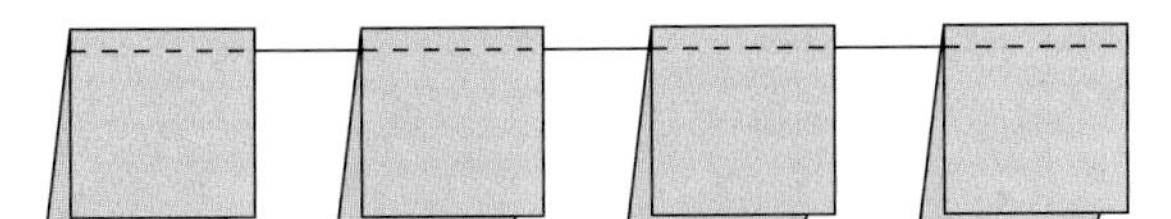

Figure 4–Chain Piecing

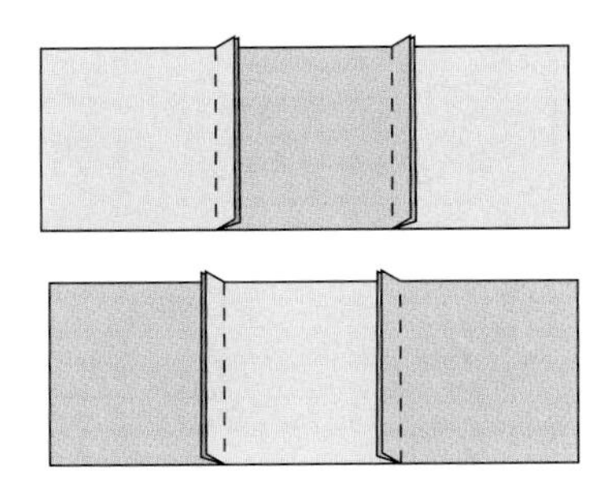

Figure 5–Pressing Seams for Machine Piecing

Hand Appliqué

Hand appliqué is the best way to achieve the look of traditional appliqué. But using freezer paper, which is sold in grocery stores, saves time because it eliminates the need for hand basting seam allowances.

Make templates without seam allowances. Trace the template onto the *dull* side of the freezer paper; cut the paper on the marked line. Make a freezer-paper shape for each piece to be appliquéd.

Pin the freezer-paper shape, *shiny side up*, to the *wrong side* of the fabric. Following the paper shape and adding a scant ¼" seam allowance, cut out the fabric piece. Do not remove the pins. Use the tip of a hot, dry iron to press the seam allowance to the shiny side of the freezer paper. Be careful not to touch the shiny side of the freezer paper with the iron. Remove the pins.

Pin the appliqué shape in place on the background fabric. Use one strand of sewing thread in a color to match the appliqué shape. Using a very small slipstitch (*Figure 6*) or blindstitch (*Figure 7*), appliqué the shape to the background fabric.

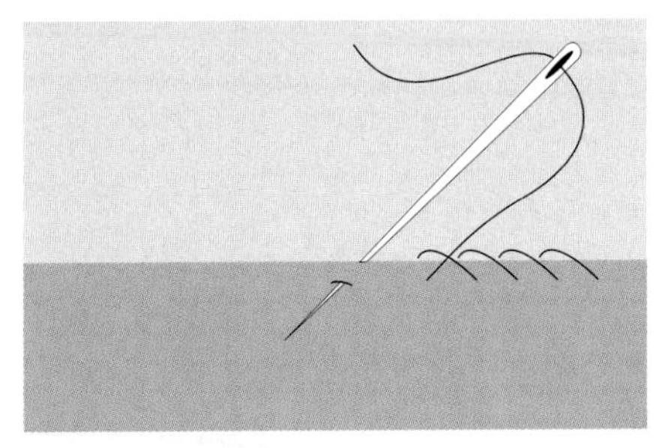

Figure 6–Slipstitch

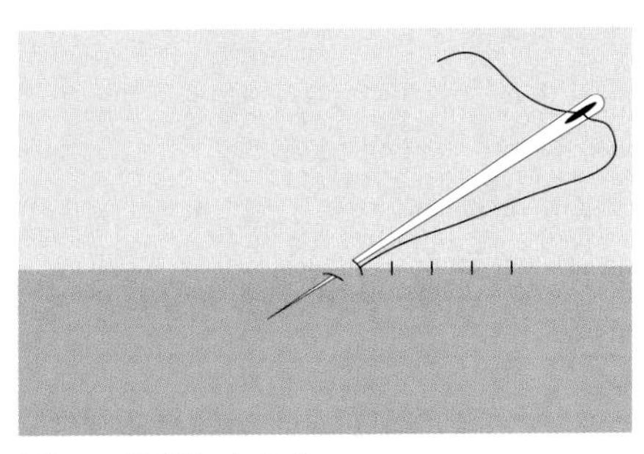

Figure 7–Blindstitch

When your stitching is complete, cut away the background fabric behind the appliqué, leaving ¼" seam allowance. Separate the freezer paper from the fabric with your fingernail and pull gently to remove it.

Mitering Borders

Mitered borders take a little extra care to stitch but offer a nice finish when square border corners just won't do.

First, measure the length of the quilt through the middle of the quilt top. Cut two border strips to fit this length, plus the width of the border plus 2". Centering the measurement on the strip, place pins on the edge of each strip at the center and each end of the measurement. Match the pins on each border strip to the corners of a long side of the quilt.

Starting and stopping ¼" from each corner of the quilt, sew the borders to the quilt, easing the quilt to fit between the pins (*Figure 8*). Press seam allowances toward border strip.

Measure the quilt width through the middle and cut two border strips to fit, adding the border width plus 2". Join these borders to opposite ends of the quilt in the same manner.

Fold one border corner over the adjacent corner (*Figure 9*) and press. On the wrong side, stitch in the creased fold to stitch a mitered seam (*Figure 10*). Press; then check to make sure the corner lies flat on the quilt top. Trim seam allowances.

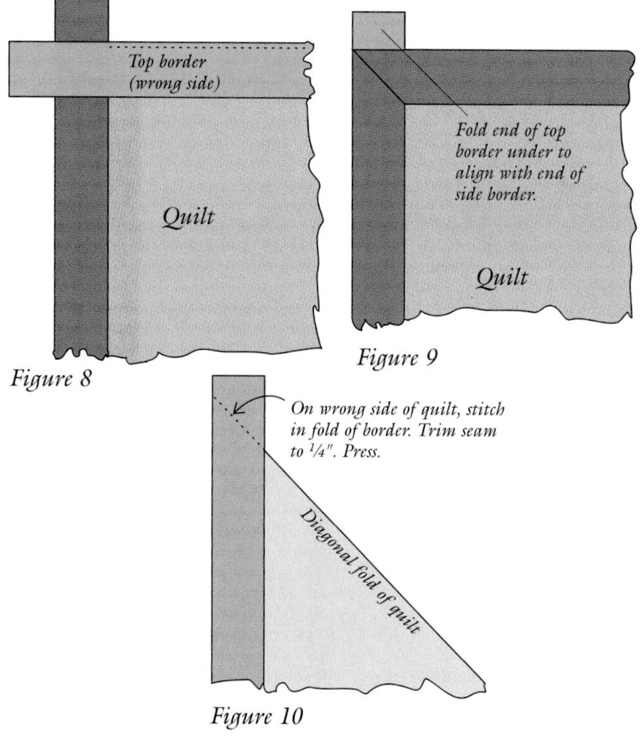

Mitering Borders

Marking Your Quilt Top

When the quilt top is complete, press it thoroughly before marking it with quilting designs. The most popular methods for marking use stencils or templates. Both can be purchased, or you can make your own. You can also use a yardstick to mark straight lines or grids.

Use a silver quilter's pencil for marking light to medium fabrics and a white chalk pencil on dark fabrics. Lightly mark the quilt top with your chosen quilting designs.

Making a Backing

The instructions in *Great American Quilts* give backing yardage based on 45"-wide fabric unless a 90"-wide or 108"-wide backing is more practical. (These fabrics are sold at fabric and quilt shops.) Pieced or not, the quilt backing should be at least 3" larger on all sides than the quilt top.

Backing fabric should be of a type and color that is compatible with the quilt top. Percale sheets are not recommended, because they are tightly woven and difficult to hand-quilt through.

A pieced backing for a bed quilt should have three panels. The three-panel backing is recommended because it tends to wear better and lie flatter than the two-panel type, the center seam of which often makes a ridge down the center of the quilt. Begin by cutting the fabric in half widthwise (*Figure 11*). Open the two lengths and stack them, with right sides facing and selvages aligned. Stitch along both selvage edges to create a tube of fabric (*Figure 12*). Cut down the center of the top layer of fabric *only* and open the fabric flat (*Figure 13*). Press seam allowances toward center panel.

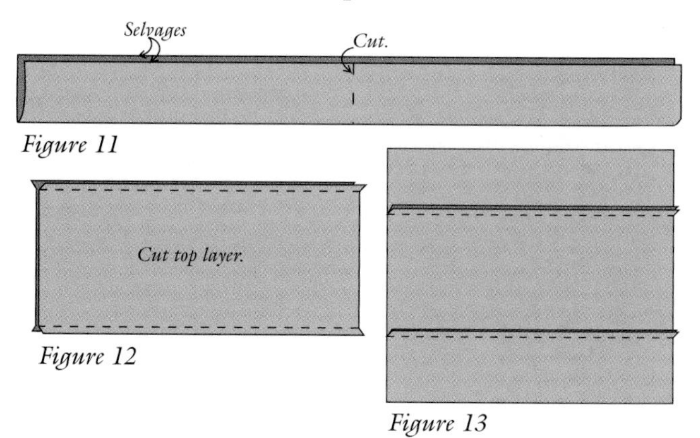

Making a Three-Panel Backing

Layering and Basting

Prepare a working surface to spread out the quilt. Place the backing on the surface, right side down. Unfold the batting and place it on top of the backing. Smooth any wrinkles or lumps in the batting. Lay the quilt top right side up on top of the batting and backing. Make sure backing and quilt top are parallel.

Use a darning needle for basting, with a long strand of sewing thread. Begin in the center of your quilt and baste out toward the edges. The stitches should cover enough of the quilt to keep the layers from shifting during quilting. Inadequate basting can result in puckers and folds on the back and front of the quilt during quilting.

Hand Quilting

Hand quilting can be done with the quilt in a hoop or in a floor frame. It is best to start in the middle of your quilt and quilt out toward the edges.

Most quilters use a thin, short needle called a "between." Betweens are available in sizes 7 to 12, with 7 being the longest and 12 the shortest. If you are a beginning quilter, try a size 7 or 8. Because betweens are so much shorter than other needles, they may feel awkward at first. As your skill increases, try using a smaller needle to help you make smaller stitches.

Quilting thread, heavier and stronger than sewing thread, is available in a wide variety of colors. If color matching is critical and you can't find the color you need, you can substitute cotton sewing thread if you coat it with beeswax before quilting to prevent it from tangling.

Thread your needle with a 20" length and make a small knot at one end. Insert the needle into the quilt top approximately ½" from the point where you want to begin quilting. Do not take the needle through all three layers, but stop it in the batting and bring it up through the quilt top again at your starting point. Tug gently on the thread to pop the knot through the quilt top into the batting. This anchors the thread without an unsightly knot showing on the back.

With your non-sewing hand underneath the quilt, insert the needle with the point straight down in the quilt about 1/16" from the starting point. With your underneath finger, feel for the point as the needle comes through the backing (*Figure 14*). Place the thumb of your sewing hand approximately ½" ahead of the needle. When you feel the needle touch your underneath finger, push the fabric up from below as you rock the needle down to a nearly horizontal position. Using the thumb of your sewing hand in conjunction with the underneath hand, pinch a little hill in the fabric and push the tip of the needle back through the quilt top (*Figure 15*).

Now either push the needle all the way through to complete one stitch or rock the needle again to

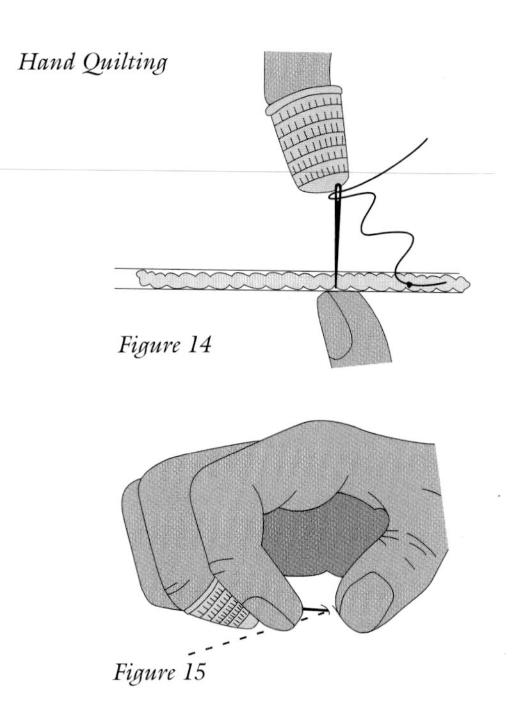
Hand Quilting

Figure 14

Figure 15

an upright position on its point to take another stitch. Take no more than a quarter-needleful of stitches before pulling the needle through.

When you have 6" of thread remaining, you must end the old thread securely and invisibly. Carefully tie a knot in the thread, flat against the surface of the fabric. Pop the knot through the top as you did when beginning the line of quilting. Clip the thread, rethread your needle, and continue quilting.

Machine Quilting

Machine quilting is as old as the sewing machine itself; but until recently, it was thought inferior to hand quilting. Fine machine quilting is an exclusive category, but it requires a different set of skills from hand quilting.

Machine quilting can be done on your sewing machine using a straight stitch and a special presser foot. A walking foot or even-feed foot is recommended for straight-line quilting to help the top fabric move through the machine at the same rate that the feed dogs move the bottom fabric.

Regular sewing thread or nylon thread can be used for machine quilting. With the quilt top facing you, roll the long edges of the basted quilt toward the center, leaving a 12"-wide area unrolled in the center. Secure the roll with bicycle clips, metal bands that are available at quilt shops. Begin at one unrolled end and fold the quilt over and over until only a small area is showing. This will be the area where you will begin to quilt.

Place the folded portion of the quilt in your lap. Start quilting in the center and work to the right, unfolding and unrolling the quilt as you go. Remove the quilt from the machine, turn it, and reinsert it in the machine to stitch the left side. A table placed behind your sewing machine will help support the quilt as it is stitched.

Curves and circles are most easily made by free-motion machine quilting. Using a darning foot and with the feed dogs down, move the quilt under the needle with your fingertips. Place your hands on the fabric on each side of the foot and run the machine at a steady, medium speed. The length of the stitches is determined by the rate of speed at which you move fabric through the machine. Do not rotate the quilt; rather, move it from side to side as needed. Always stop with the needle down to keep the quilt from shifting.

Making Binding

A continuous bias or straight-grain strip is used to bind quilt edges. Bias binding is especially recommended for quilts with curved edges. Follow these steps to make a continuous bias strip:

1. Start with a square of fabric. Multiply the number of binding inches needed by the cut width of the binding strip (usually 2½"). Use a calculator to find the square root of that number. That's the size of the fabric square needed to make your binding.

2. Cut the square in half diagonally.

3. With right sides facing, join triangles to form a sawtooth as shown *(Figure 16)*.

4. Press seam open. Mark off parallel lines the desired width of the binding as shown *(Figure 17)*.

5. With right sides facing, align raw edges marked Seam 2. Offset edges by one strip width, so one side is higher than the other *(Figure 18)*. Stitch Seam 2. Press seam open.

6. Cut the binding in a continuous strip, starting with the protruding point and following the marked lines around the tube.

7. Press the binding strip in half lengthwise, with wrong sides facing.

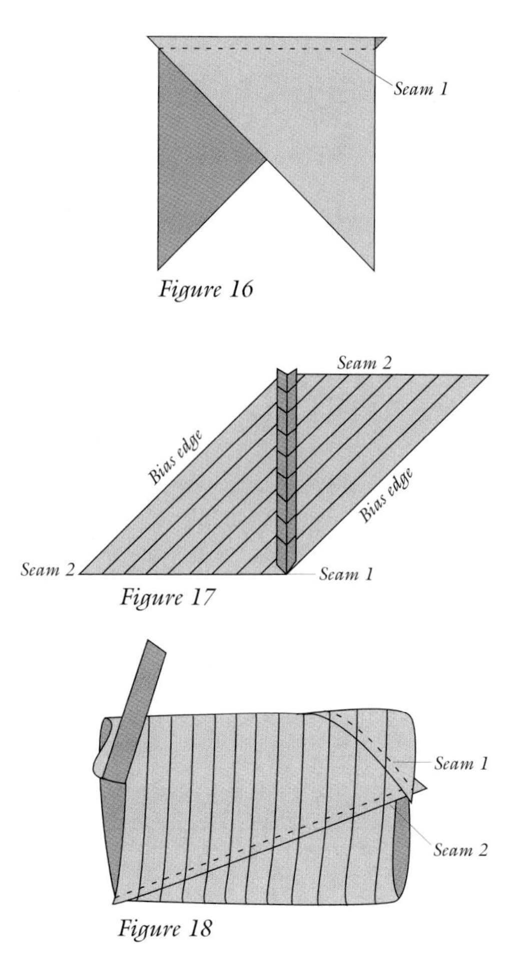

Continuous Bias Binding

Attaching Binding

To prepare your quilt for binding, baste the layers together ¼" from the edge of the quilt. Trim the backing and batting even with the edge of the quilt top. Beginning at the midpoint of one side of the quilt, pin the binding to the top, with right sides facing and raw edges aligned.

Machine-stitch the binding along one edge of the quilt, sewing through all layers. Backstitch at the beginning of the seam to lock the stitching.

Stitch until you reach the seam line at the corner, and backstitch. Lift the presser foot and turn the quilt to align the foot with the next edge. Continue sewing around all four sides. Join the beginning and end of the binding strip by machine, or stitch one end by hand to overlap the other.

Turn the binding over the edge and blindstitch it in place on the backing. At each corner, fold the excess binding neatly to make a mitered corner and blindstitch it in place.